Italian Guitar Music of the
Seventeenth Century

Eastman Studies in Music

Ralph P. Locke, Senior Editor
Eastman School of Music

A complete list of titles in the Eastman Studies in Music series
may be found on our website, www.urpress.com.

Italian Guitar Music of the Seventeenth Century

Battuto and Pizzicato

Lex Eisenhardt

UNIVERSITY OF ROCHESTER PRESS

versity of Rochester Press gratefully acknowledges the support of the
atorium van Amsterdam.

ılished 2015
d in paperback 2019

ty of Rochester Press
Hope Avenue, Rochester, NY 14620, USA
ıress.com
1ell & Brewer Limited
9, Woodbridge, Suffolk IP12 3DF, UK
ːdellandbrewer.com

er ISBN-13: 978-1-58046-533-5
ːk ISBN-13: 978-1-58046-957-9
)71-9989

∙ of Congress Cataloging-in-Publication Data

dt, Lex, 1952– author.
. guitar music of the seventeenth century : battuto and pizzicato /
ıhardt.
es cm — (Eastman studies in music, ISSN 1071-9989 ; v. 130)
.es bibliographical references and index.
8-1-58046-533-5 (hardcover : alkaline paper) 1. Guitar music—Italy—17th
–History and criticism. 2. Guitar—Italy—History—17th century. I. Title. II.
astman studies in music ; v. 130.
15.G9E38 2015
ˀ0945'09032— dc23   2015028032

ılication is printed on acid-free paper.
n the United States of America

Contents

Illustrations

Audio Examples

The audio examples are available online at http://lexeisenhardt.nl/audio/. All tracks are performed by the author on chitarra spagnuola (after Antonio Stradivari by Bert Kwakkel) or chitarra battente (after Giorgio Sellas by Sebastian Nuñez).

1 Giovanni Paolo Foscarini, *Il primo, secondo e terzo libro della chitarra spagnola* (ca. 1630), Capriccio sopra la ciaccona. Lex Eisenhardt (chitarra spagnuola). Etcetera Records, 2002, KTC1316. http://lexeisenhardt.nl/audio/1.

2 Domenico Obizzi, *Madrigali et arie a voce sola* (Venice, 1627), "Hor che vicin mi sento." Maria-Luz Alvarez (soprano), Lex Eisenhardt (chitarra battente). Etcetera Records, 2002, KTC1316. http://lexeisenhardt.nl/audio/2.

3 Domenico Obizzi, *Madrigali et arie a voce sola* (Venice, 1627), "E pur di novo, ahi lasso." Maria-Luz Alvarez (soprano), Lex Eisenhardt (chitarra battente). Etcetera Records, 2002, KTC1316. http://lexeisenhardt.nl/audio/3.

4 Domenico Obizzi, *Madrigali et arie a voce sola* (Venice, 1627), "Rompi, rompi mi core." Maria-Luz Alvarez (soprano), Lex Eisenhardt (chitarra battente). Etcetera Records, 2002, KTC1316. http://lexeisenhardt.nl/audio/4.

5 Giovanni Paolo Foscarini, *Il primo, secondo e terzo libro della chitarra spagnola* (ca. 1630), Toccata. Lex Eisenhardt (chitarra spagnuola). Etcetera Records, 2002, KTC1316. http://lexeisenhardt.nl/audio/5.

6 Giovanni Paolo Foscarini, *Il primo, secondo e terzo libro della chitarra spagnola* (ca. 1630), Corrente. Lex Eisenhardt (chitarra spagnuola). Etcetera Records, 2002, KTC1316. http://lexeisenhardt.nl/audio/6.

7 Giovanni Paolo Foscarini, *Il primo, secondo e terzo libro della chitarra spagnola* (ca. 1630), Gagliarda la passionata. Lex Eisenhardt (chitarra spagnuola). Etcetera Records, 2002, KTC1316. http://lexeisenhardt.nl/audio/7.

8   Martino Pesenti, *Arie a voce sola* (Venice, 1633), "Io non raggiro il piede." Maria-Luz Alvarez (soprano), Lex Eisenhardt (chitarra spagnuola). Etcetera Records, 2002, KTC1316. http://lexeisenhardt. nl/audio/8.

9   Giovanni Pietro Berti, *Cantade ed arie* (Venice, 1624), "Giovanete ascoltate" (ritornello: *Pavaniglia* by Francesco Corbetta), Maria_Luz Alvarez (soprano), Lex Eisenhardt (chitarra spagnuola). Etcetera Records, 2002, KTC1316. http://lexeisenhardt.nl/audio/9.

10 Stefano Landi, *Il quinto libro dárie* (Venice, 1637), "Tu vedi alato Arcier." Maria-Luz Alvarez (soprano), Lex Eisenhardt (chitarra spagnuola). Etcetera Records, 2002, KTC1316. http://lexeisenhardt.nl/audio/10.

11 Giovanni Paolo Foscarini, *Il primo, secondo e terzo libro della chitarra spagnola* (ca. 1630), Toccata. Lex Eisenhardt (chitarra spagnuola). Etcetera Records, 2002, KTC1316. http://lexeisenhardt.nl/audio/11.

12 Giovanni Paolo Foscarini, *Il primo, secondo e terzo libro della chitarra spagnola* (ca. 1630), Corrente. Lex Eisenhardt (chitarra spagnuola). Etcetera Records, 2002, KTC1316. http://lexeisenhardt.nl/audio/12.

13 Giovanni Paolo Foscarini, *Il primo, secondo e terzo libro della chitarra spagnola* (ca. 1630), Sarabanda. Lex Eisenhardt (chitarra spagnuola). Etcetera Records, 2002, KTC1316. http://lexeisenhardt.nl/audio/13.

14 Francesco Corbetta, *La guitarre royalle* (Paris, 1671), Prelude in A minor. Lex Eisenhardt (chitarra spagnuola). Verbena, 2003, CDR2003-1. http://lexeisenhardt.nl/audio/14.

15 Francesco Corbetta, *La guitarre royalle* (Paris, 1671), Allemande in A minor. Lex Eisenhardt (chitarra spagnuola). Verbena, 2003, CDR2003-1. http://lexeisenhardt.nl/audio/15.

16 Francesco Corbetta, *La guitarre royalle* (Paris, 1671), Courante in A minor. Lex Eisenhardt (chitarra spagnuola). Verbena, 2003, CDR2003-1. http://lexeisenhardt.nl/audio/16.

17 Francesco Corbetta, *La guitarre royalle* (Paris, 1671), Sarabande in A minor. Lex Eisenhardt (chitarra spagnuola). Verbena, 2003, CDR2003-1. http://lexeisenhardt.nl/audio/17.

18 Francesco Corbetta, *La guitarre royalle* (Paris, 1671), Gigue in A minor. Lex Eisenhardt (chitarra spagnuola). Verbena, 2003, CDR2003-1. http://lexeisenhardt.nl/audio/18.

19 Francesco Corbetta, *La guitarre royalle* (Paris, 1671), Menuet in A minor. Lex Eisenhardt (chitarra spagnuola). Verbena, 2003, CDR2003-1. http://lexeisenhardt.nl/audio/19.

20 Francesco Corbetta, *La guitarre royalle* (Paris, 1671), Caprice de chaconne in C major. Lex Eisenhardt (chitarra spagnuola). Verbena, 2003, CDR2003-1. http://lexeisenhardt.nl/audio/20.

21 Angelo Michele Bartolotti, *Secondo libro* (Rome, c. 1655), Prelude in E minor. Lex Eisenhardt (chitarra spagnuola). http://lexeisenhardt.nl/audio/21.

22 Angelo Michele Bartolotti, *Secondo libro* (Rome, c. 1655), Allemande in E minor. Lex Eisenhardt (chitarra spagnuola). http://lexeisenhardt.nl/audio/22.

23 Angelo Michele Bartolotti, *Secondo libro* (Rome, c. 1655), Courante in E minor. Lex Eisenhardt (chitarra spagnuola). http://lexeisenhardt.nl/audio/23.

24 Angelo Michele Bartolotti, *Secondo libro* (Rome, c. 1655), Sarabande in E minor. Lex Eisenhardt (chitarra spagnuola). http://lexeisenhardt.nl/audio/24.

25 Angelo Michele Bartolotti, *Secondo libro* (Rome, c. 1655), Gigue in E minor. Lex Eisenhardt (chitarra spagnuola). http://lexeisenhardt.nl/audio/25.

26 Angelo Michele Bartolotti, *Secondo libro* (Rome, c. 1655), Passacaglia in E minor. Lex Eisenhardt (chitarra spagnuola). http://lexeisenhardt.nl/audio/26.

27 Francesco Corbetta, *La guitarre royalle* (Paris, 1671), Passacaille in G minor (excerpt). Lex Eisenhardt (chitarra spagnuola). Verbena, 2003, CDR2003-1. http://lexeisenhardt.nl/audio/27.

28 Francesco Corbetta, *La guitarre royalle* (Paris, 1671), Passacaille in G minor (excerpt). Lex Eisenhardt (chitarra spagnuola). Verbena, 2003, CDR2003-1. http://lexeisenhardt.nl/audio/28.

29 Francesco Corbetta, *La guitarre royalle* (Paris, 1671), Sarabande et sa Passacaille in G minor. Lex Eisenhardt (chitarra spagnuola). Verbena, 2003, CDR2003-1. http://lexeisenhardt.nl/audio/29.

Preface

What is your tuning? This question is asked whenever you show up with a baroque guitar. It almost seems as if there are only two major issues with regard to this instrument: what role has it played in basso continuo and the question of appropriate stringing, with or without low bass strings (*bourdons*). The impatient reader may be tempted to jump to chapter 6 immediately, to find out about my views on the latter. However, as will be argued in chapter 5 (on counterpoint), we should know more about the use of the guitar in different musical genres in order to understand the advantages of having—or not having—the bass register, provided by the bourdons, for the realization of contrapuntal textures. This issue seems particularly relevant for thoroughbass accompaniment.

My activities as a performer on the baroque guitar and my concern for its continued identity confusion have encouraged me to begin practice-based research into the Italian solo repertory and *alfabeto* song. Probably the most characteristic feature of seventeenth-century Italian guitar music is the mixing of two distinct methods of playing: chord strumming (*battuto*) and the plucked lute style (*pizzicato*). I supposed that exploring the background of this dichotomy would provide a key to understanding the development of the repertoire and how it is notated. Moreover, I hoped to learn more about the upward mobility of the popular guitar dances (or dance songs) that became part of the sphere of "high art" music. An obvious example is the chaconne, supposedly imported from the New World. It appeared in Europe around 1600, as a simple four-chord progression on the guitar that can be found in countless Italian guitar books and manuscripts. About a century later, in 1735, the chaconne formed the grand orchestral finale of Rameau's *Les Indes Galantes*—bringing back the dance, symbolically, to its assumed origins. But how, exactly, would the original dance have sounded, in the hands of a guitarist from the popular tradition? And why, for example, is there no music notation at all for the "Gittars Chacony" in the score of Purcell's *Dido and Aeneas*?

I started writing this book very early in the twenty-first century. The sheer length of the process has given me the time to gather a wealth of information, by just keeping an open eye; it offered me the opportunity to discuss an array of related subjects with colleagues and students, scholars, and performers. Some of them have commented on parts of the manuscript; I wish to thank

Jacques Boogaart of the University of Amsterdam, and Thérèse de Goede and
Fred Jacobs of the Conservatory of Amsterdam for their invaluable comments.
I should mention the editorial committee of *The Lute* (the journal of the Lute
Society), and Christopher Goodwin in particular, who, in a very early stage of
my research, encouraged me to write about the subject of the stringing of the
five-course guitar. Gary Boye has closely read the final manuscript, and given
very detailed comments. Johan Herrenberg has transformed my cumbersome
syntax into readable English, and on many occasions suggested more concise
formulations, which, as far as I can judge, have greatly improved the text.

This work has been made possible with the support of the Conservatorium
van Amsterdam. I am indebted to Michiel Schuijer, head of research of the
Conservatory, for his tenacity and his commitment to my project. He brought
my manuscript to the attention of University of Rochester Press. Ralph Locke,
editor of the Eastman Studies in Music, responded the same day, encourag-
ing me to write a book proposal. And then everything went smoothly, thanks
to Sonia Kane, Julia Cook, and Ryan Peterson of the press, who helped me to
prepare the book for publication. Finally, copyeditor Carrie Crompton meticulously worked through the manuscript and helped me to solve some remaining issues. Her familiarity with the subjects of early music and plucked strings
made it easy to work together. Any remaining errors are entirely mine; and,
unless otherwise noted, all translations are my own.

Amsterdam, 2015
Lex Eisenhardt

Introduction

The Guitar in Seventeenth-Century Italy

The heyday of the five-course guitar in Italy was halfway through the seventeenth century. In a brief span of time, composers such as Giovanni Paolo Foscarini, Francesco Corbetta, Giovanni Battista Granata, and Angelo Michele Bartolotti created a repertoire of considerable size that would be completely forgotten in the next century. Since then, most sources have lain unused in libraries and museums, which is why few people in our time have been in the position to form an opinion on the quality of this music.

The greatest success came in the era in which the lute, once the queen of instrumental polyphony, lost favor. Lute tablatures were no longer printed in Italy after about 1650, and only the new chitarrone, the bass instrument soon to be known by its nickname *tiorba*, could keep up with the fashion for grand operatic spectacle and the *stile rappresentativo* of celebrated singers. In the shadow of the heights of the *seconda pratica* flourished another, more modest vocal genre that gave expression to less distinguished emotions. The guitar, as an exponent of oral traditions, seemed exactly the right instrument to support songs about amorous shepherds, satyrs, and nymphs; and within a short time, singing to guitar accompaniment became immensely popular.

The rise of the *battuto*, or strummed style, was decisive in the guitar's success. It enabled anyone to master the instrument in a perfectly functional way. Long before the turn of the century, a notational system had been developed, called *cifras* in Spain and *alfabeto* in Italy (literally the ABC, representing the most elementary principles of guitar playing), in which the chords to be played are indicated in shorthand (see ex. I.1). Once alfabeto notation had taken its definitive form, it was used virtually unaltered for more than a century. According to James Tyler there are more than 250 extant Italian sources with alfabeto, which justifies the supposition that there must have been many hundreds—if not thousands—of guitar players.[1] The very first instruction book for the five-course guitar, *Guitarra Española* by Joan Carles Amat from 1596, was reprinted (with some supplements) until the second decade of the nineteenth century, and the popular collections of simple dances of Pietro Millioni were also reissued time after time.

Example I.1. Alfabeto chart, Carlo Milanuzzi (1622).

Although chords were treated differently in later times (as repeated arpeggio patterns, like in much of the classical and romantic repertoire), the strummed style of playing quickly regained lost ground in the twentieth century. The accompaniments of modern-day pop songs are often not very different from what Benedetto Sanseverino did in 1622 (see ex. I.2a). The left-hand patterns have not changed at all, apart from the fact that the guitar had five courses, instead of six single strings. The same uniform repetitive rhythms are still in use today. In this "Aria detta del gran duca" only the text is given, because the melody was well known (and most amateurs were not able to read staff notation).[2]

In much the same way that jazz evolved from blues, guitar music in the seventeenth century developed an increasingly complex musical language that preserved the idiosyncrasy of battuto. Around 1630 Giovanni Paolo Foscarini started mixing battuto chords into lute-style (pizzicato) textures. An imaginative solo repertoire of toccatas, preludes, and dances arose, with all kinds of surprising idiomatic effects and capricious harmonic turns. Occasionally, the melodies are rather inchoate, more melodic scraps than anything definite. After the deaths of Girolamo Frescobaldi (1583–1643) and Johann Hieronymus Kapsberger (ca. 1580–1651) only a few works were published for other solo instruments, such as harpsichord or lute. In contrast, between 1630 and 1660 more than twenty-five guitar books with music in the new battuto-pizzicato style were printed in Italy. It was the time when Bartolotti published his little masterpieces for the guitar—the perfectly crafted polyphonic gigues and the fantastic preludes from the *Secondo libro* (ca. 1655)—in which instrumental technique is pushed to its utmost limits.[3]

In Italy, the economic downturn and the reascendency of the Catholic Church worsened prospects for instrumentalists and a secular genre like opera. Many Italian musicians moved to Paris, the new epicenter of the arts, to shelter under the wings of the powerful Cardinal Mazarin. From the end of

Example I.2. (a) Benedetto Sanseverino (1622), "Aria del Gran Duca." (b) For the most part, no more than four chords of the alfabeto are used: A (G major), B (C major), C (D major), and D (A minor).

(a)

the 1640s, Foscarini, Corbetta and, somewhat later, Bartolotti too, tried their fortunes there. The great success of the guitar in France, however, came only after 1670, and Foscarini and Bartolotti probably had to provide for themselves as theorbists. Then, in the space of no more than fifteen years (1671–86), eight books with guitar music were published.[4]

In Spain there was a true revival of instrumental music inspired by folklore, with the appearance of works by Gaspar Sanz (1674), Lucas Ruiz de Ribayaz (1677), and Francisco Guerau (1694). In Italy, the fiery love for the guitar was reduced to a simmer in the last decades of the century, with publications by local (Bolognese) figures such as Francesco Coriandoli (1670), Francesco Asioli (1674 and 1676), and finally Lodovico Roncalli (Bergamo, 1692). By 1700 the popularity of the guitar had passed its peak. The fact that two of the great monarchs of Europe, Louis XIV and Charles II, had a special liking for the instrument in their younger days could not prevent the guitar from losing ground. By the end of the century, the general public had turned its attention to newer instrumental genres. It was the time of virtuosic music for the violin by Archangelo Corelli and the mature works of the French harpsichord school of the Couperins and d'Anglebert.

In the first decades of the eighteenth century, there were some manuscripts that looked back to the Golden Age of the five-course guitar. Around 1730, Jean-Baptiste de Castillion collected works in mixed battuto-pizzicato style by seventeenth-century composers such as Francesco Corbetta, Robert de Visée, Gaspar Sanz (whom he called Gaspar Sanchez), Lelio Colista, and Nicolas Derosier. In *Passacalles y obras* by Santiago de Murcia, another manuscript from about the same date, we find compositions by Corbetta, Visée, and François Campion, next to works (notably the *passacalles*) that were probably written by de Murcia himself. Halfway through the eighteenth century, a transition to melodic playing on the five-course guitar emerged in the works of composers such as Giacomo Merchi (ca. 1730–after 1798). The battuto-pizzicato style was abandoned, and tablature was gradually replaced by staff notation. At about the same time, the instrument regained a role accompanying light songs (such as *vaudevilles* or *brunettes*) in galant style, with arpeggiated—rather than battuto—chords.

Renewed Interest

At present, solo works for five-course guitar from Italy are seldom performed. Countless arias with alfabeto are waiting to be rediscovered. There are various reasons why performers are still hesitant: unfamiliarity with certain aspects of performance and notation plays a role, coupled with uncertainty about what tuning was used. The most salient feature of this repertoire probably is the abundant use of strummed chords. To reach a historically informed reconstruction, it is necessary to understand how these were performed. The present appreciation of seventeenth-century guitar music is probably influenced quite heavily by the image of amateurism evoked by the strummed style. One could unjustly assume that this is no more than folkloric music, after all. An uncontrolled strumming of chords could seriously hinder a well-founded assessment of the battuto-pizzicato repertoire.

Another obstacle is the unusual notation. Two different systems are merged in the so-called mixed tablature: the chord alphabet for strummed harmonies and the Italian tablature (with numbers) for plucked sections. Alfabeto primarily provides information for the left hand, making clear which chord patterns are to be played at a given moment; however, it often tells you nothing about the actions of the right hand—for instance, whether to play strokes or arpeggios. In tablature (which predominated from c. 1630 onward), there is more information for the right hand, but what was *not* written becomes a source of confusion: notes to be played on open strings were often not indicated, to save labor and engraving costs. What we find on paper can often be understood only with the guitar in hand; the use of a variety of tunings, together with the sometimes cryptic notation of battuto chords, makes it almost impossible to form a proper idea of the music from the scores alone.

There were, in Italy, two different ways to string the guitar: one with bass strings (bourdons) on the fourth and fifth courses, and one without. We have to assume that there was a connection between the use of the instrument and its tuning. The stylistic development of the compositions cannot be treated as a separate issue, because the presence or absence of bass strings has far-reaching consequences; along with the manner of playing (battuto or pizzicato), it is decisive for the rendition of the counterpoint.

If we wish the baroque guitar to earn a position in the ranks of instruments with a solo repertoire appreciated by a broader public, a larger proportion of the repertoire must be played. The music from Italy in particular deserves more attention, if only for the sheer quantity of the compositions. Performance is indispensable for getting an idea of the quality of each individual work. Only on the basis of the audible results can we gain a better understanding of the musical language of the seventeenth-century guitarists, and only thus may we discover the true gems of the repertoire. It is the aim of this book to contribute to the understanding of how the use of battuto and pizzicato affected the development, performance, and notation of seventeenth-century guitar music.

The first part of this book will shed light on the historical background of the guitar. The social position of the instrument can be pictured from sources such as the treatises of Vincenzo Giustiniani (1629) and Pierre Trichet (1640) and reports of the performances of famous singers and players. The diary of Samuel Pepys and the highly informative and diverting letters of Constantijn Huygens help illustrate the mixed reception of the guitar in educated circles. In the middle section we will take a closer look at the role of the instrument in accompanying the voice, as well as the development of the style of the Italian solo repertoire. The final section will review the theoretical issues of the tuning and basso continuo and trace the clues that can lead to a better understanding of a peculiar, idiosyncratic harmonic idiom, made even more obscure by a sometimes inaccurate notation. This section considers contemporary observations on repertoire, tuning, and performance from prefaces to seventeenth-century guitar books and other relevant sources.

Recent publications on the five-course guitar very often make reference to *The Early Guitar* (1980) by James Tyler. A second monumental handbook by the same author, *The Guitar and Its Music*, was published in 2002. Tyler has treated the history of the instrument in a thorough and comprehensive manner, with a wealth of details. This book, however, aims to follow the more modest path of just one idea: the birth of the battuto-pizzicato repertoire, seen from the perspective of emancipation from the boundaries of the strummed style. Battuto has been a decisive factor since its earliest days. For a long time, the instrument's main function was to accompany lighter vocal genres and dance, as well as theatrical performances of the commedia dell'arte and opera. This had a great influence on the style of playing and the tuning and on how chord inversions and voice leading were treated.

Various aspects of the repertoire have been researched since the 1970s, and this book owes much to the work of a number of writers. Richard Hudson studied the diffusion of forms that have their origins in guitar music—such as the chaconne, sarabande, and passacaglia—in the repertoire of the guitar and other instruments.[5] To understand the enormous popularity of the guitar, it is important to realize how easy it is to play these dances. Their accessibility can be compared to that of certain styles of modern pop or dance music. Richard d'Arcambal Jensen (1980) has described the guitar technique and performance practice of the battuto repertoire in the first half of the seventeenth century. We will explore in more depth the shaping of the accompaniment in battuto, with regard to the position of the bass, and the permanence of battuto as a determining structural principle in the later developments, which set the guitar apart from the lute.

The guitar has been employed as an instrument of accompaniment in different ways. Initially there were only alfabeto chord symbols, included with a great many songs. Despite the simplicity of this notation, it is not always entirely clear how justice can be done to the style of the early baroque. Today we often hear a form of battuto executed as a percussive strumming, with right-hand patterns that seem to come from folk-rock or flamenco. It seems as if the prominent battuto element obscures our view of how things were four hundred years ago. Besides, many aspects of music changed considerably as time went on, and it certainly makes sense to distinguish between the styles of accompaniment of different periods, since figured-bass realizations in treatises from the second half of the seventeenth century bear a strong resemblance to the mature battuto-pizzicato style of the contemporaneous solo repertoire.

Nina Treadwell (1995) mapped out the role of the instrument in the accompaniment of solo arias at that time.[6] She concluded that the guitar was frequently used on its own, without another instrument to provide a true bass. But it was used mostly for the lighter, strophic, dance-like songs; more dramatic arias were usually accompanied by either the chitarrone or the harpsichord.

Robert Strizich (1981) discussed the use of the guitar as a basso continuo instrument at a time when this was still unexplored territory.[7] He was one of the first to point out the problem of the position of the bass in relation to chord strumming. He also drew attention to harmonic conflicts caused by the use of alfabeto chords, specifically in the works of Hieronymus Kapsberger. Recent research by Alexander Dean (2009) shows that there were different strategies in different genres for finding appropriate chords to a song. The guitar was used in traditional dance songs from the late sixteenth century with standard harmonic progressions, but there are also collections of three-voice (polyphonic) *villanelle* like Kapsberger's, where an accompaniment with simple alfabeto chords is often problematic. And finally there are the later collections of solo songs, from the 1620s and '30s, in which the harmonic language became more robust, and alfabeto settled into a more comfortable place.[8]

The social (and even political) backgrounds of the song repertoire with alfabeto are reviewed in a dissertation by Cory Michael Gavito (2006).[9] Gavito makes it clear that singing to a guitar happened on a large scale, and was fashionable among all levels of society. This way of music making was accessible to almost everyone, and the guitar was seen as a perfectly natural and authentic vehicle of expression; however, the way it was used in this repertoire is in conflict with contemporary theoretical premises of counterpoint and mode.

The fact that the bass (as an integral part of the composition) is in many cases completely neglected is often seen as proof of a trivial musical practice. Gavito argues that the reach of this repertoire—both geographically and socially—must not be underestimated, notwithstanding the theoretical objections one could have to editions where the bass line is left out, considering the broad involvement with this movement in even the most educated circles. Obviously, it was perfectly possible for them to relish the most refined musical utterances, such as opera and polyphonic madrigals, and at the same time idealize the intuitive approach of the music of shepherds and artisans living in an unspoiled, Arcadian world.

Differing opinions have been put forward in books and journals on the subject of the stringing of the five-course guitar. More specifically, the presence of bourdons on the fourth and the fifth courses has been subject to dispute, from the moment Sylvia Murphy's groundbreaking article "The Tuning of the Five-Course Guitar" appeared in the in *The Galpin Society Journal* (1970).[10] Many arguments have been presented, and widely divergent conclusions reached. We will look into this important issue, and follow the line of thought of some of the contributors.

Finally, we will touch on the distinctly national developments. Nowadays Spanish composers such as Sanz and Murcia get much more attention than the Italians. This is probably because of the accessibility of their music. Spanish works are predominantly in *punteado* (pizzicato). The music, accurately notated in tablature, leaves the performer in no doubt as to its execution, in contrast to the mixed tablature of the Italian battuto-pizzicato style. The difference between Italy on the one hand and Spain and France on the other is that in the former there was a great flowering of alfabeto. A considerable number of books with dances were published there, first in alfabeto and later in the mixed style. In Spain, very little music was published during the seventeenth century; in France the rise did not occur before 1670. For this reason, the maturation of the typical battuto-pizzicato style took place almost exclusively in Italy. In France, the influence of the Italian virtuosi—and of Francesco Corbetta in particular—was so pervasive that we can safely say that Robert de Visée could not possibly have written his well-known suites had he not known Corbetta's work.

Iconography, an Aural Tradition Portrayed

The guitar has always been a rewarding subject for the visual arts, and we can learn much from the ways in which it has been depicted. Examining the iconography of the guitar in the seventeenth century, a comparison with the lute is unavoidable. One important difference is that the five-course guitar does not turn up before 1600, by which time the lute already had a respectable history as an attribute of angels and gods in biblical and mythological scenes. We hardly ever encounter guitars, other than the noble vihuela in Spain, in such contexts. In Italy the rise of the guitar can be followed step by step, beginning with drawings and engravings of characters from the commedia dell'arte. There are the amusing pictures by Jacques Callot from Nancy, who published his *Balli di Sfessania* circa 1621 in Florence, and Carnival scenes by Sebastian Vrancx.[11] Engraved portraits of well-known guitarists (Foscarini, Pesori, Bartolotti, Corbetta, and Granata) were included in their books of guitar music. Only few Italian guitar paintings from the beginning of the century have been preserved, such as *The Concert* (Bologna, c. 1615) by Leonello Spada.[12] The fact that the guitar was rarely depicted in early-seventeenth-century paintings, in spite of its great popularity, probably confirms the lesser status of the instrument; unlike the lute, the guitar was seldom to be seen in the hands of aristocrats or members of the higher classes. This would change over the years.

Several different schools of painters from the Low Countries played an important role in the iconography of the guitar. First, there were those artists who traveled to Rome in the 1620s to study the Italian style, like Theodoor Rombouts from Antwerp (fig. I.1) and Gerrit van Honthorst from Utrecht. Under the influence of Caravaggio's *chiaroscuro*, they started to paint Italianate scenes in which the newly fashionable Spanish guitar makes an occasional appearance. Later, from the 1640s onward, depictions of everyday folk with guitars—peasants and shepherds playing in public houses or in the open air—experienced a surge in demand. These imaginary rustic scenes were painted frequently by Antwerp masters like David Teniers III, Joos van Craesbeeck, and David Rijckaert. Only in the second half of the seventeenth century did Flemish artists create the genre of portraits of "dames de qualité" playing the guitar. An early example of the instrument in the company of wealthy citizens is the *Family Group by a Fountain* by the Flemish master Gonzales Coques, from about 1655, in which the elegant daughter of the house is playing the guitar.[13] Group portraits by Coques and others show that the guitar became increasingly accepted in higher circles, as well. The difficult question is what music all these peasants, shepherds and young ladies played, since musical sources from the Low Countries are very rare. Only Corbetta's book of 1648—in Italian mixed tablature dedicated to Archduke Leopold Wilhelm of Austria—was published in Brussels. The dedicatee was the governor of the Spanish Netherlands from 1646 to 1656; as an important patron of the arts, he assembled a great collection of Dutch and Italian paintings.

During the Golden Age of the Dutch Republic, a few portraits of ladies (mostly young) with guitars were produced by Johannes Vermeer and Caspar Netscher. Only one Dutch manuscript with guitar music, belonging to Isabel van Langhenhove, has been preserved.[14] Around 1690, Nicolas Derosier published one of his books in Amsterdam. Besides the guitar, the small wire-strung four-course cittern was much in use for accompaniment. A considerable number of paintings from the middle part of the century, by Pieter de

Hooch, Gabriel Metsu, Cesar van Everdingen, and Johannes Vermeer, represent wealthy young women with this small instrument. In higher circles, there was a lively interest in the cittern, which was used in chordal song accompaniment and was strummed like the guitar (sometimes with a quill). The cittern is also often depicted in the hands of peasants, or hanging on the walls of public houses and brothels. In the first decades of the seventeenth century, there were printed collections of songs with accompaniment for cittern, now considered lost. The only book to have been preserved is the *Nederlandtsche gedenck-clanck* from 1626 by Adriaen Valerius.[15] The absence of later sources is an indication of its waning popularity. It is not entirely clear if the guitar ousted the cittern in the Netherlands, as it seems to have replaced both the lute and the cittern in England. John Playford complained about this state of affairs in the preface to his *Musick's Delight on the Cittern* (1666). Only in France did the lute manage to keep a firm position during the whole of the seventeenth century, with an extensive solo repertoire of very high quality.

In Italy the lute gradually became less common as an instrument of popular music. During the sixteenth century, there were lutes in many commedia dell'arte scenes, but after 1600 we consistently see guitars in pictures of Scapino, Buffetto, and Scaramouche. In this genre, the guitar took over completely from the lute. In a more serious context, however, the lute is frequently seen accompanying singers, or as part of an instrumental ensemble. Many people also sang to the guitar, as the open mouths and the music books show, but only very seldom is the guitar depicted being played with other instruments, as it is in a company of *putti* around the portrait of Francesco Corbetta that appears in his book of 1648. This supernatural gathering is an idealized one, and it is doubtful if such a representation conformed in any way to performance practice in the real world. In paintings with a romanticized pastoral subject matter, a genre which was very much in demand, the guitar is sometimes shown in duet with a duct flute.[16] It is quite likely that the performers in these paintings were understood to be playing the popular dance standards of the time, possibly of Italian or Spanish provenance, with the guitar providing the battuto chords.

There are remarkably few images in which the guitar and the lute are actually played at the same time. In some scenes (by Theodoor Rombouts and Evaristo Baschenis, for instance), the lute symbolically lies face down on the table while the guitar is being played. Iconography suggests that the two instruments did not have a repertoire in common. It is often assumed that there were continuo groups consisting of guitars and chitarrones or theorbos, but there is little to support this with evidence from the visual arts. *The Music Lesson* by Theodoor Rombouts (fig. I.1) is particularly intriguing in this respect, because at the time this painting was created, guitarists did not play from tablature, just as lutenists did not play from alfabeto. Yet most of the alfabeto (battuto) solo repertoire consists of popular dances that had been the backbone of the lute

Figure I.1. Theodoor Rombouts (1597–1637), *The Music Lesson*. Perhaps the players are having a discussion about battuto and pizzicato. Bayerische Staatsgemäldesammlungen. © bpk, Berlin.

repertoire of the last part of the sixteenth century. Rombouts's picture shows how players of the two instruments, the ancient lute and the new guitar, may have communicated, with a music book on the table as central subject. But, given that the tunings of the two instruments are different, if the music were notated in lute tablature, it would be difficult for the guitarist to decipher.

On a symbolic level, the lute often represented harmony (musical harmony, interpersonal harmony, but also the *harmonia mundi* or the music of the spheres),[17] whereas the guitar suggested frivolity, amusement, or worldly pleasures. Later, though, the guitar became an emblem of amateur artistry in the domestic sphere, portrayed in the hands of virtuous young ladies in paintings from the Netherlands, France, and England. By around 1700 the guitar had taken the place of the "old-fashioned" lute. Both are intimate solo instruments, in contrast to the more detached harpsichord. Stringed and wind instruments presume ensemble playing and a more extrovert performance, which drastically disrupt the tranquillity of the representation in portraits. Now that we have seen a first glimpse of the guitar (see also figs. 2.1, 2.2, and 6.2a), in the next chapters we will turn our attention to the guitarist and his musical world.

Chapter One

The Rise of the Five-Course Guitar in Spain and Italy, 1580–1630

The Emergence of the Rasgueado Style

Before 1600, the guitar was not always used for strumming. When Juan Bermudo published his *Declaración de instrumentos musicales* in 1555, there were two different tunings of the four-course guitar: the old (*temple viejo*) and the new (*temple nuevo*) tuning.[1] According to Bermudo, the old tuning was adequate for "romances viejos" and "musica golpeada"—simple homophonic music. The fourth course was tuned a fifth below the third, instead of the usual fourth, and was probably used to produce the continuous fifth of a bourdon or drone, but there are no examples left of such a repertoire for the four-course guitar.[2] The new tuning, in which the first four courses were tuned like those of the later five-course guitar, was used in complex polyphonic *fantasías* by Alonso Mudarra and Miguel de Fuenllana; the change of the tuning of the fourth course may have prompted them to compose for the guitar. At about the same time in France, several composers began to write for the instrument. Bermudo described the various tunings of the vihuela and also that of the five-course guitar (with the intervals fourth–fourth–major third–fourth).[3] A tuning with the same intervallic structure was used in Fuenllana's *Orphenica lyra* (1554), in music for the *vihuela de cinco ordenes*, a five-course vihuela. According to Bermudo, however, there was not much difference between the two instruments, apart from the size and (presumably) the pitch at which they were tuned.

Early in the sixteenth century, a tendency developed toward a more homophonic style of writing, in genres like *chanson* and *romance*, which were very popular in Spain. This is reflected in the vihuela works (in dances and homorhythmic song accompaniments) of composers such as Luis Milan and Esteban Daza. A gradual move away from polyphony toward a more vertical, harmonic style becomes apparent.[4]

At some point in the second half of the sixteenth century (or perhaps even earlier), guitarists from Spain began to accompany vocal music, making use of the *rasgueado* (battuto) technique. In the performance of music from an oral tradition especially, there is a need for an effective style of accompaniment that can be realized without too much consideration of theoretical principles. In his *Arte poetica en romance castellano* (Alcala de Henares, 1580) Sanchez de Lima observes: "Everything that is usually sung and played nowadays is in the strummed fashion and nothing is sung or played with understanding."[5] By this time, evidently, there had been a great increase in the use of rasgueado.

The new rasgueado style was marked by a careless approach to chord inversion and voice leading, as illustrated by the following anecdote from Joan Carles y Amat's *Guitarra española*:

> I would like to tell you what happened to me with some Guitarists, who pretended to be the best of Spain. They spoke freely (there were four of them) and they knew very well that I had this method of playing the guitar with every song. One night we met and one of them said with due respect: "My friend, we have heard that you know a wonderful art with which you can quickly arrange any song on the guitar." (And they did that to make fun of me, as they confessed afterwards.) "My friends and I, we beg you to show us how you do that, as we wish to use your method ourselves. If you can do that, we will be satisfied and very happy and we will be pleased to follow your example." I could read them like a book, smelling several rats, but without showing my suspicions I replied: "Gentlemen, the way I do this is of little importance and showing it to you is as a grain of mustard next to a great mountainside. May you stay with your riches and I in my misery." Not satisfied with my answer, they asked me again and I said that it was not worthwhile showing them. Finally they said: "My friend, this system that you use, maybe it can be used for three voices, but we are sure that for more voices it is false and impossible. Only to take the opportunity of finding that out we have come here." Without showing any embarrassment, I answered: "Gentlemen, the truth is that my method only consists of a very small table that I invented (although some have copied it) and with it you can arrange not only three, but four, five, six or as many parts for the guitar as you wish. And to show you that what I say is true, let us go wherever you wish to try it out, so that you will see." They were contented, thinking that it was a good occasion to make fun of me. We went to the place of one of them, who was a student of the Arts, and they gave me some pages with music of Prenestina [Palestrina] for five voices. I added ciphers to all the pieces and they handed me a guitar and each began to sing his part, together with the instrument and they saw that what I promised was true: they admired greatly what I had done, looking at each other with satisfaction. Thanks to our attempt, made easy by the table, we succeeded in what many had considered to be impossible.[6]

Obviously, the guitar was used here as the lute was in Italy, for accompaniment in a variety of vocal genres. Although lutenists sometimes wrote polyphonic intabulations of multipart scores for their own use, guitarists did not tend to; so Amat used a theoretical device (a table) for distilling the harmony from the bass and the other parts of the polyphonic texture.

Joan Carles y Amat (ca. 1572–1642), today simply called Amat (the family name of his mother), was an educated man in the best humanistic tradition. He studied medicine at the University of Valencia and settled again in his birthplace, Monistrol, in the shadow of Montserrat, not far from Barcelona. Apart from his instruction book for the guitar, which he published immediately after his university studies "because many of his friends asked for it"[7] (and which contains some good ideas about music theory), he wrote on other scholarly subjects and may have been the author of the *Entremés de la guitarra*, the "comedy of the guitar." He collected four hundred Catalan aphorisms in a little book that was used well into the nineteenth century in the schools of his province.[8] Amat was elected mayor of his village shortly before his death in 1642. In the following passage, he explains with self-deprecating humor his reasons for publishing his book, as well as describing the Spanish national character and the good-natured atmosphere of everyday amateurism surrounding the guitar in his time:

> The choleric temperament of Spain has caused me to make this little work see the light of day, as I noticed that no one here is phlegmatic enough to teach the art of playing the guitar. Those who desire instruction should not be surprised if after three days their masters are already tired of teaching them, because this choleric temperament weighs so heavily upon all Spaniards that anything we undertake, no matter how brief, seems interminable to us. Since there has been no author in this country who has ever written a treatise about it (as far as I know), I decided to write about the way to tune and how to play rasgueado on the five-course guitar—called *Española* because it is loved in this country more than anywhere else—and about the method to arrange any song for it. Let it serve as a teacher, so that its students will not suffer the misery that our humor causes.[9]

What was the cause and what the effect? Should the addition of the fifth course be seen as a matter of natural evolution, or did some players realize that a fifth course would create new resources for chordal rasgueado accompaniment? A parallel can be drawn with the origins of the chitarrone in Italy: at about the same time, the singer Antonio Naldi started looking for ways to improve the lute to make it better suited for accompaniment on the stage. To increase the range and tonal volume, luthiers increased the string length of the lute, which necessitated a re-entrant tuning of the highest two strings.[10] To make a chordal reduction of intabulations (as Amat did) or accompaniments to dance songs, it is convenient to have an instrument with more than four courses, as the limited range of a four-course guitar often leads to incomplete harmonies. When accompanying a singer, it is better to have the lower register of the fifth course at hand. The pitch of the first course (e′) of the guitar allows for a considerably greater string length than the g′ of the common vihuela, which helps to increase the volume of the tone. If the first string of the five-course guitar is tuned to d′, as was sometimes done, the fifth course is at the same pitch (G) as the lowest bass of the common vihuela.

One reason the vihuela is unfit for strumming is that its tuning does not allow many chords in first position, involving open strings. The first seven chords of guitar alfabeto, plus the I, O, and P chords, all need no more than three fingers, while frequent harmonies (like E, A, or F, both major and minor) are impossible to play without *barre* chords on a six-course instrument tuned in G, at least if we wish to include all courses. It raises the problem of strumming over a limited number of strings, introducing theoretical difficulties for the player.

It is not inconceivable that the vihuela was used by some players as an instrument of basso continuo, like the lute in Italy, during the first decades of the seventeenth century. After 1600, it is sometimes mentioned as an instrument of accompaniment, but tablatures cannot be found. If it was not strummed like the guitar, then maybe intavolations of polyphonic vocal compositions were played. Another possibility is that harmonies ("middle parts") were added to the bass line, as an early form of basso continuo accompaniment—sometimes referred to as pseudo-monody—to a solo voice.[11]

Nicolao Doizi de Velasco (1640) and Gaspar Sanz (1674) have ascribed the addition of the fifth course of the guitar to the poet, singer, and organist Vicente Espinel (1550–1624).[12] In the preface of his *Nuevo modo de cifra para tañer la guitarra*, the Portuguese Doizi de Velasco tells that he had known Espinel in Madrid. In his great prose dialogue *La Dorotea* (1632), Lope de Vega has one of his characters fulminate: "May God forgive Vicente Espinel, who has brought us that new [verse] and the five strings of the guitar, so that the old noble instruments are forgotten, as well as the old dances, with these wild gesticulations and lascivious movements of the [new] *chaconas*, which are so offensive to the virtue, the chastity, and the respectable silence of the ladies."[13] Although there existed a five-course guitar at the time that Bermudo published his *Declaración*, we can deduce from this passage that the great popularity of the instrument only came later, and possibly was related to certain literary circles in the Spanish capital. Espinel garnered a lot of praise for his singing and his playing of his "famosa lira" (the guitar was represented as the lyre with which Orpheus accompanied himself). Lucrecio Leonardo de Argensola, secretary to the count of Villahermosa, dedicated a sonnet to Espinel in which he expressed his admiration.

> No one doubts he could make hell
> suspend its torments and wrath
> with the sweet sounds of his famous lyre.[14]

It is not very likely that Espinel was responsible for the addition of an extra course to the guitar, but from a great number of sources it appears that he was in the forefront of using the five-course guitar as an instrument of accompaniment. The great fame he won doing that probably furthered the diffusion of this practice considerably.

The success of the *passacalle* and notably the *chacona* (originally a dance from the New World, according to Cervantes and Lope de Vega) had much to do with the accessibility of rasgueado. But not everyone was enthusiastic about this innovation. Sebastián de Covarrubias deplored the loss of the noble art of vihuela playing and the "invention" of the guitar:

> Until now, this instrument was highly valued and attracted excellent musicians, but since the guitar was invented, very few devote themselves to the study of the vihuela. This has been a great loss, because all kinds of music were played on it, whereas the guitar is no more than a cowbell, so easy to play, especially in rasgueado, that there is not a stableboy who is not a musician on the guitar.[15]

Secular Music from Spain

The genre of songs with guitar accompaniment probably came into use first in Spain and then in Italy. In Italy, a musical revolution took place; with the rise of the *stile rappresentativo* (the new dramatic style of opera), other vocal genres, like the solo madrigal and aria, also gained importance. The Spanish clung to a more traditional musical idiom, firmly linked to vernacular music, which often harked back to preexisting melodies and variations on bass patterns like *la romanesca*, *la folia*, the *passamezzo antico*, and the *passamezzo moderno*. Not much has been preserved of the early repertoire of Spanish songs with guitar. Luis de Briçeño's book of 1626 (published in Paris)—with only song texts, chord symbols, and the rhythm of the accompaniment—presupposes well-known melodies, orally transmitted.[16] In both countries, the guitar enjoyed a growing interest; and initially, the application of rasgueado and battuto was the same in both. But later, as we will see, the national practices began to diverge.

In the first half of the seventeenth century, vocal works were seldom, if ever, printed with basso continuo parts in Spain—in contrast to Italy, where song collections normally were edited in that way.[17] The increasing independence of harmony, to which the practice of basso continuo leads, presumably contributed to a greater liberty in the choice of alfabeto chords in the Italian repertoire. Theorbists in particular were involved in the accompaniment of vocal genres in the new style, and many played the guitar as their second instrument. Italian players like Foscarini, Pellegrini, and Bartolotti thus came into contact with a progressive harmonic language, and this exerted an influence on their guitar compositions. The *chaconas, villanos, folias, vacas* and other dance songs from Spain (see ex. 1.1), on the contrary, make use of stock progressions that are more or less fixed.

The innovations in the field of performance and the refined expression of the seconda pratica did not, in general, take root in Spain. Within the all-powerful Church, polyphony remained part of the liturgy, and there was not much development in secular music, either, which was the domain of the guitar. While the courts in Italy played an important part in creating favorable conditions for musical inventiveness, the conservative, centralistic line of the Habsburg dynasty (and, in imitation, the *Grandes de España*), with its strong emphasis on frugality and religious severity, may have hampered new artistic impulses. In Italy, patronage of the arts flourished; local princes added lustre to their power with exuberant theatrical performances; and they were surrounded by musicians (singers, instrumentalists, and composers), artists, and poets. Spain, in contrast, did not have a strong civic identity, and there was not much of a middle class. A career in the army or the Church was held in higher esteem than doing business or plying a trade. The permanent state of war, on many fronts, was the reason the great influx of silver from the New World did not bring the country much prosperity. When Philip II died in 1598, he left a debt of 100 million ducats. The seventeenth century brought increasing poverty; bad governance and military failures dragged the nation into a lasting state of inertia and stagnation.

Composers could not find work under those circumstances: almost no music was published in Spain during a period when the production of printed music in Florence, Rome, and Venice reached unprecedented heights. In a country of soldiers and priests, a secular genre like the opera simply could not prosper. Italy, very differently, was fragmented into small states and basked in the glory of an idealized classical antiquity. Here ancient philosophy and literature were revitalized under the influence of humanism, and the gods and goddesses of Greek and Roman mythology made a triumphant return. In Spain the inspiration came either from biblical themes or from satirical/realistic treatments of subjects such as the wanderings of roguish heroes and the grandeur and misery of empire. It was the time of picaresque novels by Lope de Vega, Vicente

Example 1.1. Luis de Briceño (1626), fol. 6r, "Gran Chacona."

LA GRAN CHACONA EN ÇIFRA

V 3 2 5 2 3 2 5 2
Ida vida. vida bona. vida bamonos a chacona.

3 2 5 6 4 2 3 2 5 2
Vida vida. vidita vida. vida bamonos a castilla.

ROMANÇE DE LA CHACONA.

Espinel, and Miguel de Cervantes. It is telling that Don Quixote identified himself with the faded romanticism of the knight errant. Spanish arts were first and foremost literary, and there was more interest in comedy than in a novel musical genre like opera.[18]

Later in the seventeenth century, however, an original Spanish genre of music theater, the zarzuela, came into existence, with largely conservative music, indebted to popular culture. According to Louise Stein, the extravagances of the theatrical *stile recitativo*, the dramatic style that takes a central place in Italian opera, hardly grew to any maturity in Spain. A typical Spanish variant was developed instead, the *recitado*, remaining close to the moderate, traditional style of the early *romances*:

> The antecedents for *recitado* come forth very clearly in the late sixteenth century, in the performance practices of the Spanish *romances*, which belonged to a large, constantly circulating, orally transmitted repertory that was at once "high" courtly music, preserved in written polyphonic songbooks and popular music performed by everyone from the skilled improviser to the amateur at home and from street musicians to professional actors and actresses. In the latter mode of performance, the *romances* were declaimed or recited with simple melodies to occasionally polyphonic but mostly chordal accompaniments played on the *vihuela* and, later, on the Spanish guitar.[19]

It is worth noticing that all known accompaniments on the vihuela are contrapuntal, with plucked textures and often a homophonic character. In contrast, not one plucked chordal accompaniment for the guitar has come down to us from the first half of the seventeenth century.

The guitar was used so much for accompanying that in the *Entremés del rufián viudo*, a comedy by Cervantes, there is a stage direction for two musicians to enter "sin guitarras"—without guitars. The instrument, used for song and dance in Golden Age Spanish drama, especially in the successful pastoral intermezzi, gained ever more prestige in musical life. We even encounter the guitar in important court performances, together with the harp or keyboard instruments (and less often the lute and theorbo). The theorbo, which had been linked from the beginning with vocal monody, occupied only a marginal place in the musical world of early seventeenth-century Spain. The instrument was mainly used by a few professional musicians, such as Juan Blas de Castro and Filippo Piccinini, at court.[20]

"Cantare alla Spagniuola"

On the face of it, it may seem as if there was a clash of the high culture of Renaissance polyphony with the popular song tradition. In Italy, a heated debate arose between the champions of innovation and theoreticians who wished to hold on to established rules that were seen as an expression of musical perfection.[21] As happens often in musical history, though, genres that first have been considered to be trivial and of little value may reinvigorate tradition. In his *Dialogo della musica antica, et della moderna* (1580) Vincenzo Galilei, a lutenist-composer and theorist who formed part of the Florentine Camerata, stood up for music for one voice, accompanied by simple harmonies, in contrast to the mannered polyphonic style. Only when performed like this could the text be fully understood. According to Galilei, this is done best with the accompaniment of a plucked instrument: "Singing in unison was introduced . . . after the use of consonances and this is when one sings solo to the instrument, of which many strings are struck, among which is the part of him who sings at the same time, arranged so that between them they produce diverse consonances."[22]

One of the main reasons to support the voice with just one instrument is probably that the singer can accompany himself, voice and instrument coinciding perfectly, whereas an accompaniment by more instruments (let alone with percussion) forces the singer to adapt to the ensemble. The guitar seems admirably suited to Galilei's purpose, as the way the instrument was played made it possible to concentrate primarily on the poetry sung. On the other hand, we can assume that for a theorist like Galilei, the coherence of bass and treble was still a fundamental principle, while the disregard of the bass was characteristic of the guitar in this period.[23]

The fashion for singing *villanelle* or *canzonette* to the guitar probably emerged in the south, first in the Kingdom of Naples, which was under Spanish rule, and only later in Rome and Florence. In the last quarter of the sixteenth century, Italian commedia dell'arte troupes visited Spain; a 1581 contract in Madrid recorded that two local musicians were hired to play the guitar and sing in the Castillian manner, which was probably unknown in Italy at that time.[24] Very soon the guitar gained a permanent place on the expanding international stage of commedia.

In his book about musical life at the court of Cardinal Montalto in Rome, John Walter Hill gives us an insight into the evolution of monody and the broad acceptance of the guitar in the highest circles of that city around 1600.[25] In the first printed guitar book from Italy, *Nuova inventione d'intavolatura*, published in Florence in 1606, Girolamo Montesardo speaks of "sonare, e cantare alla Spagniuola," playing and singing in the Spanish style.[26] A real craze for everything Spanish arose, for which there was a fertile soil in the second half of the sixteenth century, particularly in Rome and Florence. In certain regions of the Apennine Peninsula, the Kingdom of Naples, and Milan, the political orientation was strongly Spanish, and the Medici, the Grand Dukes of Tuscany, had close political and family ties with the house of the Habsburgs. Spanish song and dance found a place in the musical performances and spectacular events they organized. As late as 1628, Vincenzo Giustiniani could describe in his *Discorso sopra la musica* that Italy preferred Spanish clothing over every other. About the change of customs in vocal music, he remarked:

> Having abandoned the past style, which was quite rough, and also the excessive passage work with which it was ornamented, they now cultivate, for the most part, a recitative style embellished by *grazia* and by ornaments appropriate to the conceit, along with an occasional melismatic passage drawn out with judgment and articulation and with appropriate and varied consonances, marking the end of each period, within which the composers of today are [otherwise] apt to produce boredom with excessive and frequent cadences. Above all, they make the words well understood, applying to each syllable a note now soft, now loud, now slow and now fast, demonstrating with their face and in their gestures the conceit that is sung, but with moderation and not excessively. And one voice, or at most, three voices sing to the accompaniment of one's own instrument: a theorbo, guitar, harpsichord, or organ, according to the circumstances. Furthermore, within this style there has been introduced singing *alla Spagnola* or *all'Italiana*, similar to the foregoing but with more artifice and ornament, as much in Rome as in Naples and Genoa, with the invention of new *arie* and of new ornaments, for which composers strive, for instance in Rome the German theorbo player named Johann Hieronymus [Kapsberger].[27]

Traditional *romances* (ballads) and *villancicos*, with their largely syllabic text-setting and short musical phrases, relatively untouched by the advance of melodic embellishment of the *stile recitativo*, seem to ask for a moderate approach which, probably, was the distinctive feature of Spanish performance.[28] The guitar played a central role in the rapid emergence of a comparable song repertoire in Italy, which was similarly pervaded by a sense of melancholy and a longing for a lost natural world, even though it used newly composed melodies and harmonies different from the traditional, endlessly recurring chord progressions of Spanish dance. But the idiosyncracy of the battuto style kept the *chitarra spagnuola* somewhat aloof from the musical mainstream, which perhaps even contributed to a desired image of otherness.

Songs with Alfabeto

Chordal (alfabeto) guitar accompaniment for the voice is not based on the rules of counterpoint, like basso continuo on other instruments, yet these practices share similarities. A figured (or unfigured) bass can also be used—certainly on a theorbo—to decipher the chords and standard cadences one has to play. Applied like that, it is not really the foundation for extemporizing truly independent "middle voices," although it is sometimes presented as such in theoretical observations. To be able to realize an accompaniment in parts, a player would need a sound theoretical knowledge—which few amateurs would have had.

For the performance of basso continuo, harmonic instruments like organ, harpsichord, lute, and theorbo seem to have had their own sets of rules. Lodovico Viadana, for example, wrote in 1602 that the organ is never obliged to avoid subsequent fifths or octaves in an accompaniment.[29] While on other instruments the accompaniment was essentially contrapuntal, guitarists probably often just played harmonies that sounded plausible in combination with a melody. The alfabeto of the guitar seems consistently to shun all rules of counterpoint. Having obligations to a bass is not a very comfortable situation for a guitarist to be in, so a new method was invented. The instructions for alfabeto, to be found in many song collections, always begin with a chart of chords to accompany a *scala per B quadro* and a *scala per B molle* (see ex. 3.3). These charts served one purpose only: to provide an efficient overview of chords compatible with each bass note.[30] It goes without saying that a modest system like this, not observing the interdependence of the different voices, does not always result in a proper harmonization of the melody. We will see examples of that in chapter 3. Yet, there are interesting implications for the expanding idea of tonality behind this highly pragmatic modus operandi.[31] These "scale triads" of alfabeto accompaniment did most likely function as an early form of tonality based on scale degrees, a first step on the way to the later "rule of the octave."

It is telling that many composers did not let formal objections stand in the way and had their collections of solo arias edited with alfabeto. Clearly, the advantage of an easily realizable accompaniment outweighed the sin of abandoning theoretical principles, at least within this genre. It is not for nothing that battuto experienced an enormous rise in Italy and that distinguished composers, including Marini, D'India, Pesenti, Grandi, Landi, and Kapsberger, became involved with it. In some years between 1620 and 1640, more than half of the editions of secular music published consisted of collections with arias, or *villanelle*, in which alfabeto was included.[32] It seems as if, the yoke of the contrapuntal theory of dissonance treatment having been lifted, composers and publishers celebrated with a flood of songs that required no more than the slight support of chords produced by an instrument that happened to be available. Often, that would have been the practical chitarra spagnuola, found in many a household. Less frequently, it would have been the theorbo, an instrument more difficult to play (and more costly), reserved for a smaller group of professionals and educated amateurs. In Vicenzo Giustiniani's *Discorso* we can read about the rise of the theorbo and the guitar at the expense of the lute:

> Playing the Lute was also much practiced in past times: but this instrument has been almost entirely abandoned since the Theorbo has been introduced. It, being more suitable for singing even moderately well and with a poor

voice, has been eagerly accepted generally in order to avoid the great amount of labour needed to learn to play the Lute well. At the same time the Spanish Guitar was introduced throughout Italy, especially in Naples. Together with the Theorbo, it appears to have conspired to banish the Lute altogether and it has almost succeeded; just as the mode of dressing *alla Spagnola* in Italy prevails over all the other fashions.[33]

In cities like Rome and Venice, there developed a lively trade of collections of songs with alfabeto. Many of these were cheap editions with only text and chord letters. Perhaps the best known were those of Remigio Romano, who published at least four of such collections, all of which were reprinted more than once.[34] Such songs circulated in all kinds of guises, printed and in manuscript (text only; text and alfabeto; melody in staff notation with basso continuo, with or without alfabeto). The many concordances of melodies or texts that appear in different anthologies show that there was a broad repertoire of popular songs. Arrangements of arias by respected composers were also included, often without being edited. Anonymous poetic texts were used, probably often written by the composer himself. From Cory Michael Gavito's research, it is evident that composers sometimes borrowed texts (or even just single lines) for their own songs.[35] A lively practice of oral transmission must be assumed, of texts and (newly composed) melodies dressed up in different harmonizations, comparable to how people nowadays like to think up their own easy-to-play or simplified guitar chord progressions to hit songs. Silke Leopold remarks:

> Within a few years solo song had developed from being an intellectual game played by esoteric circles into a broad movement. On the way, some of its compositional refinement was lost, but much in the way of formal completeness and melodic agility was gained. The new melodies had to be pleasant, clearly structured, and logically built, so that they were easy to remember. Now, anything that was "catchy" had a chance of survival, even without being preserved on paper.[36]

Praetorius in 1619 defined the aria as "eine hübsche Weise oder Melodey, welche einer aus seinem eignen Kopffe also singet," a pretty tune or melody, sung by heart.[37] The questions that remain to be answered are: where could one hear these songs and who were the singer-guitarists responsible for the dissemination of the newest *arie*? Their popularity suggests that one could listen to them over and over again (and this in an era with no sound recording or electronic distribution), so that at least the words and the melody could become familiar. We can speculate, for instance, about informal public appearances of trained singers who were employed at the San Marco at the time that Claudio Monteverdi was the maestro di capella there, such as Giovanni Pietro Berti or the young Domenico Obizzi, performing alfabeto repertoire, including their own songs.[38]

In his preface to Kapsberger's *Libro secondo de villanelle*, the compiler Ascanio Ferrari expressed his thoughts on the uncontrolled diffusion of these compositions: "The villanellas, which sprang with such grace and beauty from your [Kapsberger's] pen, are now being passed around in a thousand ragged and impoverished disguises, stripped of their glory. In an act of sympathy and love I have now gathered them all together and, as far as possible, I have reclothed them in their original splendour."[39] Although the composer probably approved of this edition, sometimes some of the alfabeto chords included seem not well chosen. We will return to that subject in chapter 3.

Unwritten Practices

The battuto practice suited the simplicity of the villanella repertoire perfectly. The plainness of alfabeto notation can give rise to the assumption that what is indicated on paper is only the proverbial tip of the iceberg, a sketchy code of a performance, standing firmly with one foot in unwritten traditions.[40] Editions like Remigio Romano's take for granted a familiarity with the melodies of the songs; they do not give more than the two cues one needs: text and chord symbols. Even the notation of the rhythm is lacking.[41] Therefore it is often supposed that the letters of alfabeto were no more than pointers to highly intricate strumming patterns (of which, however, there exist no contemporary notated examples) and elaborate melodic improvisation.

Music from an aural tradition as a rule does not appear on paper—or at least not in any definite form—and this raises the question if (and how) we can get a more complete picture of it. For a better understanding, we should probably look at the more advanced solo compositions from the same period. There must have been a connection between extemporization and the music that we find in the many guitar collections. Two different styles of improvised performance might have been involved.

First, one could speculate about a continuo practice that departs from the given bass (figured or not). This presupposes a well-developed lute-style approach, of which, however, we find no examples at all in the solo repertoire of the time.[42] Precisely because he did not perform the bass line himself, the guitarist would have needed a thorough knowledge of music theory to be able to follow the implied harmony from which to derive the accompanying "parts." This is not corroborated by what is known of the chronology of the developments. The time of the greatest success of alfabeto song was between 1615 and 1630, preceding the battuto-pizzicato sytle that was introduced by Giovanni Paolo Foscarini in his *Libro terzo* of about 1630. As Foscarini observed, music completely in pizzicato—which goes one step further—belonged to the domain of the lute.

Second, one can imagine that the guitar was used as a melody instrument, since it would have been relatively easy to extemporize over the harmonic foundation of an ensemble.[43] But in that case, too, the conjecture of such an improvisatory practice needs to be backed up by existing notated examples of melodic play. Surprisingly, there is almost no trace of melody to be found in the entire guitar repertoire of the first decades of the seventeenth century. Moreover, in Foscarini's works of the 1630s in battuto-pizzicato style, the guitar is never treated as a pure melody instrument on which to play single lines. In his instructions for basso continuo, which can be found in the *Quinto libro* of circa 1640, Foscarini gives examples of harmonies derived from the bass line, but without any melodic elaboration.[44]

In his treatise *Del sonare sopra il basso* (1607), Agostino Agazzari discusses the role of different instruments of accompaniment. About the lute he writes: "He who plays the lute . . . must play it nobly, with much invention and variety, not as those who, because they have a ready hand, do nothing but play runs and make divisions from beginning to end, especially when playing with other instruments which do the same, in all of which nothing is heard but babel and confusion, displeasing and disagreeable to the listener."[45] Agazzari did not refer to the five-course guitar as one of the instruments of harmonic foundation, and what he said about the lute certainly does not apply to the chitarra spagnuola.[46] It is not known if he saw alfabeto as a good way to accompany the voice, or if he had encountered the battuto practice, which was just emerging at that time, close enough to have a well-founded judgement. Yet everyone knew the plucked style of the lute, and the distinction between the two must have been clear. There were several families of stringed instruments, and different ways to set the strings in motion. Some were played with a bow, others (like the cittern) with a quill. Some were hand-plucked, and others were strummed. For Benedetto Sanseverino, who published at least three books with songs and dances, battuto was the proper way to play the guitar: "Finally, it seems to me that the Spanish guitar ought to be played with full strokes and not otherwise, because playing it with diminutions, suspensions and dissonances would be rather more appropriate to playing the lute than the Spanish guitar and playing diminutions on such an instrument not only takes away its own natural and ancient style but also completely deprives it of harmony."[47] This makes it perfectly clear why Sanseverino thought that the guitar should not be used for melodic improvisation, nor for plucked accompaniment in lute style.

The Guitar and Theatrical Performance

Although the Spanish way of singing to the guitar came to have great influence in Italy, this does not mean that the instrument was fully accepted everywhere. In opera, which took the country by storm at the beginning of the seventeenth century, the guitar probably was used only in very specific scenes.[48] For stage performance the theorbo was developed, at first only to accompany lower male voices.[49] There was an urgent need for a plucked instrument able to perform the bass line (and simple harmonies) of the solo aria. Apart from that, the theorbo could fulfill the emblematic role of Orpheus's lyre (the chitarrone was sometimes presented as a descendant of the ancient *kithara*), preferably played by the singer himself.

In 1589, the Spanish guitar literally entered the stage in Florence, in the hands of soprano Vittoria Archilei, performing in the musical *intermedi* for Girolamo Bargagli's comedy *La pellegrina* at the wedding of Ferdinando I de' Medici and Christine de Lorraine. The music for these intermedi was written by various composers—e.g., Giulio Caccini, Jacopo Peri, and Emilio de' Cavalieri. Star soprano Vittoria Archilei ("la Romanina") played one of three guitars that were brought from Naples (a city under Spanish rule) shortly before the festivities.[50] Apparently the instrument was not yet very common in other parts of Italy at that moment, and the novelty of the performance would have added to the spectacle.

In the preface to Cavalieri's *Rappresentatione del anima e del corpo* of eleven years later (Rome, 1600), we can find a stage direction for the character Pleasure: "PLEASURE and his two companions, it will be good if they have instruments in their hands, while they sing and play their ritornelli. One can have a chitarrone, another a *chitarrina alla spagnuola* and the third a *cimbaletto con sonaglie alla spagnuola* [a Spanish tambourine], making some noise. They leave the stage while playing the last ritornello."[51] Exactly in such light-hearted situations, the guitar was welcome on the stage. The instrument was preferred by singers and dancers, as it was easy to manage and very practical for providing a chordal accompaniment with a lively, rhythmic pulse. Apart from that, the guitar could be seen as an emblem of simplicity of heart, associated with man in pastoral ("natural") surroundings, free from societal conventions. This is also mirrored in the prominent place of the instrument in commedia dell'arte. Specifically, the guitar became identified with the uncomplicated love song and was often employed for that in the theater, as part of the symbolic language expressing the different passions.[52]

Cory Michael Gavito argues that a true ideology of pastoral realism was developed—an intentional and systematic idealization of natural knowledge (and intuitive gifts of music)—in which concepts like historic authenticity and simplicity of mind play a central role.[53] Stress was laid on the opposition between a "harmonious rural world" and urban civic society. Aristocratic rulers like the Medici in Florence sponsored plays (and their pastoral intermezzi) to further the image of their entourage as a part of an authentic and natural order, which added to the legitimacy of their position.[54] Parallel to that, an idealization of rustic life took root among broad layers of society, in cities like Rome, Florence, and Venice. The guitar and alfabeto song took a prominent place in this movement. Both from the lyrics and the presentation of the books, a longing for an Arcadian world is apparent.[55]

As long as it was played battuto, the guitar could be used in the theater for dance and dance songs. At the same time, the style of battuto does not conform to the premises of the seconda pratica. Giulio Cesare Monteverdi, the brother of the celebrated composer, speaks of the primacy of poetry: "By Second Practice . . . [my brother Claudio] understands the one that turns on the perfection of the melody, that is, the one that considers harmony not commanding, but commanded and makes the words the mistress of the harmony."[56] Elaborate melismatic embellishment, applied to heighten the musical expression of the poetry, is characteristic of the stile recitativo, as expounded by Giulio Caccini in the preface to his *Nuove musiche* of 1601, a collection of solo arias (not including alfabeto), that contributed vitally to the image of the new monodic style.

In contrast to through-composed recitatives and solo madrigals, most alfabeto songs have uncomplicated (but catchy) melodies built out of short phrases, with predominantly syllabic text-setting. The same melody is used time after time, without any written-out ornamentation, and the battuto accompaniment for the various stanzas remains practically unaltered. Alfabeto chords are uniform by definition, precluding any harmonic subtleties and thus incapable of communicating nuances of the text. Moreover, strumming inhibits the rhythmic freedom of the accompaniment, thus making alfabeto an impediment to the *passaggi* in solo madrigals.

The guitar is also ill-equipped for accompanying recitative, which demands sonorous basses, imposing, great arpeggios, and dramatic harmonies. As we shall see in chapter 7, the guitar was capable of producing surprising dissonances, but these were always linked to the very specific playing technique of the instrument and could not be delivered exactly as and when a composer of vocal monody might need them. On the whole, the strummed accompaniment of the guitar cannot provide the foundation of a real bass, indispensable in the slow harmonic progression of recitative. The good points of the guitar—fast repetition or changes of chords, and a clear, dancing pulse—appear only to full advantage in lighter genres, when the movement is steady, ongoing, and not too slow. Thus, what remains for the guitar is mainly a decorative role on the stage. It is telling that any indication (in staff notation or alfabeto) of a guitar part is lacking from opera scores like Cavalieri's *Rappresentatione*. Apparently, opera composers did not care overmuch what was played on the instrument.

The list of singers and instrumentalists participating in the performance of *Il tempio della pace* (1608) by composer Santi Orlandi—an *intermedio*, performed between the acts of Michelangelo Buonarotti's comedy *Il giudizio di Paride*—contains the names of the sopranos, the *donne*, including Vittoria Archilei and Francesca Caccini, who probably accompanied themselves on the guitar.[57] From this early period, there are several reports of the use of the instrument by female singers.

Also, at a later stage, the guitar is mentioned in an operatic context. In Stefano Landi's *Il Sant'Alessio* (Rome, 1634) there is a pastoral scene, in which a guitarist appears on stage.[58] It is noticeable that the guitar does not participate in the *sinfonia* at the beginning, when the instrumentation of the orchestra is given in the score: three violins for the upper voices; harp, lutes, theorbos, violones, and harpsichord for the basso continuo.[59] In the scene in question, the guitar was probably played by one of the theorbists—often players were equally skilled on both instruments—or by a singer. At the Paris premiere of Luigi Rossi's *L'Orfeo* in 1647, there were two guitars. The complete instrumental ensemble, including the guitars, played in the prologue and at the end of the acts.[60] It is questionable, however, what the significance of such an instrumentation is, and whether the guitars fulfilled any special musical role. It seems more likely that it was the aim to produce as much sound as possible with all available forces.

In theatrical performances in Spain, the guitar had a more prominent place, as we can learn from, for example, the letters of the Italian stage designer Baccio del Bianco, which presumably were addressed to his former patron Mattias de' Medici in Florence.[61] Del Bianco was involved in the staging of court plays by the celebrated dramatist and poet Pedro Calderón de la Barca. For these performances he often collaborated with composer Juan Hidalgo, as in the opera *La púrpura de la rosa*. From del Bianco's letters, an image emerges of unsophisticated performances in the theaters of Madrid— by the musicians in particular—that were very different from what he was used to in Italy. He is clearly disconcerted that guitars are allowed to figure prominently in certain scenes:

> The mishaps that occurred in this play are not fewer than those of last year. . . . It was not possible, in an apotheosis of the Gods, to avoid [the inappropriate arrival onstage of] the four rogues dressed in the usual black with Spanish guitars, cape, and sword, just as the twelve signs of the Zodiac, which were twelve women, were at the point of falling from the sky, and got all out of order; and then the same four [onstage] turned their backs to the public, the custom in this place, such that when I tried to eliminate this habit, they nearly crucified me, claiming that it is impossible to dance without the four guitars behind them; in short, the refinement of the scene and the precision of movement on the stage are not observed here.[62]

In his letter of March 3, 1656, del Bianco is very critical of a musical intermezzo (to accompany a scene change) in Ulloa y Pereyra's pastoral play *Pico y Canente*, performed by an ensemble of guitars, *violone*, violins, and a keyboard instrument. The first performance took place in the Salón of the Buen Retiro palace, but owing to its overwhelming success, performances continued in the larger Coliseo theater. About this performance del Bianco remarks: "Then the guitars, the *violone*, and the four violins with a keyboard instrument played [a sinfonia], each one going his own way and playing according to his own taste. After this pig-headed symphony, the scene changed from the garden to the wood."[63] In the ballets and operas of Lully, finally, that after 1653 set the tone in France, we regularly encounter guitars. In the performance of *Alcidiane*, in 1658, "huit esclaves maures" (eight Moorish slaves) appeared on stage with guitars.[64] Here, too, there is no indication in the score of what the guitarists played, so we have to assume simple battuto patterns. With the Italian Lully, the use of the guitar is always confined to pastoral, comical or exotic scenes. Sometimes commedia dell'arte characters, like Scaramouche, are featured. In a sense this practice is a continuation of a theatrical tradition that has its origins in Italy and Spain. Lully's own background as a dancer and guitarist no doubt played an important role.

The Habitat of the Guitar

To what extent did the guitar participate in the developments of the musical mainstream of the first decades of the seventeenth century? Because of some of its characteristics, the world of the guitar stood apart from the leading musical culture. At the start, the instrument had a solo repertoire that, quite unusually, knew hardly any melody, while there were both melody and a bass in even the simplest works for the lute. Guitar music was determined by the unique style of battuto—thus, strictly harmonic and (motoric) rhythmic. Besides, the instrument had its own notational system, the alfabeto, prescribing the action of the hands. Essentially, alfabeto has very little connection to other systems of notation, even to lute tablature.

The guitar normally did not participate in heterogeneous ensembles, so players did not come into regular contact with other instrumentalists; however, in several alfabeto books there are battuto dances for ensembles consisting of two to four guitars, each tuned to a different pitch.[65] Although the amateur guitarist was largely isolated from the sphere of influence of the musical mainstream, or at least from the innovations in certain genres, through alfabeto accompaniment he could at least come into contact with the newest strophic arias of renowned composers. Admittedly, leading players such as Foscarini, Pellegrini, and Bartolotti, who were all active as theorbists, too, were certainly not cut off from outside impulses. Still, taking into account the extended repertoire of very simple dances from the many alfabeto collections, it seems safe to conclude that for the most part, the population of *dilettanti* was not oriented toward high art music. From the preface to Luis de Briçeño's *Metodo* (Paris, 1626) we get a richly detailed view of the place of the guitar in society:

> The guitar is the most favorable instrument for our times that has ever been seen, because, if today one wishes to save money and labour, the guitar is

at centre-stage theater of this economy. Besides this it is well suited and appropriate for singing, playing, dancing, jumping, jigging and foot-tapping. Singing and expressing with its aid a thousand passions of love while strolling, it is a sauce for happiness, banisher of pains and cares, pastime for the sad, comfort for the lonely, joy for the melancholic, moderation for the choleric; it makes the mad sane and the sane mad. It is [not] a slave of the weather, nor offended by any of the inconveniences that the delicate lute fears; there is no smoke, heat or damp that bothers it. It is like the rose, always alive, if it goes quickly out of tune, it is very quickly tuned again, if it is broken, with two *sueldos* [i.e. with little money] it is repaired, and so, in my opinion, and that of many others, it has a great advantage over the lute, because, to keep it [the lute] in order, a good many things are needful: it must be [a] good [instrument], well played, well strung, and listened to with concentration and in silence, but the guitar, my Lady, whether well or badly played, well or poorly strung, makes itself heard and listened to, tempting the minds of the busiest with the brevity and ease of learning it, and making them leave higher exercises in order to hold it in their hands.[66]

The contrast with the lute was often explicitly underlined. That instrument became more and more regarded as outdated and associated with complicated theoretical issues, while the guitar conjured up the image of artlessness and spontaneous musicality. It is noteworthy that two of the composers who had won their spurs on the lute, Foscarini and Bartolotti, included works in their guitar books entirely in pizzicato. The fact that they could identify themselves with both instruments probably kept them from reacting against the manner of playing of the lute.

Richard Jensen emphasizes the popular role of the guitar, assuming that in the first decades of the seventeenth century the guitar was played almost exclusively by dilettantes.[67] Apparently, there was not much change after that. From a *registro de discepoli*, included by Stefano Pesori in his books of 1648 and circa 1675, it becomes evident that he had students from all layers of society. On the list there are *nobili veneti, marchesi, conti, dottori, religiosi, gentilhuomini, capitani, cittadini, mercanti,* and *tedeschi* (Germans), with the *ebrei* (Jews) bringing up the rear. If we take into account that the music from Pesori's books is of utmost simplicity, it gives an inkling of the general level, which will not have been much higher than in the time of Girolamo Montesardo, half a century earlier. Only a small proportion of the guitar books was directed at advanced players. Domenico Pellegrini, for instance, remarked in the preface to his *Armoniosi concerti* of 1650 that his book was not for beginners, but for those who are "esperti in questa professione."

Also according to Jensen, the guitar was often seen as an instrument of the younger generations.[68] Stefano Pesori began the introduction of his *Galeria musicale* (1648) with: "alla virtuosa gioventù . . ." and Montesardo issued his 1606 collection "in order to please the light-hearted and noble youth."[69] Chord strumming to popular songs is probably indeed something that fits *gioventù* best. One can imagine the chords of songs and dances being played—even sometimes without being actually sung or danced—just for the pleasure of the (inner) ear, exactly as the guitar is used in our own time. Today, too, it is (mainly) young people who play the chords of popular songs, daydreaming. And in our time, too, chord symbols are used that have meaning only for the guitarist, representing no more than the left-hand patterns. Alfabeto makes the guitar the perfect instrument to accompany the voice, through the simplicity of the action—there is no need to pay attention to the notes of a bass line, voice leading is not an issue, and the rhythm is a result of ongoing motoric movement. Singing and supporting yourself on the guitar is essentially a relaxing activity, to be practiced at home, whereas the ready ear of a continuo player (even if he or she is just an accompanist) inevitably teases a performance from the singer. Another good feature of the guitar is its portability: it can be played in the open air at all kinds of festivities, and for serenades. Most strophic arias are love songs, and it is understandable that the guitar came to stand as a symbol of worldly pleasures, both in the theater and in painting.

We can hardly say that the composers of alfabeto songs were generally very young at the time of publication, but there were some, like Domenico Obizzi, who published his wonderful *Madrigali et arie a voce sola* (1627) at the early age of fifteen. Carlo Cantù, a boy soprano at the cathedral in Milan who later became a famous *commedia dell'arte* actor, was only about eleven years old at the time that Benedetto Sanseverino dedicated his *Aria sopra vezzosetta* to "Signor Carlo Cantù, gentilissimo soprano, nel duomo di Milano." Giuseppe Fachoni reports from Rome in a letter, dated May 9, 1609, to Vincenzo Gonzaga in Mantua that the young Neapolitan soprano Adriana Basile (born c. 1580–83) knew over three hundred Italian and Spanish songs by heart, which she performed to her own accompaniment on either the harp or the guitar.[70] The duke of Mantua, Carlo II Gonzaga, was only fourteen when Corbetta dedicated the *Varie capricci* to him in 1643; and Louis XIV, too, started to play the guitar at a tender age.

Chapter Two

Italian Guitarists at Home and Abroad

Venice and Bologna

Venice suffered severely from the devastating plague of 1630, and in the year that followed, music publishing was suspended almost completely. Between 1620 and 1630 many collections of songs with alfabeto had been printed every year, but there are no such publications at all from 1631 and 1632. After the plague, the demand for songbooks recovered to some extent, and in 1633, printer Alessandro Vincenti started to add titles to his catalogue again. Yet the downturn of this genre could not be stopped.

The former success of the guitar in accompaniment did not immediately lead to the creation of a solo repertoire in the new mixed style. Alfabeto books had been printed mainly in a few geographic centers—Florence, Rome, Milan, and Venice—while books with music in the new battuto-pizzicato style mostly came from Rome and Bologna. It was not Venice but Bologna that gave birth to a school of guitar music. While *la Serenissima*, the mercantile republic of Venice, was the place of frivolous carnival disguises, singing, and dancing, Bologna was host to the oldest university of the Western world. Its cultural climate was much more intellectual and serious, and there was a keen interest in the study of musical theory. The city was under papal rule and the Church was omnipresent, which could explain a lesser focus on the lighter genres of secular monody.

There was no single aristocratic family governing Bologna and acting as dominant patrons of the arts, like the Medici in Florence or the Gonzaga in Mantua. The city was governed by a senate, almost like a republic. Nine senators, called the Anziani della Signoria, were chosen from the Bolognese aristocracy for a two-month term.[1] These influential families sponsored performances, both public and private, of dramas, comedies, operas, and oratorios.[2] Less prestigious genres profited as well from this constellation, and the publication of works for instrumental ensembles and solo instruments such as the guitar thus found ready support. The *cappella musicale* of the church of San Petronio employed distinguished instrumentalists. It contributed to the city's fame as a center of vocal and instrumental music. Unlike most of the literary academies of the renaissance and baroque, the Bolognese academies, in particular the Accademia Filarmonica (earlier, from 1633 to 1666, known as the Accademia dei Filaschisi), were institutions primarily under control of professional musicians, providing both theoretical and practical training for their members. Domenico Pellegrini, who composed cantatas as well as guitar music, belonged to the Accademia dei Filomusi, founded by Adriano Banchieri.

The conditions for the rise of guitar music were favorable. Bologna had been a great center of lute making in the sixteenth century, in particular with the workshop of Laux Maler (ca. 1485–1552) and his heirs. Later, there was the workshop of Gasparo Franchi (Caspar Frei). In his inventory of 1627 there were listed "50 chitare alla spagnola."[3] In the early seventeenth century, a small number of books for the lute was printed here, notably two by Alessandro Piccinini. Throughout the seventeenth century there was a strong tradition of theorbo playing in Bologna, especially in the role of basso continuo.

In addition, scholars and students came to the university, the *alma mater studiorum,* from all over Europe. In this climate of intellectual independence, many well-educated young men were seeking diversion, and there must have been a considerable demand for musical activity. The guitar, as an instrument of dilettanti, could take advantage of a trend toward individual music making. As the lute had gradually been falling out of favor since c. 1630, the guitar remained the only popular chordal instrument, with a rapidly growing solo repertoire. In the preface to *Nuovi souavi concenti di sonate musicali,* Granata's opus 6 (1680), it reads: "I had the good fortune to serve as a Master many Signori from all parts of the world, who flocked to Bologna to study."[4]

Performers and Teachers

The city of Bologna was home to the most prolific publishing house for guitar music, that of Giacomo Monti. His publications of works by Corbetta, Calvi, Granata, Pellegrini, Coriandoli, and Asioli account for roughly a third of all battuto-pizzicato guitar music from Italy.[5] Around 1630 Giovanni Paolo Foscarini had published a book in Rome with a tablature with both battuto and pizzicato music for the guitar.[6] The first book for guitar published by Monti was Francesco Corbetta's *De gli scherzi armonici* (1639), in the same year that he (posthumously) printed Piccinini's second book for the lute. It is likely that Corbetta lived in Bologna for some time, as the dedications to his patron Conte Odoardo Pepoli and other noblemen imply that he had been active there as a guitar teacher. His first book consists mainly of alfabeto, with only a small number of pieces in the mixed style.[7] In 1646, Monti published a book by Giovanni Battista Granata and a collection of dances in alfabeto and tablature compiled by Carlo Calvi. The music in this book was partly taken from Corbetta's first publication—it is unknown if Corbetta agreed to this or not; it is even not clear if he was still in Bologna at that time. Granata filled the gap, publishing six more books (in c. 1650, 1651, 1659, 1674, 1680, and 1684, the last four again with Monti). He must have had a close relationship with the printer. Later Francesco Asioli published two books with Monti, and Domenico Pellegrini and Francesco Coriandoli published one each.

Angelo Michele Bartolotti, one of the great players of the time, was probably born in Bologna. Nevertheless, his *Libro primo di chitarra spagnola* (1640) was not printed there, but in Florence, with a dedication to the Conte de Salviati. James Tyler remarks: "The wording of the dedication makes it clear that he was in Salviati's service, and the fact that the copy preserved in London (GB-Lbl) once belonged to a certain Giulio Medici invites speculation that he was the guitar teacher of other members of the Florentine aristocracy as well."[8] Also published in Florence, in 1640 and 1643 respectively, were two books by Antonio Carbonchi, the first of which, *Sonate di chitarra spagnola con tavolatura franzese*, is dedicated to Mattias de Medici. There are several possible reasons for the fact that Bartolotti's book was not printed by Monti in Bologna. All Monti's guitar books used movable type for tablature (he may have been the only printer with the requisite technology at hand to produce mixed tablature), while Bartolotti's books are engraved. Engraving is a more advanced technique with regard to details such as slurs, fingerings and battuto signs.[9] Francesco Corbetta also opted for the flexibility of engraved tablatures for his second book (1643). It may not be a coincidence that two of the best composers made use of this technique. Engraving later became, the standard format for printing guitar music in Italy and in France and Spain as well. However, Giacomo Monti stuck to his movable types until 1684. The flood of Monti's publications reached its highest point in the 1670s, long after Bartolotti and Corbetta had left. In total, Monti printed not fewer than eleven books between 1639 and 1684.

The question arises how to value Monti's continual outpouring of publications and the guitar books by lesser figures such as Coriandoli and Asioli. Although some of the works are technically somewhat demanding, the content of these books is often rather bland. It can be safely assumed that, though some of the composers enjoyed only local fame, the publications by Granata, Carbonchi, Corbetta, Asioli and Bartolotti had patrons from the highest ranks in society. What we do not know is how many copies were printed of every title. It is quite conceivable that the printing of guitar music was to some degree a form of "vanity publishing," sponsored by rich dilettantes. The number of copies printed was probably modest and paid for by a patron, or even by the composer himself. In the case of engraved tablatures, a composer even could cut expenses by engraving his own music.

On the other hand, a real market for student repertoire probably did exist. Guitar teachers of renown provided the necessary material themselves, so that their pupils had more at their disposal than just collections of songs with simple alfabeto. The output of Monti's press could have been meant for them in the first place. Asioli's books contain dedications to the individual students of the *collegio de Nobili* in Parma (Asioli, 1676); Granata's *Soavi concenti* (1659) proudly lists the names of the highborn members of the *collegio di Francesco Xaverio della compagnia di Giesù*, Jesuits from the Veneto and the Emilia Romagna regions. In this way composers gained control over a local market. The preface to *Nuovi souavi concenti di sonate musicali*, Granata's opus 6 (1680), states that "Every sort of person, having some knowledge of tablature and the way this instrument is played, can be instructed." It is his wish to serve the reader: "Wherever my books are sold, my voice instructs and my hands show how to play these compositions."[10]

In the first half of the century, the guitar did not have much of a solo repertoire to be performed publicly. Only some of the compositions by Giovanni Paolo Foscarini and the passacaglias and dance suites from Bartolotti's *Libro primo* (1640) and Corbetta's *Varii capricci* (1643) were suitable for that purpose. Listen to Foscarini's *Capriccio sopra la ciaccona* (audio ex. 1). The repertoire will mainly have been useful for the many amateur players; from all that we know of musical life of the seventeenth century, there is not much reason to suppose that guitarists could obtain posts as professional performers. The exception was Corbetta, whose fame grew rapidly and who soon took his first steps into the society of the great rulers of Europe. He dedicated his *Varii capricci* to Carlo II Gonzaga, the duke of Mantua. The Gonzagas had close family ties to the house of Hanover. Corbetta was on the payroll at the court in Hanover in 1652–53.[11] His is one of the very few documented engagements of a guitarist, apart from the official post of "maître de guittarre du Roy" in France. This is significant when compared to all the positions that were held by singers, organists, and string and wind players in virtually every major city in Europe. There is no information about what Corbetta had to do in return. It is quite possible that he worked at court as a guitar teacher, but his playing would certainly have been warmly received. Around 1653 he headed for Paris, like many other musicians from Italy.

Professional theorbists like Foscarini and Bartolotti also published guitar books and may have supplemented their income with guitar lessons. While the guitar was not the sort of instrument with which to earn money as a performer, a theorbist could participate in ensembles and theatrical performances. Some players who were trained on both instruments may have had a more or less regular income from this combination. There are reports of Granata's attempts in 1652–53 to obtain an engagement as a lute player (probably to play continuo on the theorbo, or even on the theorboed guitar) at the *Concerto Palatino* of the church of San Petronio, a post that had been previously held by guitarist and composer Domenico Pellegrini.[12] Apparently Granata's earnings from playing and teaching did not suffice; from the preface to his *Soavi concenti* (1659) it becomes evident that Granata embarked on a second career as a barber-surgeon: "If I have been occupied because of the diligence which my profession of surgery demands, from which I was able to concede less time than I would like to apply to playing [an instrument], I hope nonetheless that I have had printed the most harmonious and unusual pieces that I have yet composed."[13]

Bartolotti was involved as a theorbist in performances of operas by the best composers, such as Francesco Cavalli (1602–76), and he worked with singers and instrumentalists of great fame. The contrast with the amateur world of the guitar could not have been greater. His exceptional skills are reflected in the remarkable quality of some of the compositions from his *Secondo libro* for guitar, printed circa 1655 in Rome. There are movements from his dance suites comparable to works by Denis Gaultier for the lute and Johann Jacob Froberger for the keyboard, for example the *courante* or *gigue* from the Suite in E Minor (audio exx. 23 and 25). For the average guitarist, however, this repertoire must have been out of reach. Such virtuosic pieces probably were seen as music for professional players only, something that caused Granata to state that "rumours have been spread that my compositions for the chitarra spagnola are difficult to play and that they are not for beginners, but only for *maestri*."[14]

Around 1652, Bartolotti had obtained a post as a theorbo player at the Swedish court, in the service of Queen Christina. After her abdication—she converted to Catholicism—Christina resided in Rome and became its most influential patroness of the arts. In 1655–56, Bartolotti most likely was also in Rome, since his *Libro secondo* was printed there, bearing a dedication to the Queen of Sweden. Like Foscarini and Corbetta, Bartolotti left Italy. Around 1660 he took part in performances at the court in Paris. In France, he had various engagements, most likely always as a continuo player. As far as we know, Bartolotti never cared to publish another book for the guitar. In the 1650s and 60s there were perhaps better prospects for performing as a theorbist in Paris than for publishing guitar music.

The decline of the guitar as a solo instrument was perhaps inevitable. We can surmise that, as in more recent times, the guitar was played mainly by a group of dedicated amateurs. Its immense but short-lived popularity had started with a role in vocal accompaniment. To sustain this momentum in a new solo repertoire was possibly too much for such a limited instrument. The guitar is incapable of producing cantabile lines, and it lacks the range of keyboard instruments to perform full scores. The first attempts by Foscarini, Corbetta, and Bartolotti to create a genuine guitar style, incorporating lute-style elements into battuto, shows the instrument freeing itself from its restrictions. They added a more intellectual component to a genre that originated in an unwritten transmission of harmonic schemes and right-hand strumming formulae. We can compare this to the evolution from blues to jazz, or from the basic chord patterns of rock to the very advanced electric guitar solos that emerged afterward. The innovations of Corbetta must have brought more variety to the guitarists' menu, but only for as long as the fashion for the instrument lasted. The decline of the lute in Italy proved (as shown by the dramatic slump in printed matter) that plucked instruments were not fit to meet the requirements of the new energetic, expressive style. The last part of the seventeenth century was the time of expanding instrumental virtuosity, typified by the abundance of sonatas for the violin and cello.

With the waning interest in alfabeto songs and the sparse opportunities for performance in solo and ensemble, some of the best players sought opportunities abroad as professional theorbists. The charismatic Corbetta managed to move in court circles of France and England as a society figure, a gamester, and a virtuoso guitarist. Those who stayed behind in Italy, composers such as Giovanni Battista Granata, Francesco Coriandoli or Giovanni Bottazzari, stuck to a somewhat archaic battuto-pizzicato style. The last book from Italy is *Capricci armonici* (1692) by Lodovico Roncalli.

Actors, Dancers, and the Guitar

During the festivities for the wedding of Ferdinando I de' Medici and Christine de Lorraine in Florence in 1589, a performance took place of the comedy *Zingana*, by a commedia dell'arte company called I Gelosi (the Jealous Ones), on the same stage where *La Pellegrina*, with the famous musical intermezzi mentioned earlier, was played.[15] This company enjoyed the support of the Medici family. Such troupes mainly employed professional actors. Although sometimes supposed to be of low descent, the actors were held in high esteem. Some actually were of noble birth, like Flaminio Scala (1547–ca. 1620), a member of Verona's leading aristocratic family.

Since the beginning of the seventeenth century, the guitar had played a role in commedia. Michael Praetorius saw the guitar as an instrument of "Ziarlatini und Salt'in banco," comedians and clowns.[16] Singing to guitar accompaniment was one of the ingredients of the game of truth and illusion of the commedia dell'arte and also of the annual masquerade of Carnival, which had a great influence on artistic developments. The first theaters where a paying audience could attend performances of the commedia dell'arte were in Venice, a genre which, in its turn, contributed significantly to the success of opera. The fame of guitar-playing actor-singers certainly added to the instrument's popularity in Italy and abroad. Several characters from the commedia dell'arte are always portrayed guitar in hand, like Buffetto, a creation of Carlo Cantù (ca. 1607–76). The former boy soprano Cantù, whose picture is shown in figure 2.1, was one of the stars in the Italian cast of the epoch-making Parisian premiere of Francesco Sacrati's Venetian opera *La finta pazza* in 1645.[17] The performance took place at the Palais du Petit-Bourbon and was attended by the young Louis XIV and his mother, Anne of Austria, who had become Regent of France after

Figure 2.1. Stefano della Bella, *Portrait of Carlo Cantù in Paris*. In Cantù, *Cicalamento in canzonette ridicolose, overo trattato di matrimonio tra Buffetto e Colombina Comici* (1646). In the background right, the Pont Neuf and the Notre Dame cathedral. Reproduced by permission from Österreichische Nationalbibliothek, Wien.

Louis XIII's death in 1643. In *Cicalamento in canzonette ridicolose*, the autobiographical story of Buffeto's matrimony with the actress Isabella Biancolella (Colombina in commedia dell'arte), Cantù speaks of a letter sent by the Queen Mother to his patron Odoardo Farnese, Duke of Parma, with the request to have him join the Italian comedy troupe in Paris.[18]

Another main commedia character, Scapino, created by Francesco Gabrielli, was likewise inseparable from his guitar.[19] Unlike the old Orpheus, Scapino holds the distorting mirror of human motivations before us.[20] In Remigio Romano's *Seconda raccolta di canzonette musicali* (Vicenza, 1618), there is the song "Fermeve sù":

Stop, O whistlers!
Give up, O ignoramuses,
Go to whistle at the shore,
Evil little goat-skins!
Two-bit hustlers,
Throw yourselves into the river.

You are those, who despise us
Who don't know that in Venice
Scapino remembers
Who is strong, and who is lazy,
Who is rich, and who is wicked,
And who is insolent.

O how many are whistling,
Who should not be;
And if they know their business
They have their summer coats
Patched
With the greasy backside.

He who is noble born,
May not be insolent;
But the vagabond
Cannot help but be
Or be made fun of
By all the world.

But I conclude, and say,
Take care not to proclaim
Yourself Scapino's enemy;
For he will sing your name,
Your clothing, and your surname,
With the guitar.[21]

By 1640, the time of the greatest success of the commedia dell'arte in Italy had come to an end. With the deaths of some of the most important actors of the time, Giovanni Gabrielli (Scapino), Tristano Martinelli (Arlecchino), Flaminio Scala (Flavio), and Pier Maria Cecchini (Fritellino), the troupes had lost their most prominent characters. The next generation found employment and economic security in the richly variegated cultural environment of the French capital, where an invasion of Italian musicians and actors took place under the protection of Cardinal Mazarin (1602–61), born Giulio Mazarini. One of the most celebrated actors was Tiberio Fiorelli. Louis XIV (1638–1715) had come into personal contact as a child with Fiorelli's jokes and guitar-playing as Scaramouche when the commedia dell'arte was summoned at court to amuse the Dauphin. This Scaramouche was always portrayed with a guitar.

The guitar had played a part in French court ballets since the 1620s, e.g., the *Ballet des fées des forests de St. Germain* (1625), in which Louis XIII himself danced on the stage. This ballet features an entrée of the *chaconistes espagnols*. Before the influx of musicians from Italy had started, around 1645, the instrument was probably often in the hands of Spanish players from the entourage of Louis XIII's wife, Queen Anne of Austria, daughter of Philip III of Spain. Later there were Spaniards in the household of her younger niece, Marie-Thérèse (1638–83), the first wife of Louis XIV. The colorful lifestyle associated with the guitar became more appealing than the image of erudition projected by the lute, and some regretted, not without bitterness, that the guitar gradually took over the preeminent position of that instrument, as Pierre Trichet did in 1640:

> The guiterre or guiterne is a musical instrument widely used by the French and Italians, but still more among the Spanish, who were the first to make it fashionable and who know how to play it more madly than any other nation, using it particularly for singing and for playing their sarabands, galliardes, espagnolettes, passemezes, passecaglias, pavanes, allemandes, and romanesques with a thousand gestures and body movements which are so grotesque and ridiculous that their playing is bizarre and confused. Nevertheless even in France one finds courtesans and ladies who turn themselves into Spanish monkeys trying to imitate them, demonstrating that they prefer foreign importations to their own native products. In this they resemble those who, though they could dine well at their own table, would rather go out to eat bacon, onions and black bread. For who is not aware that the lute is what is proper and suitable for the French and the most delightful of all instruments? Still there are some of our nation who leave everything behind in order to take up and study the guitar. Isn't this because it is much easier to perfect oneself in this than in lute-playing, which requires long and arduous study before one can acquire the necessary skill and disposition? Or is it because it has a certain something which is feminine and pleasing to women, flattering their hearts and making them inclined to voluptuousness?[22]

In Charles Sorel's *Nouveau recueil des pièces les plus agréables de ce temps* (1644) there is an amusing dialogue of the Lute and the Guitar with their Master, which gives insight into how these instrument were viewed: "THE LUTE. It is generally known that the Guitar is an imperfect instrument that cannot come to an agreement with the others, and it is more involved in cohabiting than in marriage. Let us leave her with her voluptuousness. While she is used to serve buffoons, she is not entitled to spread gossip about me and speak badly of me."[23] At that time probably only dances and accompaniments in battuto were played, of which very little is preserved on paper. The French did not make much use of alfabeto, which raises the vexing question: how was this music transmitted, even if it involved no more than the strumming of simple chord sequences? Whatever the answer, the repertoire must have had a strong similarity to the ciacconas, sarabandas, passacaglias, and Ruggieros, for which the guitar was liked so much in Italy; apparently chordal reductions of well-known popular dances, which could easily be learnt by imitation, had great appeal. In both countries there was a fad for the exotic habits and clothes from the Iberian Peninsula and these dances belong to that same foreign world. At the same time there was not as much of a market in France for printed battuto music as there was in Italy, which soon led in the creation of a solo repertoire. In 1640, Foscarini, Corbetta, and Bartolotti had already made important contributions. The step forward to publishing music in the battuto-pizzicato style was taken in France some thirty years later.

The influential composer Jean-Baptiste Lully (1632–87), born as Giovanni Battista Lulli in the vicinity of Florence, started his career in Paris as a dancer and actor in theatrical ballets, in which also Louis XIV participated. He had been playing the guitar from an early age:

> Lulli started out on this instrument. The guitar being the most fashionable of all instruments in Italy, and which is there played the best, he became familiar with it first. The rest of his life he always liked to play it. . . . Whenever he saw a guitar, at home or elsewhere, he amused himself hitting that kettle, out of which he got much more than others. He composed at least a hundred minuets and a hundred courantes, which he didn't keep; as you'll understand: all lost.[24]

In 1653, aged twenty-one, Lully was appointed as the court *compositeur de musique instrumentale*. In 1661 he danced to his own music in the role of Scaramouche in the *Ballet de l'impatience*, guitar in hand, together with the King.[25] The music was in the new French style, the libretto written by Isaac de Benserade. Such ballets were constructed as a sequence of comic dance scenes interspersed with short dialogues, inspired by the Italian theater. The musical outline consists of short, well-formed phrases and melodies that are easy to sing. The whole is a festive show meant to dazzle and entertain, striving for effect like a Broadway musical today. Francesco Corbetta, almost twenty years Lully's senior, took part

Figure 2.2. *Guitarist and Woman with Castanets.* Anonymous seventeenth-century picture. Museum Boijmans van Beuningen, Rotterdam. © Studio Buitenhof, Den Haag.

in one or more of these ballets as a guitarist (and most likely as a dancer, too), performing alongside the eighteen-year-old King, who danced in Lully's ballet *La galanterie du temps* (1656). Louis XIV's predilection for humorous situations from the commedia dell'arte and for dance and guitar music created favorable conditions for the instrument in the higher circles of Paris. The guitar became a regular attribute of some of the supporting characters in the many theatrical performances of the day: figures from the Italian theater, but also Egyptians (Gypsies), Spaniards, and Moorish slaves. Their popularity was great among the dilettanti, mostly courtiers, who could playfully identify themselves with them. Sometimes this identification seems to have been taken to extremes, spilling over into real life, so that some enthusiasts may actually have behaved, as Trichet put it, like "Spanish monkeys" (fig. 2.2).

Just as in Italy half a century earlier, the guitar was now a highly fashionable cultural icon in France; and there, too, the image of a pastoral world was cultivated, with music making presented as first and foremost a matter of intuitive knowledge. Toward the end of the seventeenth century, the guitar became utterly indispensable, as many paintings of imaginary outdoor scenes by Antoine Watteau suggest. In the more official musical world of instrumental solo and ensemble music, the instrument occupied only a marginal position. Although there are quite a few references to the use of the guitar in opera and ballet performances, there is almost nothing to be found in the scores. We can assume that for the most part, well-known Spanish and Italian dances were played in battuto. In Lully's *Hercule amoureux* (1662) there is a section called "Concert de guittares." It is a composition for string ensemble (*les petits violons*) in five parts. In the score there is no clue at all as to what the guitars were playing. It is likely that the dancers strummed simple chords to supplement the harmonies of the orchestra.

In 1673, Scaramouche Tiberio Fiorelli went to London. The famous actor, already sixty-eight years old, was a guest at Whitehall. Sir Richard Bulstrode reported in a letter to Lady Harvey:

> There is arrived Scaramouchy, ye famous Italien comedian with his crew, to act again, & are to have ye King's Theatre in Whitehall for their use during their stay and all people allowed to come there & see them, paying as they doe at other houses, so now a Papist may come to Court for halfe a crowne. This is not much lik'd by other players, for it will half break both our houses.[26]

In his diary of 1675, John Evelyn wrote: "I saw the Italian Scaramucchio act before the King at Whitehall, people giving money to come in, which was very scandalous and never so before at Court diversions." He continues: "Having seene him act before in Italy, many yeares past, I was not averse from seeing the most excellent of that kind of folly."[27] Three of the principal figures, who had been acquainted at the French court some decades before, met here again: Scaramouche, the King, and the guitar virtuoso Signor Francesco.[28] Charles II was notorious for his patronage, and both (Catholic) Italians presumably belonged to the circles of his favorites.

The Guitar at the Royal Courts of Paris and London: Corbetta and His Followers

In 1663, the first book of French guitar music was published: François Martin's *Pièces de guitairre*. Although it can be assumed that a virtuoso like Francesco Corbetta performed on his instrument when he visited Paris, it is not known when guitar tablatures began to spread on a somewhat larger scale (after all, most manuscripts are undated). Since Foscarini and Corbetta were in France long before 1660, it is likely that certain circles would have already been familiar with their music. Between 1671 and 1686, eight books came out in rapid succession, by Antoine Carré, Francesco Corbetta, Rémy Médard, Henry Grenerin, and Robert de Visée. Some interesting handwritten tablature collections have been preserved from the last decades of the century, including the voluminous, richly varied "Gallot" manuscript.[29]

The music from Corbetta's *Guitarre royalle* collection of 1671, one of the first guitar tablatures published in France, can be considered an instant high point of the French "school." As the Italian Lully defined the style of French opera in the second half of the century, so Corbetta lay the foundations of the French guitar style with his two *Guitarre royalle* collections, published in Paris. He transformed the unpolished battuto-pizzicato from his homeland into a style with *agréable*, fluent melodies and a rich chromaticism, which greatly influenced the works of all later French composers of guitar music. The Italian battuto-pizzicato became the standard way of playing in France, though in Spain, as far as we can tell from the sources, there was a preference for *punteado* (pizzicato). A number of manuscript collections from the last decades of the century contain compositions by Granata, Bartolotti, and Corbetta. Rémy Médard stated that Corbetta was his example: "I affirm to have followed the manner of the famous Francisque Corbet completely . . . with this difference that I found in my pieces an easiness which he never troubled himself to seek."[30] Corbetta's influence is also unmistakable in the works of Grenerin and Visée, who largely continued his approach to both technique and composition. The main distinction is that the phrases in Visée's compositions are always clearly structured and balanced (and somehow more predictable).

Corbetta's wanderings illustrate the quest for (and the uncertainty of) the means of support that a guitarist could acquire through his playing. It has been supposed that Corbetta first came to Paris in the late 1640s. He probably visited Brussels in 1648, when his *Libro quarto* was printed, and dedicated it to Leopold Wilhelm, archduke of Austria and governor of the Spanish Netherlands.[31] As we have seen, a few years later (1652–53) Corbetta was employed at the court in Hanover in the service of Duke Johann Friedrich of Braunschweig-Lüneburg.[32]

Cardinal Mazarin, who had become Chief Minister of France, sent to Italy for a guitarist to teach the future king, Louis XIV, still a young child.[33] In his *Essai sur la musique ancienne et moderne* (Paris, 1780), Benjamin Laborde relates that Corbetta was sent to Louis XIV by the count of Mantua. However, Laborde was describing an event that had taken place some 130 years earlier and it is not clear when exactly this took place.[34] All in all, there is not enough evidence for us to state that Corbetta was the teacher of the Dauphin of France. (And it is not very likely that if Corbetta had such an honorable position, he would have left it for a position at the remote court of Hanover.) Still, as for many Italians, the political upheaval of the *Fronde*, in the years 1649–53, may have been a reason for Corbetta to keep out of the French capital. It is known that the official post of "maître de guittarre du Roy" was occupied by Bernard Jourdan de la Salle from Cádiz, from the early 1650s (when Louis XIV was approximately twelve years old) until the end of his life in 1695.[35] Of course, it is possible that the King received occasional instruction in guitar playing from

Corbetta. Later Jourdan was succeeded by his son Louis, who held this post until his death in 1719. He was followed by Robert de Visée. Visée must have been over sixty by then, and in his capacity as teacher of the King, he probably had to give guitar lessons to the young Louis XV (born 1710), who had succeeded his great-grandfather Louis XIV as King of France in 1715.

In the 1680s Robert de Visée could build on the foundations of Corbetta's work. In the spring of 1686, he was ordered by His Majesty to play in the royal apartments at courtly gatherings before supper. In these months the king spent much time in bed, as he was weakened by physical discomfort.[36] The Marquis de Dangeau, who for more than thirty years kept a diary in which he meticulously described the daily routine at Versailles, reports: "Saturday 11 [May 1686] à Versailles: . . . In the evening His Majesty went out for a long walk in the gardens. He takes a nap every day at eight, and has supper in bed at ten. Usually he orders Vizé to play the guitar at nine. Monseigneur, Madame la Dauphine, and all the royal court are with him until his supper."[37] In Versailles there was always music, and the King's interest went far beyond the fashion of the ephemeral guitar. He had lessons on the lute and the harpsichord from a young age, and there were always virtuosi around to entertain the court. In 1716, in the preface to the *Pièces de theorbe et de luth mises en partitions*, Visée looked back on successful court performances of his works for lute and theorbo. There are reports of his concerts (most likely on the theorbo) together with famous players such as Forqueray, Marais, Couperin, and Rebel. His books with guitar music date from an early stage of his career (1682 and 1686), and it is likely that his activities as a guitarist lessened after about 1690.

Around 1660, the year of the Restoration, when Charles II reclaimed the crown of England, the circumstances for Corbetta were probably more propitious there than in France. Although Paris was a rich musical environment, with many ballets, theatrical performances, and operas in which guitarists could perform, there were so many other famous musicians at court that no more than a marginal role was given to Corbetta. We know that he played (and probably danced) in a comical scene in Lully's *Galanterie du Temps* in 1656. But it can hardly be maintained that he had a successful career as a performing musician. Corbetta's *La guitarre royalle* (1671) was dedicated to the King of Britain, and yet most of the text of its preface is addressed to the great monarch of France. According to his obituary, published in the *Mercure galant* in 1681, Corbetta made two or three journeys to Paris in the 1670s, to have his books printed. It is not known if he visited France between 1660 and 1670.

In that country, the fashion for the guitar as a solo instrument perhaps came into full swing only after 1670, considering the almost complete lack of publications until then. Corbetta already had moved to London, where he was in a privileged position. There he had free access to the royal apartments and he most likely gave guitar lessons to Charles II, his brother James, and their sister Henrietta Anne, the duchess of Orleans.[38] Perhaps a guitarist was not allowed to have an engagement as a performer at all; but in any case, a great rage for the guitar soon started, very much due to the presence of Corbetta. Listen to Corbetta's Suite in A Minor (audio exx. 14–19). In his *Diary* Samuel Pepys described the contact "Signor Francisco" had with the aristocracy. Pepys, a passionate amateur on the lute, was not initially a devotee of the guitar: "After done with the Duke of York and coming out of his dressing-room, I there spied Signor Francisco tuning his gittar and Monsieur de Puy with him, who did make him play to me, which he did most admirably . . . , so well as I was mightily troubled that all that pains should have been taken upon so bad an instrument."[39] In 1674 Pepys took guitar lessons with the Italian Cesare Morelli, and a number of songs with guitar accompaniment have been found in the inventory of his belongings. Apparently he, too, had been infected by the guitar fever at court and had put aside his objections: "I followed my Lord Sandwich, who was gone a little before me on board the Royall James. And there spent an houre, my Lord playing upon the gittarr, which he now commends above all musique in the world, because it is base enough for a single voice and is so portable and manageable without much trouble."[40] According to Richard Pinnell, the example of Henrietta Anne as an amateur was of great importance for this craze. Just as her brother-in-law Louis XIV had done, she made the guitar acceptable, and for women, too. It became especially fashionable for young ladies to play the instrument. In 1677, in the evening of his life, Corbetta was named royal guitar master to Charles II's niece, Princess Anne.[41] The *Easy Lessons on the Guittar for Young Practitioners*, now lost, date from the same year.[42]

The lack of elbow room that Corbetta must have initially experienced as a performer in London obviously was compensated for by his success in gambling. He held a privilege from the King in 1661 for the game of *l'oca di Catalonia*. This lucrative trade came to an end in 1664, when under the pressure of public opinion, Charles II put a ban on certain games and lotteries.[43] After that time we hear more about Corbetta in connection with the guitaromania that was rapidly spreading in court circles—and the preference of the King for his music. In the *Mémoires du chevalier de Grammont* (Paris, 1713) we read:

> There was a certain Italian at court, famous for the guitar: he had a genius for music and he was the only man who could make anything of the guitar: his style of play was so full of grace and tenderness, that he would have given harmony to the most discordant instruments. The truth is, nothing was so difficult as to play like this foreigner. The King's relish for his compositions had brought the instrument so much into vogue that every person played on it, well or ill; and you were as sure to see a guitar on a lady's toilet as rouge or patches. The Duke of York played upon it tolerably well and the Earl of Arran like Francisco himself. This Francisco had composed a saraband, which either charmed or infatuated every person; for the whole guitarery at court were trying at it and God knows what an universal strumming there was.[44]

Corbetta is one of the very few guitarists of whom it is documented that they performed for an audience, even if it was in an informal setting. We may assume that almost every guitarist we know by name, if they earned money with their instrument at all, would have been mainly giving lessons. Where other musicians could find employment in ensembles (*collegia*), at courts, churches, or in festivities, guitarists very seldom would have played in "chambres" or other groups of professional musicians.[45] Only a few, like Foscarini, Bartolotti, Grenerin, and Visée, who found work as theorbists in the many theatrical performances in Paris, could hope to make a living. For Corbetta, who stated in the preface to *La guitarre royalle* (1671) that he did not play the lute at all, there was not a lot to do in all those productions. There are only a few reports of his playing.[46] A guitarist could attain a certain fame with occasional performances in the houses and palaces of the high society and by teaching the aristocracy. In London, the Italians Francesco Corbetta, Pietro Reggio, and Cesare Morelli, and possibly also Nicola Matteis, were sought after as guitar teachers by the elite.

"That Miserable Instrument"

One highly informative source illuminating the position of some of the leading professional guitarists is the correspondence of the Dutchman Constantijn Huygens (1596–1687). Huygens was for some time one of the most influential men in Holland, as the secretary of the stadtholder Frederik Hendrik (1584–1647) and his son Willem II (1626–50). The Calvinist Huygens was also a writer-poet and an ardent amateur musician who played the lute, viola da gamba, harpsichord, and guitar. He was in correspondence with statesmen as well as musicians, and a significant portion of his letters is preserved. They give a surprisingly clear picture of his encounters with well-known players. Huygens was in contact with three of the greatest Italian guitarists of the time, Foscarini, Bartolotti, and Corbetta. Bartolotti and Foscarini appear in his letters only as theorbists, and it is not possible to tell if he knew them in their capacity as guitarists, as well. He exchanged letters with Giovanni Paolo Foscarini, who had been in Flanders long before, in the service of Archduke Albert of Austria.[47] Foscarini was in Paris in 1647–49. In a letter to Huygens of July 26, 1647, he offered his services as a musician for the planned new Chapel Royal in The Hague.[48]

Noble Sir and patron,

Now that I am in France, commanded by the Queen [Anne of Austria] to make myself of use in an opera which was performed this winter [*L'Orfeo*], and because of my intention to assemble a book titled *L'armonia del mondo*, with which I take the courage to publish an Italian work in France, and because I have chanced to meet a competent person named Mr. Walter Krieger, living where you live, who has told me about your exceptional merits and abilities, and because of my plan to place the work with the title *L'armonia* under your protection, which work I hope you have received in a package, entrusted to Mr. Krieger, taking into consideration that, above all your other qualities, you are a protector of music, I take the liberty to send you some of my compositions, enclosed with this letter. If I can succeed in having you accept these benevolently, I will continue my work, no matter how insignificant it may be, and send you more according to your demands. Therefore I ask you to accept this humble proof of my infinite reverence, and while I am certain that I will be able to take my place among the servants of His Highness, your Master, I will meet you at some moment, which will be a good occasion to leave this place, as I will henceforth be under your protection and patronage. And now, to not expatiate any further, I humbly kiss your hands and express you my respect.[49]

Your devoted and most obedient servant
Gio. Paolo Foscarini.

Due to changed political circumstances, notably the death of William II in 1650, the royal chapel was never founded. Foscarini appeared in the premiere of Luigi Rossi's opera *L'Orfeo* in 1647 in Paris, which took place one year after the successful performances of *La Finta Pazza*.[50] Both operas were staged on the initiative of the influential Mazarin, and many musicians from Italy were engaged. In Paris Foscarini could oversee the printing of his treatise *Dell'armonia del mondo, lettioni due*.[51] Presumably, he found employment in France in his capacity as a theorbist; he seems to have printed no guitar music after 1640.[52]

In a letter to Huygens in 1649, he said that he would take part in a musical performance for the coronation ceremony in Madrid of Maria Anna of Austria, who became the second wife of Philip IV of Spain later that year.[53] Foscarini intended to travel in her retinue from Italy to Madrid, but most likely he was not able to, due to his desperate economic situation. From a series of four letters to Huygens from the first quarter of 1649, it appears that Foscarini got stuck in Paris, wanting to flee the civil war of the *Fronde*. His allowance from the court was suspended.[54]

Noble Sir and patron,

On 1 January I answered your kind letter of 10 December and in addition sent you a dialogue in three parts, which I hope has not displeased you. After that I went to Mr. Tassin, in accordance with your commission. He is the reason that I am deprived of all means here in Paris; with all the insurrection, I have been obliged to sell everything I had to survive, as I have to do without my income from the court. All my prospects are lost. If Mr. Tassin had handed me immediately what you by your innate kindness allowed me, I could have traveled to Lyons, where I could have devoted myself to necessary business. I received twenty-five écus last Monday from said Mr. Tassin, to whom I have given a receipt. What remains for me now is the obligation to send you a book with *ariette* for one, two, and three voices, fifty in total, that I mentioned in my last letter, which I have not yet sent for lack of money to pay for copying.

I feel ashamed writing about the miserable state I am in, because, if I still enjoy your appreciation, I would ask you for a special favor: to send me some more money to help me out, so that I can go to Lyons with my family, in compensation of which I offer to send you my five lutes from Bologna, as soon as I have arrived in Italy. And if you have a friend to whom I can hand them over, I will not forget to do that at my arrival and on my word of honour, I promise to send two lutes of the model of Ans Frai [Hans Frei] as well, which are very beautiful and have a wonderful varnish. For the love of God, I ask you to pardon me for the great liberties I take, but I assure you that it robs me of my soul, as I have used the little that I had and we have been in danger of life here, about the rest you can guess. Therefore I ask you not to leave me in this misery, so that I will be obliged to you for all time, next to the compensation I promised you.

I handed Mr. Tassin some [instrumental] works, with the scores, which are well-crafted compositions and have a wonderful effect when they are played on viols and are admired in the academies of Rome. I told him that the book with the *ariette* for one, two, or three voices was all there is, but there is also an interesting piece about an amorous madwoman ["La pazza amorosa"], which you will like. I intended to have it printed and to send it to you in print. The barricades of Paris have spoiled all this. Please receive my good intentions with this manuscript, I hope you will like it anyway, with the assurance of as much of my humble devotion as my faint health allows.

I ask forgiveness for my audacity, confident of your generosity, to which I feel eternally obliged. You will excuse me for not having written with my own hand, I have an inflammation in my arm, caused by a great melancholy that has come over me since I have been from home for three years. I have not been able to acquire anything of more value than a drink of water. I leave the rest to your consideration. I will await your benevolent answer. To conclude, I express you my reverence and I kiss your hands. Paris, 29 March 1649.[55]

Your devoted and most obedient servant
Gio. Paolo Foscarini.

In his letter to Huygens of April 29, 1649, Foscarini says that he has made a booklet for the theorbo—*al modo di Francia*, with *preludii, alemande, corente, gigi, sarabande, ciacone*, and *passacaglii*, and that he has decided to leave Paris before the end of the next month.[56] It is the last sign of life we have of the composer.

Later that year, political tensions increased with the imprisonment, by order of Mazarin, of the the prince of Conti, the Prince de Condé, and the duke of Longueville. The Cardinal had also raised taxes; some of his opponents in Parliament linked these to the grandiose performances of Rossi's *L'Orfeo*, which made unprecedented use of new stage machinery of Italian design. Such extravagance was a thorn in the flesh of the opposition, who incited riots in the streets. Many burlesque satirical leaflets (called *Mazarinades*) were printed, ridiculing the Cardinal. In a manuscript with songs and dances from about 1649, owned by "Monsieur Dupille, commissaire des guerres," there is a *chanson pour boire* (a drinking song) with guitar accompaniment:

No more war, no more war
We have had enough.
Paris and Saint Germain
Have made many fools.
A good drinker, La, la, la
Makes a good Frondeur.

They are burning, they are burning
The government.
And Mazarin
As well as parliament.
A good drinker, etc.

Study, study
Prince of Conti
Now you are at rest.
You have not to worry
And you can, La, la, la
Read Macchiavelli.[57]

It is almost symbolic of the cultural gap between the French and Italian traditions that the accompaniment for this *chanson pour boire* requires a guitar in re-entrant tuning (ex. 2.1), because most Italian newcomers probably used the bourdon tuning from their homeland.[58]

One of the Italian immigrants was Angelo Michele Bartolotti, who also settled in Paris, possibly in the late 1650s. His two books of guitar music were published in Italy, but other works of his appear in handwritten collections from France, for instance in the "Gallot" manuscript. Bartolotti worked as a professional theorbist in the opera. He published a manual for playing basso continuo on the lute, and a few of his solo works for the theorbo are preserved in manuscript.[59] As far as we know, he published no solo music for this instrument. Apparently the situation for the guitar in France was not auspicious enough in the years before 1670 to warrant publication of a third guitar book, although Bartolotti was still active as a musician for about fifteen years after the appearance of his *Secondo libro* (ca. 1655). Huygens reported that they had met in Paris, in the home of the celebrated Italian singer Anna Bergerotti:

Example 2.1. Collection of Monsieur Dupille (F-Pg MS 2344), "Point de guerre," an *air a pinser* in which the single melody is plucked, interspersed with occasional chord strums. The letter *a*, the d′ of the open fourth course, tuned in the high octave, belongs to the melody.

[My] compositions for the theorbo are reminiscent of the style of Mr. Angelo Michel, with whom I got acquainted in Paris. I regret not asking him for music during the time I met and conversed with him at Signora Anna's. But in those days I did not care for the theorbo very much, except for voice accompaniment. Since then my fancy took wing, and now I have written more than sixty compositions for it myself, with a broad variety and in different keys, of which herewith I humbly send you some examples to scrutinize.[60]

Huygens kept pace with the literature for the lute that was published in France. He also acquired copies of music by composers of all sorts, many of whom he knew in person. Not much is known of Bartolotti's life in Paris. We can deduce from the dissemination of his works outside his first two guitar books that he was known in France as a guitarist. The "Gallot" manuscript alone contains a number of beautiful preludes attributed to "A. M.," of which no other source is extant, that resemble the music from the *Secondo libro*. We cannot rule out the possibility of a third book.

In a letter of May 7, 1660, Huygens writes to Lady Swann: "I hope, you shall have your eares feasted at Breda with the excellent guitarre *del Signor* Corbetta [my italics], which is indeed worth your hearing and admiration, as I can testifie by the favor of her Royall Highness."[61] Corbetta was in the retinue of Charles II when it stayed in the Dutch town of Breda. Presumably this was the first time Huygens ever heard a performance on the guitar at this level. He took up the guitar only at a very advanced age, entirely self-taught, in the early 1670s.

In a word, after and many times between business belonging to my employment, I use, as I did, to fiddle myself out of a bad humour, either upon a viol, or a lute, or a theorba or a paire of virginals, which in my cabinet I doe find still ready about me. And as if upon all those instruments I had not spoiled and spent good hours enough, since a yeare hence I am become a notable guitarre-man, having produced above a thirty peeces of all sorts and tunes upon that miserable instrument. So that there wanteth almost nothing more but that I should be exalted to be a trumpeter at the head of our troops.[62]

In a letter to Sébastien Chièze, a diplomat who helped him acquire guitar and lute music, he made a similar remark: "I have become a guitarist by accident and I have composed some thirty works for this miserable instrument, which I only have on loan."[63] Chièze stayed in Madrid for several years as the ambassador of the Prince of Orange. Huygens repeatedly asked him to send tablatures and songs. What would this repertoire have been? At the time of their correspondence, the only printed guitar music, with a couple of exceptions, would have come from Italy. Judging by his complaints about the "inverted" tablature, it must have been music by Spanish or Italian composers. Huygens objected to the fact that the tablature was upside down ("leur sotte tablature, qui met tous dessous dessus"), without mentioning his unfamiliarity with alfabeto.[64] However, every book from Italy (other than alfabeto collections) has mixed alfabeto tablature, while Spanish solo music was normally written in tablature without alfabeto chords. This makes it even more likely that he was thinking of tablatures from Spain, notwithstanding the fact that there is no printed music known from before 1674 (the year that the *Instrucción* by Gaspar Sanz was published). Chièze must have sent him music in manuscript, and Huygens reacted with mixed feelings:

> I am very pleased to see these Spanish songs in musical notes, in which the true genius of the nation can be found, strongly African in my opinion, and which can never shed *de Punicum et Lybicum* [the Punic or Libyan influence] from overseas. With respect to the guitar tablature: I will one more time (*y no mas* [and no more]) take pains to translate this sottish way of notating *sotto sopra* [upside down] in good letters of the alphabet, in hopes of finding something worthwhile to figure out. You could say that this is a tablature for the antipodes. These gentlemen would oblige me very much, if they would express themselves in the ways of this side of the Pyrenees, which would be easier for them than for me. *Miraremos* [We will see] if the game is worth the candle.[65]

Huygens became more and more critical of Spanish music for the guitar: "My most acid invectives are directed against the [solo] guitar music of your murderers of harmony, because some of the songs are tolerable."[66] With the vocal repertoire, we should think of the *tonos humanos* (secular songs) of a composer like José Marin, without doubt among the best that Spain produced in the seventeenth century.[67] But Huygens was disappointed by the quality of Spanish music in general, and with mordant sarcasm he described how the famous lutenist Gautier (probably Jacques Gautier "d'Angleterre") was treated at the court in Madrid:

Let's see if they have alemandes, courantes or sarabandes that are worth-while to listen to, because what they have put into your hands now are *niñe-rias* [childish pieces] and the poorest. Gautier has told me that after having played for two hours on his superb lute in the Cabinet of the King in Madrid, *los Grandes d'España—grandes aselli*—said: *Pity he doesn't play the guitar*, which tempted him to give them a box on the ear with his lute. Still, this makes me believe that there must be a connoisseur who knows how to make this instrument [the guitar] produce something good.[68]

Chièze still could see the charm of the music of his host country, when per-formed by Spanish singers with the support of a typical Spanish continuo group: "The songs, Sir, are very Greek, yet in the throat of musicians over here, with their confused and impassioned eruptions, they don't lack charm, espe-cially when they are supported by harps, vihuelas, and shawms, of which there are some celebrated players here. About the cifra of the guitar I will say no more, I will try to find a sensible virtuoso, to show him the compositions you have sent."[69] Huygens's comments are of no uncertain kind:

> I have received the *tonos humano-bestiados* [human-bestial songs] and they suf-fice *ad nauseam* to see how far the beautiful genius of Spain has degenerated, that used to inspire the great minds of people like Seneca, Lucan, and the rest of the demigods I have mentioned to you before. I do not understand what is supposed to be *humano* in this music, or is it that the beasts will sing the rest?[70]

> Your latest [letter] of 13 September brought me the last of your *tonos* and I am very happy that it is the last, for I notice more and more what point of bes-tiality these half-Africans have reached. Who has ever heard of a *villancico*—something I would consider a gigue or vaudeville—*al santissimo Sacramento*? And then, instead of singing a motet or a most serious church piece, to let it roll on with *fa, la la la*. What devil has turned around the spirit of those cous-ins of Seneca, Lucan, and many other luminaries from antiquity?[71]

On October 3, 1673, Huygens wrote that he had to return the guitar he had borrowed for life (*inter vivos*) from Mrs. Catherina Smith from Amsterdam. A few years later however, he apparently had ordered a guitar from Madrid:

> Herewith I send a sketch of the guitar I promised to you, Sir, and descriptions from the hand of the man who is charged with the task of making one for you, which must be to your taste, because he says he is one of the best artisans of Europe. The guitar is ready, but he wishes to keep it here for this winter in order to, in case the wood becomes warped, remedy that *y assentar la obra* [and finish the job]. As recompense they ask only for your judgement of the pieces [of music] included and perusal of some of yours and of those that you can get out of France, *con advertencia* that the tablature enclosed is Italian.[72]

In Huygens's estate there was a "tablature de guitarre par Franc. Corbetta."[73] It is not known which book it was. It is doubtful if Huygens ever got over his aversion to Italian tablature, and there is no way of telling if he would have joined in the style of battuto, given the great worth he attached to music theory. In the two *Guitarre royalle* collections by Corbetta (1671 and 1674), however, there is only music in French tablature, which he had mastered.

There is a late report of the decline of the guitar, written in 1730, from the hand of Jean-Baptiste de Castillion. Castillion collected music of the great guitarists of old, Giovanni Battista Granata, Francesco Corbetta, and the Roman composer Lelio Colista, but also of Gaspar "Sanchez," Nicolas Derosier and François Lecocq. Three large manuscripts have been preserved, containing a great number of works of composers of the seventeenth century.[74] Castillion gave a concise survey of the history of the guitar. As is evident from his selection of pieces, he was very knowledgeable about the whole of the repertoire, also copying works that can only be found with him, by Michel (Miguel?) Perez de Zavala, Lelio Colista, and Francesco Corbetta. It is clear that he had tablatures at his disposal that now are considered to be lost. Remarkably, Bartolotti is absent from his collections, which could mean that his books had only a limited distribution.

> In those of Mr. Francis Corbet we find much gravity. Mr. Lelio made his with a pleasant sweetness. Michel Perez Zavala from Spain and master of my honored Father in Madrid around 1690, clearly has imitated those two well. The pieces of Mr. Gaspar Sanchez, also a Spaniard and of Mr. Jean Baptiste Granata, Italian, have their merits: the chaconnes and passacailles of the latter must be considered well-made. Mr. Robert de Visée was famous in all France for the frequent honour of playing for Louis XIV, that great King, and for having dedicated to him his livre de Guitare in 1682, a work that distinguished him for many years. Mr. Saint-Luc in turn was also of high repute, he played the guitar with great skill. Finally, Mr. Nicolas Derosier, well-grounded in music, Ordinaire de la Musique of Her Highness the Electress Palatine, devoted an entire study to the guitar and to make it more perfect, he invented the *Guitarre Angelique*, with eight more courses than usual. He published a book for each in the year 1692.[75]

In the first part of the large manuscript B-Bc Ms. S5615, now in the Conservatoire in Brussels, there is a vast collection of works by François Lecocq. This virtuoso lived and worked in the southern Netherlands at the turn of the century. As a guitar teacher to the highest aristocracy, he played a role comparable to Corbetta decades before in London.

> The famous François Corbet introduced it to the Low Countries and after he had dedicated his book [*Varii scherzi di sonate per la chitara spagnola* (1648)] to the Archdukes Albert and Isabelle, all the nobility in Brussels took a pride

in playing it. And at the end of the last century and at the beginning of the present, I saw that the guitar alone was fashionable still and that Madame l'Electrice of Bavaria took lessons from Mr. François Le Cocq, today a retired musician of the Chapel Royal of the Court.[76]

The closing words of Jean-Baptiste de Castillion's preface give a sad impression of the solitary position of the guitarist: "As in this world all is subject to changes of fortune, it seems that the great King, Louis XIV, was the last who learned to play it, and at present it is the turn of the guitar to languish. [May] heaven allow this book after my death to fall into the hands of some amateur, able to play from my efforts."[77]

Chapter Three

Accompaniment

The Guitar and the
Early-Seventeenth-Century Canzonetta

Musicologists and performers have long neglected the song repertoire with alfabeto, although it was certainly not unknown that a great number of collections from the first half of the seventeenth century were published in this way. Only recently have serious attempts been made to arrive at a reconstruction, taking into account the historical position of the guitar in this repertoire. The chord alphabet of the guitar seemed an inferior alternative to the "real" basso continuo of the harpsichord. It has even been assumed that the addition of alfabeto was primarily a commercial ploy by printers such as the Venetian Alessandro Vincenti.[1]

Beginning in the 1980s, the lute (or often, the theorbo) was increasingly used in historically informed performance practice; the guitar, however, was not at that time deemed a serious continuo instrument. Many still assume that the songs with added alfabeto are ideally performed with theorbo or harpsichord. The guitar, it is suggested, could easily serve as an alternative, but it should be supported by at least one bass instrument. James Tyler remarks about alfabeto practice: "Certainly, its tunings often prevent it from sounding the true bass note; however, an idiomatic continuo accompaniment for guitar can be stunningly effective when combined with a lute or theorbo playing the true bass line."[2] Nevertheless, there are reasons to suppose that the guitar was used as an independent instrument for accompaniment in many situations.[3] In "The 'Chitarra Spagnola' and Italian Monody 1589 to circa 1650," Nina Treadwell gives an overview of the different genres where the guitar provided an accompaniment—often light, strophic arias like villanelle, canzonette, and ariette. There were also composers, however, who included alfabeto in their more dramatic works—through-composed arias or solo madrigals. Songs with alfabeto were published by such renowned composers as Sigismondo d'India, Stefano Landi, Girolamo Kapsberger, Biagio Marini, and Martino Pesenti. In her article "Remigio Romano's Collections of Lyrics for Music," Silke Leopold remarks:

The more complicated the setting, the more difficult the ornament, then the smaller was the chance that a composition would appeal to even a medium-sized audience. And so the situation appears to be turned on its head—that ephemera tend to be the expressive, recitative, declamatory monody, while the little arias were on everyone's lips. Our conception of this period, based as it is on the impression made on us by the harmonic summersaults [sic] of a Saracini, the declamatory finesse of a Peri, the demands on vocal technique of a Monteverdi, is a little distorted. We can only understand the development of vocal music in the second half of the century if we take this repertoire seriously. When confronted with a popular strophic song, we should not automatically agree with the only theoretician of the time, the conservative Giovanni Battista Doni, that music was in decline. For these little songs are in some ways a step ahead of recitative monody, with their formal and rhythmical periodicity, not modelled on dance patterns but arising as it were naturally from the basis of the metrical structure of the text, in pure, simple harmonic relations.[4]

Alessandro Vincenti published many collections in which a bass line is provided for continuo as well as alfabeto. Often an instruction for the guitar alphabet is included, which shows that he wished to reach the beginner. Indeed, it is not certain whether or not the composers themselves always included the chords. In most cases, the front page states that the songs can be accompanied by chitarrone or harpsichord, or other similar instruments: "Commode da cantarsi nel Clavicembalo, Chitarrone, & altro simile Stromento. Con le Lettere dell'Alfabetto per la Chitarra Spagnola."[5]

Although it is often supposed that the choice to include alfabeto was not made for primarily artistic reasons, there are indications that in certain genres the use of the guitar was a serious option and sometimes even the only one. There are descriptions of performances by celebrated singers like the Neapolitan sopranos Ippolita Recupito and Adriana Basile accompanying themselves on the guitar. Then there are editions and manuscripts with nothing more than song texts and alfabeto, like the *Prima racolta di bellissime canzonette musicali* published by Remigio Romano in 1618. In succeeding years, Romano edited a number of anthologies containing arias by several composers with only text and alfabeto. These editions must have served for singing well-known melodies to guitar chords.

In Biagio Marini's *Scherzi e canzonette* (1622), there are villanelle for two voices, with alfabeto but without a separate continuo bass. One could plausibly assume that the lowest voice in example 3.1 was played on an instrument like the theorbo to reinforce the lowest notes. And yet, the question remains: why didn't Marini provide an instrumental bass line, as he did with the solo songs? This curious omission makes it more likely that it was performed by only two singers and that one of them—the soprano—played the alfabeto chords, which were put above the upper staff for ease of readability. Although we cannot

Example 3.1. Biagio Marini (1622), "Il più bel fiore," a villanella without a basso continuo. The third line is a transcription of the alfabeto.

exclude the possibility that the bass voice was sometimes performed on a theorbo, it does not seem to have been the prime intention of the composer here. The rhythm of the lower voice, following the syllabic text placement, points more toward an all-vocal performance. However, at the final cadence there are the figures "7–6" in the bass, indicating that if this part is supported with a harmonic instrument, a suspension is to be played. In the alfabeto accompaniment, this tenor cadence iv⁶–V is replaced by two parallel harmonies E♭ and D (alfabeto M and C) on the guitar, different from what was customary on other continuo instruments.[6]

Editing the music in a way that leaves open different options for performance is exactly in line with what Biagio Marini said about his intent to accompany the voice in different ways: "You will find in some places in this work that the alfabeto is not in concord with the bass. The intention of the composer is to have the voice accompanied in as many [ways] as possible, do not concern yourself with the obligation to that [bass line], since the guitar cannot produce many beautiful harmonies."[7] In a similar vein, Carlo Milanuzzi explained: "I admit that, in many places, I have altered the chords for Spanish guitar with respect to the basso continuo, because when these ariette are accompanied, the Spanish guitar gives a different effect from that of the Chitarrone or Spinetta. In making these alterations I seek to give greater charm to the music."[8] It is no great wonder, then, that these songs appear in different guises. The famous "Amarilli, mia bella" by Giulio Caccini, for instance, the classic example of a solo madrigal, has been found in versions for four to six voices and in *contrafacta* and instrumental arrangements all over Europe. Although Caccini was anxious to assert that his songs were conceived for a solo singer from the start, like many other composers he may not have disdained the practice of arranging his own works, both from solo song (not provided with alfabeto, however) to multipart versions and vice versa.[9] The liberty with regard to the choice of instruments for the accompaniment reveals just another aspect of the context of domestic music making. One of the functions of a chordal instrument was to fill out the harmony, and that is what the guitar does in Marini's "Il più bel fiore," the bass part being provided by one of the singers. It is quite conceivable that the composer himself added the alfabeto symbols to songs such as these.

The Hieroglyphs of the Guitar

To realize a continuo from a bass line on a keyboard or theorbo, normally the rules of counterpoint were followed. Because the guitarist did not have the bass to hang on to, the application of these rules was sketchy. The chords of standard alfabeto do not have prepared dissonances or delayed resolutions, and thus they function as block harmonies, and not so much as horizontal polyphony. We can deduce from how many songs are provided with alfabeto with a chord on almost every single bass note that whoever edited the alfabeto (the composer, the compiler, or the printer) often was not able to work out a proper accompaniment for the guitar with respect to both the treble and the bass. The idea of harmony (in contrast to counterpoint) as an independent force in music was only just awakening. What began to take shape as harmonic relations, in a repertoire of sixteenth-century dances, sometimes led to a defective result in the less formalized environment of guitar accompaniment, or in freely composed newer dance types such as the *courante francese.* Here the nearly unlimited choice of alfabeto chords that he had at his disposal put the guitarist in the position of a sorcerer's apprentice.[10] Occasionally we can speak of downright incorrect harmonies. If there is no fixed succession of chords, nor any structuring cohesion between bass and soprano, randomly chosen chords can be placed one after another, related to just one of the voices instead of both.

In an article published in 1981, Robert Strizich described a passage in Kapsberger's "Voi pur mi prometteste" (ex. 3.2), where there is an alfabeto chord in root position placed on every note of the bass.[11] This clumsy use of alfabeto results on some occasions in a harmonization that is in sharp conflict with the vocal melody as well as with the lute part. It is the effect of a decidedly

Example 3.2. Girolamo Kapsberger (1623), "Voi pur mi prometteste," mm. 21–22. According to Kapsberger's own lute part, the first harmony in the second measure is a $^6_3$ chord on D (B-flat major), while in the alfabeto it is a D-minor chord. An even more serious conflict arises with the next harmony ("+" in alfabeto). This E-minor chord contains the note B played at the same time the singer and the lute have a B♭.

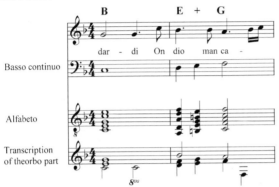

amateurish approach to basso continuo. Still, we cannot exclude the possibility that even trained musicians made such mistakes, as well. Battuto, notated in alfabeto, was a new phenomenon, and the rules for this "guitar code" were not yet widely understood. It is impossible to tell if Kapsberger—who played the guitar himself—is responsible for including alfabeto with every song or if this was the work of the editor.

Lutenist Bellerofonte Castaldi commented, not without sarcasm, on the practice of adding (often faulty) alfabeto letters of the "chitarra Spagnolissima" to every song:

> Please do not turn away because the Author, most well knowing how to do it, did not place the A.B.Cs of the Spanish Guitar above each one of these Airs, as one does according to current usage. This would have been done if one had not seen that such pedantry is of little use to those who don't know (if the letters are not discarded) of the innumerable errors that occur at the cadences because of the aforementioned hieroglyphs. He who knows how does not need to be taught.[12]

If we compare the alfabeto accompaniments made by different guitarists to the same aria, it appears that there were different levels of understanding. The song "Tirinto mio" (ex. 3.4), from Giovanni Stefani's anthology of 1620, is provided with alfabeto; since most of the songs from Stefani's collections are borrowed from other composers, some being alfabeto arrangements of preexisting three-voice Roman or Neapolitan villanelle, it is not certain that he composed this song himself. The discrepancies between it and the alfabeto chords added by Pietro Millioni, seven years later, are striking. In Stefani's print, as many root-position chords as possible are placed upon the bass notes (mostly taken literally from the *Scala di musica per B. molle* included in his alfabeto instructions, see ex. 3.3), even if this results in awkward progressions, while Millioni provides the song with a fluent and efficient accompaniment, created with very few (but well-chosen) chords, evincing a keen sense of harmony. We should consider the possibility that Millioni copied the text together with the alfabeto from an original that is now lost.[13] His version is from a booklet with text and alfabeto only, which fits with the notion that he published for amateur guitarists.[14] Since there is no bass line to reckon with, the chords are exclusively related to the (unwritten) melody. Millioni's guitar manuals, with simple alfabeto dances, are equally devoid of music in staff notation. Perhaps Millioni (or the example, either in notation or performance, he took his cue from) chose his consonances in accordance with an imaginary bass line, different from Stefani's, as in the first chord in the penultimate measure of example 3.4.

Biagio Marini was among the first to introduce new chords for alfabeto. In his instructions for the guitar from the *Scherzi e canzonette* (1622), there are eight examples of cadences, with suspensions—a horizontal element—produced by new alfabeto chords. This makes it clear that Marini was well aware of the possibilities of the instrument, and we may assume that he included the alfabeto in the songs in this book himself. The well-chosen harmonies, without unnecessary changes with every movement of the bass, shows that he had a good understanding of how an accompaniment in battuto is best shaped. Marini managed to synthesize the rigid simplicity of alfabeto and an implicit harmonic ground plan of the songs, being aware that the guitar requires a different application of the rules.[15] The two ways of realizing the same aria—with figured bass for keyboard or theorbo and alfabeto for the guitar—give very different results in some spots. Example 3.5 shows that Marini could express himself very well in both ways. In the second measure of example 3.5a, we see a typical cadence (.A.A. - B), as described in Marini's own instructions. In example 3.5b, an interesting harmony (a C-minor chord with an added ninth) has been inserted for the guitar where the letter L of alfabeto is placed above the vocal staff.

Alfabeto and Genre

Nina Treadwell concludes that many composers distinguished between different genres with regard to the addition of alfabeto. In some books, only a limited number of songs have alfabeto chords. These are mostly light, strophic arias, often in triple time.[16] Domenico Obizzi, for example, gives alfabeto with what he calls "ariette" in the first part of his *Madrigali et arie a voce sola* (audio exx. 2–4), while the through-composed solo madrigals in the second part of

Example 3.3. Giovanni Stefani (1620), Scala di Musica per B. Molle.

Example 3.4. Giovanni Stefani (1620), "Tirinto mio tu mi feristi." The note F in the bass in measure 3 should probably be an F♯. On the third stave is the transcription of Stefani's alfabeto, and on the fourth stave, the alfabeto by Millioni. The stems of the notes in the transcription indicate the direction of the strum.

this book have no guitar accompaniment. The title pages of collections of several composers (e.g., Rontani, Vitali, and Sabbatini) state that alfabeto is only added to those songs that are suited to being sung to the guitar.[17] In *Il primo libro delle musiche* (1618) by Francesca Caccini (the daughter of Giulio Caccini), there are a few canzonette with alfabeto. The other works in this collection, *sonetti, madrigali, arie,* and *hinni* (hymns), partly spiritual songs, are provided with a basso continuo, but have no alfabeto.

The songs in which the stanzas alternate with instrumental ritornelli for violin and chitarrone are an interesting category. We also find those ritornelli in Marini's "Il più bel fiore" (ex. 3.1), which is remarkable, because in the all-vocal stanzas there appears to be no role for these instruments, while, conversely, there is no alfabeto in the ritornelli. Treadwell supposes that the voice would have been accompanied by chitarrone (theorbo) and guitar together, with the theorbo principally playing the bass line. In the ritornelli, the guitar would supplement the harmony at the player's discretion, since there is no

Example 3.5. (a) Biagio Marini (1622), "Il Verno." The rhythm of the guitar strums is not indicated. The bass line implies a different harmonization than the alfabeto. (b) The addition of the L chord is highly effective.

alfabeto given.[18] It is doubtful, however, if the guitarist, who always had to rely on the simplified harmony of alfabeto, would have been able to find the proper chords here. Another possibility is that the guitar remained silent in the ritornelli. This is consistent with Biagio Marini's indication that the ritornelli are meant for the violin and chitarrone. A third option can also be considered: there may have been two different ways of performing the songs, one with theorbo and violin and another with the guitar alone, as a duet or even as a solo song, in which case the ritornelli were left out. This would enable amateurs to sing and accompany the beloved works of a well-known composer.

Despite its limitations with regard to accompaniment in more dramatic works, the guitar has some qualities that enable it to support a recitative in other ways than with strummed chords alone. In Foscarini's basso continuo instructions there are examples of arpeggios which can be useful for the accompaniment of chamber monody (less so in larger rooms, since the tone of the guitar does not carry well). In several collections there are arias beginning with a short recitative; some are set up so that triple-time dance-like movements alternate with narrative sections in binary meters, like miniature cantatas. These songs can be accompanied effectively with a succession of arpeggios (pizzicato) and chord strums. Even though a guitar in accompaniment cannot produce an effect as dramatic as the theorbo, a considerable number of through-composed songs with alfabeto were published, and this raises the question of where and how the guitar was involved in performance. One possible answer could be that the main function of such a songbook format was to provide the amateur with a solid footing from which to explore a song repertoire—either well-known or new—to satisfy his curiosity. It must be taken into account that although the guitar was not the best tool for accompaniment in every genre, publishers (or composers) would have anticipated more profits by including alfabeto.

The Chronology of Alfabeto Repertoire

As demonstrated by the earliest descriptions of the use of the guitar *a lo rasgado*, from around 1580, a tradition of song accompaniment emerged in Spain in a repertoire of which not very much has survived. If a guitar dance becomes a song (or a song a dance, as was perhaps the case with "Guardame las vacas"), the chords will fit perfectly, and a number of Spanish songs from around 1600 were indeed connected to dances like *la folia*, *villano*, *Ruggiero*, and *ciaccona*. This may partly explain why singing to guitar chords at that time was seen as typically Spanish. In some cases it is possible to reconstruct the accompaniment by comparing the concordances of well-known dances with song texts.[19] However, not all Spanish songs are based on the stock chord progressions of popular dances, and only very few melodies of guitar songs have been preserved in music notation.

There are several early manuscripts of Italian provenance, such as the "Traetta" (ca. 1599) and the "Riccardiana" manuscripts from 1610–20, which contain Italian and Spanish texts with alfabeto, showing that Spanish song had set foot on Italian soil around 1600.[20] Since a number of these manuscripts can be linked to court circles, and in one case even more precisely to the Neapolitan soprano Adriana Basile, who was one of the most celebrated singers of the age, it can be assumed that this Spanish song repertoire had reached educated classes from the very start.[21] It is reported in a letter from 1609 that Adriana knew some three hundred Italian and Spanish songs by heart, a repertoire which she must have learned in the preceding years.

In Italy, unlike in Spain, an extended song repertoire with alfabeto appeared in print, starting with Kapsberger's *Primo libro de villanelle* (1611) and Montesardo's *Lieti giorni di Napoli* (1612). The rapid increase in popularity of the guitar in southern Italy correlates with the rise of the vocal genres of canzonetta and solo villanella. Taken at face value, the situation in both countries might appear very similar, but perhaps this deserves a second look.

In imitation of Spanish practice, Italian dances like the *pavaniglia*, *bergamasca*, *corrente*, *paganina*, *aria de Firenze*, and *la monica*, all dating back to sixteenth-century lute repertoire, were transcribed or reduced to alfabeto versions, and can all be found in large numbers in the early alfabeto books. The battuto style of the guitar at once made this repertoire accessible to everyone (as illustrated by the "music lesson" of figure I.1). In northern Italy, however, the craze for battuto dances possibly did not start on a large scale before the early 1620s, as the number of publications from before 1620 is very small.[22] Perhaps Sanseverino's reference to the "natural ancient style" of battuto applies mainly to the image of historic authenticity, given that the guitar was a relative newcomer in the musical world of the north. The paucity of sources suggests that at the very beginning of the seventeenth century, the guitar did not play much of a role there.

After the publication of Girolamo Montesardo's *Nuova inventione* (Florence, 1606), there was a gap of fourteen years before the first Northern Italian alfabeto tutors came out,[23] by Giovanni Ambrosio Colonna (Milan, 1620), Benedetto Sanseverino (Milan, 1620), and Carlo Milanuzzi (Venice, 1622). Between 1622 and 1640, over twenty-five similar collections were printed.[24] In all these books we find the same Spanish and Italian dance types, and in this respect the alfabeto repertoire of the guitar can be characterized as backward-looking. As the example of the "Aria del gran duca" from Sanseverino's *Primo libro d'intavolatura* (ex. I.2) shows, some of these dances could serve equally as a basis for songs, even if the lyrics are seldom included.

If a polyphonic song were to be accompanied, dance-like, with strummed chords, the two traditions, vocal polyphony and alfabeto, would not merge automatically. Nowadays it is often supposed that the style of chordal song accompaniment was simply transferred from the earlier Spanish dance song tradition to polyphonic genres. In a small number of Italian songbooks from 1610–16, such as Kapsberger's *Libro primo di villanelle* and Montesardo's *Lieti Giorni*, there are two- and three-voice villanelle in Neapolitan style with added alfabeto chords. However, Alexander Dean's research into the five-course guitar and seventeenth-century harmony has shown that in this repertoire, the guitar chords are in many places in conflict with the prevailing harmony.[25] The "alfabeto editors" of these collections, the persons responsible for adding alfabeto symbols to the music, obviously were not always able to find the appropriate chords to the (not seldom homorhythmic) polyphony. Often it seems as if the chords relate to only one of the voices, which is either the bass or the soprano. Dean characterizes these accompaniments to Neapolitan villanelle as "non-practical alfabeto," arguing: "Given the commercial motivation for alfabeto use and the apparent lack of editorial care in the guitar villanella books, of course, it can be argued that the alfabeto/text format does not accurately represent contemporary practice."[26] The inclusion of alfabeto may indeed have had another purpose here, as the association with the guitar and dance song may have served mainly to contribute to an image of spontaneous music-making.

After about 1615 a new repertoire of (mainly solo) songs began to appear, now making use of alfabeto chords which, for the most part, go well with both upper voice and bass. Examples are the song books by the Neapolitan composer Andrea Falconieri (Rome, 1616 and 1619), and those by Flamminio Corradi (1616), Carlo Milanuzzi (1622), Giovanni Pietro Berti (1624 and 1627) (audio ex. 9), and Domenico Obizzi (1627), which were all printed in Venice. Biagio Marini published his *Scherzi e canzonette* (1622) in Parma (see ex. 3.5). Many of these composers were employed as church musicians, trained in the contrapuntal style of sacred music, and skilled on other instruments, like the organ or the lute. We may assume, therefore, that finding appropriate chords on the guitar would have been no more difficult for them than composing a continuo bass. The differences in their works between the continuo line and alfabeto can probably be best explained by a thorough knowledge of the guitar, as the above-cited comments of Marini and Milanuzzi make clear. Perhaps these songs were composed with guitar in hand (and a keyboard within easy reach). The bass line in staff notation, which these collections always include, is still a good starting-point for a continuo on other instruments. It seems reasonable to suppose that in their compositions these composers already took the guitar's limitations into account, and it is very likely, too, that the simplicity of alfabeto harmony affected the style of this genre at a more structural level. Dean calls this the stage of "integrated alfabeto."

> The two basic determining features of this "integrated alfabeto" style are: (1) the use of functional alfabeto which simplifies the bass line by omitting passing tones, observing inversions, and using the kind of practical, playable chord progressions found in the alfabeto solo dance sources; and (2) the use of a dance-song style of composition that is inherently amenable to guitar accompaniment. Basso continuo lines in these pieces often use one note per harmony in combination with recurring rhythmic patterns to create strong harmonic periods that are easily adapted to strummed guitar performance. In such pieces, there is little need to simplify the bass line to make the alfabeto functional, since the compositional conception is already so close to the guitar tradition. The alfabeto dance-song tradition . . . is characterized by short periodic structures created by recurring chord patterns in combination with particular strum patterns. Similar short-term periodic structures created by harmonic and rhythmic means are also characteristic of Venetian canzonetta composition.[27]

How to Find the Chords to a Song

One of the most difficult questions to answer is how guitarists like Pietro Millioni (who may have copied from earlier sources) created an alternative alfabeto accompaniment to continuo songs, ignoring the harmonic implications of the bass (as in ex. 3.4). Here the chords of the *scala di musica* (ex. 3.3) are not helpful, and a system of harmonization with functionally related chords (a veritable "rule of the octave") was not introduced before the eighteenth century. To explain where these alfabeto harmonies come from, some writers have referred to alfabeto inscription as reflecting unwritten practices. Alexander Dean comments:

> In the Venetian usage, the alfabeto at times follows the vocal line and ignores the harmonies suggested by the more complex continuo lines. In such cases the alfabeto tends to follow the passacaglia pattern that best accommodates the voice. While these symbols may or may not represent the "wrong" harmony, it seems clear that reference to passacaglia patterns rather than analysis of notated voices became the prevailing standard in applying vertical harmonies to the solo voice and continuo texture.[28]

Dean supposes that a continuous exposure of the amateur guitarist to the standard cadential patterns of the passacaglia and the ciaccona encouraged applying the same chord progressions to the accompaniment of new songs.[29] The frequent occurrence of standard progressions of the early passacaglia (such as I–IV–V–I) does suggest that players from a popular tradition who had little knowledge of counterpoint-based harmony could have fallen back on the formulas they were used to, even if these cadences do not match the basso continuo line.[30] In some cases, as in Millioni's alfabeto in example 3.4, this can indeed be true.[31] However, the similarity between battuto dance and alfabeto song accompaniment is rather misleading: practical alfabeto makes use of only a very limited number of chords, no more than about thirteen or fourteen in total; within one song, seldom more than eight to ten different chords are used, which could explain why certain combinations appear more often than others, especially at cadence points.

Although the I–IV–V–I (or i–iv–V–i) formula was often used, we can see many other popular dance genres of the time (*ballo del gran duca, folia, villano, Ruggiero*, etc.) in the same alfabeto anthologies making use of other harmonic schemes. Besides, it should be noted that, even if dance-like rhythms are very common in these little arias, only a minority of the songs with alfabeto is based on known dances, and therefore we should be cautious not to equate the two genres, no matter how close they are with respect to form and character. Standard cadential progressions and dance rhythms, including hemiolas and syncopations (ex. 3.6, measures 3–4), which can be found in instrumental ensemble works and lute music as well, are by no means unique to the strummed style of the guitar, and even if performing them on the guitar feels very natural, they could have entered the canzonetta repertoire via a different route. Biagio Marini's *Scherzi e canzonette*, published in 1622, is this composer's first known collection of songs with alfabeto. In his *Arie, madrigali et corrente* of 1620, for example, there are a number of ariette that would have been good candidates for the alfabeto treatment, especially because Marini would have been well able to provide the chords for the guitar himself, as he did in his 1622 collection.

Within the sphere of basso continuo there is a tendency toward chordal textures, as we can glean from the early-seventeenth-century treatises of Bianciardi, Agazzari, and Viadana. In Flamminio Corradi's *Le stravaganze d'amore* (1616), one of the very first Venetian song collections with alfabeto, there is tablature for the chitarrone as well, showing a sober chordal accompaniment style. This is where the two traditions, the battuto of the guitar and the pizzicato of the lute, lead to very similar results.

The relationship between oral traditions and music preserved in any kind of notation is a complex one. Reinhard Strohm proposes to delineate the realm of unwritten music as follows:

> Perhaps the biggest mystification would be to define "unwritten music" as a specific kind of music at all. In almost any kind of music, certain elements are not usually written down ... think not only of rhythm but also tempo, dynamics, embellishments, musica ficta, instrumentation, absolute pitch or tuning. Some of these elements were, accordingly, left quite undecided by the composer. It was not "the piece" that remained unwritten, but very important aspects of it.[32]

In what sense would this apply to the alfabeto repertoire? The stereotypical chordal reductions of sixteenth-century (lute) dances that we find in alfabeto books and manuscripts give all the information one needs for performance. Insofar as the available sources from 1600–1640 are able to reveal it, the relatively new battuto style of the guitar was applied in a very specific way, given that even the rhythm of the strumming patterns shows great uniformity. With respect to the emergence of more adventurous practices in Italy, we should rather think of variant battuto versions of popular ostinatos such as folia, ciaccona, and passacaglia, the earliest examples of which can be found in manuscripts from the first decades of the seventeenth century.[33] The practice of chordal variation (as in ex. 4.2b), which the rise of alfabeto harmony and the introduction of the battuto style made possible, demonstrates once more that, in certain genres, guitarists started to explore the opportunities of harmony, while not paying much attention to the rules of counterpoint.[34] In chapter 4 we will discuss the application of chordal variation in the solo works of Foscarini and Corbetta.

As we have seen in the example of "Il più bel fiore" (ex. 3.1), Biagio Marini sometimes inscribed alfabeto chords that do not correspond to his own continuo bass. Taking into account Marini's familiarity with the guitar, it must be assumed that he had good reasons for shaping the accompaniment differently. The example of chordal variation in "Il verno" (ex. 3.5b) shows that the two traditions, basso continuo and alfabeto, could invite different harmonizations. It is here that we see that the strummed style of the guitar, linked with unwritten practices, demands an unconventional approach. Alexander Dean describes three frequent characteristic cadential figures in the "integrated alfabeto" style, which we can suppose were used to overcome the shortcomings of the alfabeto system with regard to non-triadic harmonies.[35]

First, because there are no diminished chords in alfabeto, which would be needed to play a vii^{o6}–I progression, the diminished chord (vii^{o6}) was in many cases replaced by a minor chord of the second degree (resulting in ii–I). Second, as in Marini's "Il più bel fiore," the 7–6 figure on E♭, implying a tenor cadence iv^6–V, was often replaced by a succession of two major harmonies E♭–D (VI–V). The reason for this is probably that there are no seventh chords in alfabeto. The third typical "guitaristic" is the obviously dissonant L chord, which is a C minor harmony with an added ninth (the d′ on the second course, as seen in ex. 3.5b). It concerns a simplified left hand pattern that makes it easier to connect to the G minor and D major chords with which it often is used in an O–L–C–O progression, which is a i–iv–V–i cadence.[36] A very early example of this particular minor passacaglia cadence including the L chord can be found in a Roman manuscript (I-Bc MSV 280) from circa 1614.[37] From then on the L chord formed part of standard alfabeto chord charts. The uncomplicated nature of these pragmatic solutions tempt one to speculate about an influence from unwritten traditions.

We should distinguish here between important aspects that remained unwritten, like the rhythm and the strumming patterns of the accompaniment, and elements at odds with general music theory, such as the practice of chordal variation and the systematic use of chords in unusual inversions. The use of the term *unwritten traditions* might suggest that there was a whole community of amateur guitarists only indirectly connected with the official musical world, developing a common musical language of their own. It is clear, however, that many of the composers who published alfabeto songs with these idiomatic guitar adaptations were familiar with counterpoint, so perhaps we should rather say they established a different set of (unwritten) rules for guitar composition, based on a thorough understanding of how to deal with the blank uniformity of alfabeto. Thus a repertoire was created in an "ancient style" (according to Sanseverino), a description that exposes an ambivalent attitude toward alfabeto harmony and the theory of counterpoint, an attitude which persisted for the rest of the seventeenth century, as we will see in the next chapters.

Composition and Arrangement

The impression of amateurism made by Remigio Romano's and Pietro Millioni's collections is strengthened by their modest appearance and the alfabeto-text format, which is similar to that of the "Traetta" and "Riccardiana" manuscripts mentioned before. This format serves a specific purpose. To be useful, the melodies must be sufficiently known, as the exact order of the chords could easily be forgotten. One can of course speculate that among singer-guitarists, it was customary to make one's own alfabeto accompaniment to preexisting material (text and melody). If this were true, it would imply that the performer was in the position to listen to the song—still in some original form—often enough to be able to memorize at least these two elements, as was perhaps the case with Adriana Basile, whose musical talents were nonetheless considered exceptional.

Yet, it remains possible, too, that she had learned the many songs she knew by heart, together with the alfabeto chords, from sources that are no longer extant. Even if an aria is now anonymous, one can assume that there must have been a composer first, who set the text to music and created an instrumental accompaniment, in the form of a continuo bass or alfabeto, or a polyphonic vocal setting. In the latter case, someone (an equally anonymous guitarist) could have made an alfabeto reduction of the polyphony afterward.

John Griffiths, however, argues that there are also examples of the opposite: "The fact that several of the identified composers of early seventeenth-century polyphonic songs were also renowned guitarists such as Juan de Palomares and Blas de Castro cannot be overlooked. This link suggests the likelihood that some of the preserved polyphonic songs were conceived as guitar songs and later arranged as more sophisticated polyphonic versions." Griffiths illustrates this with an example of an anonymous (undated) three-voice setting of Lope de Vega's "Ya es tiempo de recoger," arguing that the guitar may have played a central role in its composition: "Examples such as this suggest that concordant polyphonic songs are possibly more than mere concordances; they are possibly alternate versions made by the same composers but using another mode of expression."[38]

Most likely Remigio Romano and Pietro Millioni had access to manuscript or printed sources, from which they not only copied the text but, perhaps, also learned the melody in staff notation, which could have served them as an example of how to shape the harmony as well. Finding the appropriate chords to a "nontraditional" (composed) song, without recourse to an implicit model of functional harmony, requires a certain level of understanding of the underlying rules of counterpoint, the lack of which is probably the reason why there are so many faulty harmonies in alfabeto songs.

It is not known whether Romano and Millioni were trained musicians or not, since almost nothing is known of their lives and their musical careers. However that may be, the general appearance of their cheap "guitar case" editions in the very small *octodecimo* format (ca. 6.5 in. x 4 in.) creates the impression of dilettantism. In our time this can easily lead to misinterpretation, as we might be inclined to read in it an intuitive understanding of music, while perhaps it is nothing more than a deliberately cultivated image. Pietro Millioni, who published many guitar tutors, obviously had some idea of the poetic schemes the songs were based on, and, since the style of the accompaniment to *Tirinto mio* resembles the Venetian usage of "integrated alfabeto," he may have been familiar with the basic elements of music theory.[39]

It appears that Remigio Romano, on the other hand, often simply used a *scala di musica per B quadro* or *B molle*, placing root position chords on almost every single bass note, a method of arranging that often leads to faulty results (as we have seen in exx. 3.3 and 3.4).[40] Many songs from Romano's collections, however, are original works by composers such as Giovanni Pietro Berti, Alessandro Grandi, and Carlo Milanuzzi, and in his aricle "New Information on the Chronology of Venetian monody: The 'Raccolte' of Remigio Romano," Roark Miller concludes that in some cases Romano may have copied the alfabeto directly from other (printed or manuscript) sources, such as Carlo Milanuzzi's *Primo scherzo delle ariose vaghezze* (1622).[41]

Surveying the field, we get the impression of only a limited amount of strategies being employed to create an alfabeto accompaniment to continuo songs: by using a system of scale triads, by attempting to make standard chord progressions (the guitar passacaglias) fit the melody, and finally, by cleverly using the rules of counterpoint to find the proper harmonies. The latter method requires a certain degree of theoretical open-mindedness, as we have seen in the discussion of chordal variation.

The Guitar and the Change of Style

Several scholars, including Silke Leopold, Roark Miller, Margaret Murata, and Alexander Dean, have noticed an association between song texts in the new Chiabreran style of light and elegant poetry, with short lines, and the clear-cut cadential formulas of the guitar passacaglia and ciaccona.[42] The immense popularity of battuto came in tandem with the taste for simple, "standard" harmonic progressions and typical dance-like shifts in metrical accentuation (as heard in ex. 3.6, Domenico Obizzi's "Rompi, rompi, ò mio core," mm. 3–4, audio ex. 4). In the canzonette, these elements were combined with small-scale periodic structures based on sequenced melodic and rhythmic motives that mirror the formal structure of the text. It is tempting to assume a causal relationship between the popular alfabeto practice, both written and unwritten, and a more general change of style, but it would be difficult to conclusively prove that examples of alfabeto dances and passacaglias gave rise to a modular compositional style, within this particular song repertoire.[43]

To the extent that most of the alfabeto dances from the early seventeenth century are arrangements of preexisting material, the "integrated alfabeto" accompaniments can be understood as reflecting ideas that were becoming habitual, and not exclusively in the sphere of the guitar. Craig Russell argues

that "no instrument better represents this radical transformation than the guitar, which was at the forefront of the revolution from the horizontal to the vertical."[44] The opposite could also be true: a growing preference for small-scale
periodic musical structures and standard cadential formulas may have enabled
the emergence of the alfabeto accompaniment of the guitar, occasionally leading to a happy association.

"Gently Strike the Strings"

In our time, the five-course guitar is often used in ensembles to add a percussive attack to the sound, comparable to (and sometimes even more powerful than) the effect of the harpsichord. However, it is questionable whether
the instrument was used for such a purpose at all in the seventeenth century.
Another picture emerges when we examine how the battuto technique was
used in solo repertoire, full of rather subtle variations. Girolamo Montesardo
described the execution of the *trillo*, an ornamental strum that can be found
in many books from that time. He advised playing the strum "più soave," with
the right hand at the rose, or even at the neck. "To have an elegant hand on
the guitar, it is necessary to relax it and strike the strings gently with three or
four fingers in the manner of an arpeggio, not all at once, which would create
a great noise and sound crude, which is very annoying to the ear."[45] From 1630
onward, most solo music was to be performed in an alternation of battuto and
pizzicato. In the *Balletto il fedel amante* by Foscarini, for example, the complete
melody of the first phrase is played with strums.[46] In some cases the strokes
cover no more than one course; it is implausible that battuto would have been
used as a percussive technique in a situation like that.

In battuto-pizzicato solo music, dissonant pizzicato chords are often
resolved to a strummed chord. This would require that the battuto chord
be unaccented. The idea that battuto would normally have been used as
a means of obtaining strong dynamic accents may well be influenced by
superficial observation of the practice of "rhythm guitar" in popular music
and jazz, or flamenco. Of course, the battuto style involved accents as
well, as we can see in the right-hand patterns of typical guitar dances, like
ciaccona and sarabanda. Here it often is the second beat of the measure
that is emphasized most, an effect that can be achieved by strumming with
more fingers (for instance, two fingers plus the thumb). The result is a
rhythmic broadening. We can assume that downstrokes and upstrokes were
used also to obtain variation; a downstroke by nature has more weight than
an upstroke. Several guitarists, including Foscarini, have described these
battuto techniques in detail.

Strumming probably was more varied than appears from the bare
chord symbols included with so many songs. In example 4.3, a ciaccona by

Francesco Corbetta, we find the *repicci*, a battuto ornament similar to the trillo. It is a rhythmic variation (making use of sixteenth notes instead of quarter notes) of the standard strum pattern. In every measure only one of the beats is subdivided, so that an interesting differentiation emerges, as the plainness of the two other crotchets preserves the musical tension of the slow movement of the ciaccona. When executed with restraint, this type of variation can also be used to good effect in accompaniment where rhythmic variety is welcome, but a continuous staccato of semiquavers would spoil the character of the music. Doubling the strums, by striking up and down (as in Sanseverino's "Aria del gran duca," ex. I.2), was a favorite means of avoiding too much uniformity.

Battuto Accompaniment to Solo Songs

The genre and the character of a song should determine the shape of its accompaniment. A song based on the ciaccona or on another well-known dance (Ruggiero, la monica, ballo del gran duca, villano de Spagna, etc.) should preferably be accompanied by appropriate battuto patterns.[47] If, for example, a composer has added his own bass to a ciaccona song, the guitarist could decide to ignore it and just strum the dance rhythm with the proper harmonies.[48] Newly composed arias (villanelle, canzonette, and the like), on the other hand, demand an accompaniment that takes into account the implied harmonies and the rhythm of the bass.

In the second measure of 'Rompi, rompi, ò mio core' by Domenico Obizzi (ex. 3.6), for example, we see a complementary rhythm of soprano and bass. It seems undesirable for the guitar to play more strokes than there are bass notes, since it would spoil the musical effect. In a situation with syncopations or hemiolas (as in mm. 2–4), economy probably gives the best result; the guitarist can choose to provide a battuto accompaniment based on the rhythm of the bass. In Obizzi's print the alfabeto letters are placed exactly where the harmony of the basso continuo changes. At the beginning of the third measure we might consider playing only the bass line, instead of full chords.[49]

For a better understanding of the very particular harmonic language of the guitar as it appears from the examples above, a performance should be realized with only simple alfabeto chords, and without a bass instrument dictating (or even sometimes changing) the harmony. Nevertheless, in our time the guitar is mostly used in combination with other harmonic instruments, like the theorbo or harp, a practice that seems to be based on the arbitrary generalization of historical examples. The exotic ensemble of chitarrone (theorbo), guitar, and tambourine (played by Pleasure and his two companions), mentioned in the stage directions of Cavalieri's *Rappresentatione*, should not therefore be taken as the standard performance of vocal monody, but as something wholly out of

Example 3.6. Domenico Obizzi (1627), "Rompi, rompi ò mio core." In the transcription, on the guitar stave, the direction of the strums is indicated by the note stems.

the ordinary. It is a light and airy intermezzo from an early musical drama in which the stage performance is supported symbolically by the choice of the instruments. Of course, all kinds of combinations of instruments might have been tried, but the format of some editions, either with text and alfabeto only, or with a melody in staff notation with a basso continuo together with "non-practical alfabeto" (as in Kapsbergerger's "Voi pur mi prometteste," ex. 3.2), may sometimes have been an obstacle to easy cooperation.

Above all, it is valuable to know where and when such combinations were used, as significant regional and national differences may have existed. Countless reports inform us, for instance, that in Spain theater ensembles commonly consisted of harps and guitars, sometimes supplemented by the bass of a viol or theorbo.[50] It is doubtful that these groups played a proper continuo from a bass. There is almost no Spanish continuo music from the first half of the seventeenth century, so it should rather be assumed that chordal arrangements of vocal works were played on the double harp, with added cifras played on the guitar, more or less in the style of Joan Carles Amat.[51] Spanish music was written in a largely conservative style, predominantly triadic and lacking the advanced chromaticism that was characteristic of the Italian madrigal repertoire of around 1600. Only later, in the second half of the seventeenth century, came the success of the *tonos humanos*, mostly solo songs with a continuo part.

We do not encounter similar ensembles in Italy, and the fact that these instruments existed there as well does not mean automatically that the Italians were copying Spanish ensemble practice. The question is not so much whether or not this could possibly have occurred, but if there is any concrete evidence for it. Relying on available sources, we must conclude that a wider variety of instruments was used in Italy than in Spain, and that the guitar played a far more modest role in ensemble performance.

Battuto in Instrumental Ensemble Music

Very little is documented about how the guitar was involved in continuo in heterogeneous ensembles. Even the instructions for accompaniment included in guitar manuals seldom give clear information about the groups in which the instrument would have been active. One exception is a work for strings (or actually "per ogni sorte d'stromento musicale"—for any kind of instrument) by Biagio Marini, in which alfabeto is included above the bass part, a very rare example of battuto in chamber music.[52] According to a note on the title page, the guitar can participate "a beneplacito" (at will), which makes it clear that Marini (or his printer) certainly considered the guitar as one of the instruments fit for the performance of this music. Alfabeto is added to the most appropriate works in the collection, actually some of the simpler balletti, correnti, and zarabande, and on the title page it reads: "Con alfabeto alle più proprie." It goes without saying that the guitar was used along with the bass instrument (wind or bowed string), if only because the guitarist could not play both the demanding bass line—part of the polyphonic texture—and the chords, making it probably not coincidental that these are *sonate da camera* for which no true continuo instrument is required. As Eleanor Selfridge-Field remarks, "The use of plucked instruments (lute, theorbo, chitarrone and guitar) in association with the violin is heavily linked with court music by such composers as Salomone Rossi and Biagio Marini. There is no strong association toward any particular genre in publications in which the combination of violin(s) and lute(s) occurs."[53] A decisive objection to the use of the guitar as the sole continuo instrument in an ensemble (as opposed to accompanying a solo treble instrument) is that its basses do not go low enough, and, moreover, that the instrument would fall short in volume if played pizzicato, as it occasionally must in figured bass, to balance the upper voices. This does not apply to Marini's opus 22, because here the bass is provided by another instrument, and the guitar's role is to support the harmony with alfabeto chords, played battuto.

Although a wealth of ensemble music was published in Italy halfway through the seventeenth century, it almost never included alfabeto, which justifies the assumption that it was unusual for the guitar to participate. It has to be taken into account that for a long time alfabeto was the only notation from which most guitarists could play, and, as we have seen in the discussion of the alfabeto accompaniment of Neapolitan part songs, finding the right chords to work with the other parts evidently was problematic.[54] All this makes it doubtful that the vertical approach of battuto was considered compatible with the more complex, often polyphonic nature of a repertoire very different from the genre of popular canzonette or scherzi. Many sources make reference to the theorbo or (arch-) lute as the preferred instruments for basso continuo, while the guitar is hardly ever indicated.

Example 3.7. Giovanni Battista Granata (1659), *Sonata di chitarra e violino, con il suo basso continuo*. The middle stave is the five-line guitar tablature.

Only a few editions of Italian chamber music with the guitar are known. Foscarini (ca. 1640), Corbetta (1643), and Granata (1651, 1659, and 1680, see ex. 3.7) published ensemble works with a solo part in battuto-pizzicato style. In these compositions the guitar does not fulfill the role of a continuo instrument.[55]

From Alfabeto to Basso Continuo

Between 1610 and 1640, many collections of strophic arias with alfabeto were published. Subsequently, the interest in this genre diminished rapidly, as is evidenced by the sharp decrease in the numbers of printed works. Accompaniment to larger-scale serious songs is usually more demanding, the figures added to the bass implying a more complex harmony, which would expose the limitations of the guitar all the more. Originally, alfabeto was a closed system of major and minor block chords played with strums, an accompaniment which, harmonically speaking, is uniform and rather uninteresting. The whole system fails miserably, for example, if we wish to play chords in $\frac{6}{3}$ position where they are clearly needed,—for instance, when the figure of a third (of a major chord) in the bass leads to the root of a harmony on the fourth degree (I^6–IV). To do this, we have to step outside the battuto system and play some of the chords pizzicato, for which we need to read tablature.

And so, from 1640 on, brief instructions for realizing an accompaniment from a figured bass begin to appear at the end of guitar manuals such as those of Foscarini (ca. 1640), Corbetta (1643, 1648, and 1671), and Granata (1659). In fact, the approach is still ambiguous: the new pizzicato chords respect the position of the bass (for which low octave strings on the fifth and fourth courses are vital), but the chords they resolve to are mostly the usual alfabeto patterns, often not in the preferable (root) position, as required by the situation (as in ex. 5.11). The "default mode" is battuto; pizzicato is used only in places with figures at the bass, like sixth chords and suspensions (4–3 or 7–6). Application of this method does not lead to a style of continuo with the bass as the principal voice, as on the theorbo or harpsichord. In the second half of the seventeenth century, very few collections of songs with alfabeto were published, and, with the rise of the battuto-pizzicato solo repertoire, guitarists may have wished to accompany in a more learned (lute) style. In chapter 5 we will go deeper into that.

Tablature realizations of basso continuo in this hybrid style (battuto-pizzicato) are very rare, probably because the instrument was used only sporadically for this sort of accompaniment. In Corbetta's *La guitarre royalle* (1671), there are two- and three-part songs with a guitar part in battuto-pizzicato. The composer explains: "I have given an example in the three-part chansons with a basso continuo, and beneath it the same bass in tablature, to serve as accompaniment."[56] Yet in many instances the guitar does not exactly follow the line of the bass (for example, compare the parts in the last measure of ex. 5.18), as a result of Corbetta's liberal selection of inversions of the battuto chords. Moreover, the accompaniment is not exclusively strummed; a number of the chords should be played pizzicato, and therefore will be low in volume. Consequently, a second bass-line instrument (as suggested by Corbetta in this example) like a viol would be indispensable to a proper and efficient continuo. This made the guitar a less practical instrument, compared to the theorbo.

Nevertheless, from the last quarter of the seventeenth century onward, the guitar was presented as a full-fledged continuo instrument, and in the treatises of Sanz (1674), Grenerin, and Matteis (both 1680), the bass is taken as the starting point. Only with the bass as the lowest line (a basso continuo in the true sense) can full justice be done to the horizontal aspects of dissonance, suspension, and resolution. In these books there are examples of figured bass that are carefully harmonized, reproduced in tablature.[57] This approach is very different from the earlier alfabeto style, and it is a moot point if fully strummed accompaniment was still much in practice at that time, as the general style of solo music for guitar had changed to battuto-pizzicato (or just pizzicato), and the song and dance repertoire from the early alfabeto books had become obsolete.

In contrast to the detailed instructions on the application of theory, which we find in the tutors from this period, there is a tantalizing lack of information about the instruments with which the guitar would have played. Gaspar Sanz discusses the accompaniment of vocal and instrumental works, but is silent about instrumentation. Henry Grenerin, by way of exception, gives examples of the use of the guitar in *Simphonies a deux dessus de violon avec la basse, la compagnement de la guitare et le theorbe*. The tablature realization of the continuo largely corresponds to the thoroughbass figures.[58] The accompaniment of the guitar is almost identical with the theorbo part, which strongly suggests that the two instruments were alternatives and not necessarily intended to play together. Even though the tablature includes the complete bass line, the guitar cannot compete in volume with the two violins, so a second bass instrument (the *basse de viole*) is needed to counterbalance the ensemble.[59] The composer has also included a guitar continuo in his vocal works in three (and even four) parts. In these compositions the guitar broadly follows the line of the lowest voice, filling out the harmony, which is why few demands are made on the power of the instrument's bass.

Apart from a few examples in guitar tutors, probably included for didactic purposes, there is very little ensemble music preserved with guitar accompaniment in tablature. Nowadays, Nicola Matteis' explanation from the preface to the English edition of *The False Consonances of Music* (1682) is often cited to prove that the guitar had a role in the continuo:

> The guitar was never so much in use & credit as it is at this day, & finding it improved to so great a perfection, it is my present design to make it company for other Instruments. Every body knows it to be an imperfect Instrument & yet finding upon experience how agreeable a part it bears in a consort I have composed severall pieces both for ye practice & information of those that would make use of it with ye Harpsichord, Lute, Theorbo or Bass-Viol.

However, it is not self-evident that Matteis aimed at a combination of guitar and harpsichord, lute, theorbo or bass viol playing continuo together. His tutor begins with a few tablatures ("severall pieces") for the guitar as a solo instrument, to which a line in staff notation for basso continuo is added, probably to be realized on the aforementioned instruments.[60]

In his continuo exercises Matteis largely refrains from using the old alfabeto style, and likewise none of the treatises from the last part of the century reflects a practice of accompaniment, performed exclusively in battuto.[61] If we take into consideration the limited power of the plucked basses of the guitar (the diapasons of the theorbo are about twice as long), its most likely use was in the accompaniment of the solo voice, or perhaps a solo treble instrument, certainly if the guitarist took Matteis' instructions as a reference, in which many chords are played pizzicato. François Campion remarked in 1716: 'One is not prejudiced against the guitar without reason. I acknowledge, along with everyone, that it is not as strong of harmony as the harpsichord or the theorbo. However, I believe that it is sufficient to accompany one voice.'[62]

Different Types of Guitars and Their Musical Context

The question of the use of the guitar in ensemble probably should extend to organology, as there may have been different types of instruments involved, linked to different styles of playing. Agostino Agazzari remarks in his *Del sonare sopra il basso* (1607) that the chitarrina is used in a specific way in basso continuo: "As ornament we have those which, by scherzando and by counterpoint, make the harmony more agreeable and sonorous, namely the lute, theorbo, harp, lirone, cittern, spinet, chitarrina, violin, pandora and the like."[63] His words are sometimes understood to mean that all kinds of melodic improvisations were performed on the guitar, as an "ornamental" supplement to the harmony of the organ, harpsichord, lute, arpa doppia etc. Yet, it must be asked whether the chitarra spagnuola was indeed played this way, since it is completely at variance with what we know of the use of the instrument in this period. Agazzari divided the instruments into three groups. The first are the instruments that form the fundament because they can render the harmony perfectly, such as the organ, harpsichord, lute and harp. The second group consists of instruments that "have within them an imperfect harmony of the parts," such as the common cittern, lirone, and chitarrina. The instruments of the last group have no harmony at all, like the viola, violin, and pandora.[64] Some stringed instruments (violin, harp and lute) were commonly used in instrumental ensembles, while for the others (cittern, pandora, and guitar) there are far fewer indications in scores, iconography, and contemporary reports.

Was the chitarrina mentioned by Agazzari identical with the five-course guitar? Sometimes different names were used for the members of the guitar family. Pesori, Granata, and Calvi used both chitarra (spagnuola) and *chitarriglia*. In guitar ensembles a smaller type of guitar (a chitarriglia?) was occasionally used, tuned to a higher pitch, but still with the same intervals. Pesori interchanges the two terms to such an extent that one has to assume he really meant the same instrument all the time. After all, it is not illogical to use diminutives like *chitarrina* or *chitarriglia* as pet names and in contrast to the large, impressive *chitarrone*.

Carlo Calvi's book (in fact a collection of works by Corbetta and other composers) consists of two parts. The first, entirely in alfabeto, is for the chitarriglia. The second part, in tablature, is for the chitarra, but "can also be played on the chitarriglia."[65] We can deduce from this that at least the chitarriglia was tuned to the same intervals as the chitarra. The difference could be the pitch, with the chitarriglia being the smaller instrument tuned higher, or the stringing itself, with one instrument using re-entrant tuning and the other a tuning with two bourdons.[66] The question then remains why the chitarriglia would have been best suited for the music from the first (alfabeto) part of the book. Another possibility is that Calvi was referring to a different stringing, made from wire.[67] A guitar with metal strings is indeed better equipped for battuto than for pizzicato. Not much is known of the wire-strung guitar from this period. Nowadays it is generally assumed that the *chitarra battente* first came into fashion in the eighteenth century, in folkloristic music from Italy. In many cases older guitars (chitarre spagnuola) were modified to bear the higher tension of the metal strings then in use by shortening the neck and canting the top at the bridge (a drastic modification involving bending the top and modifying the sides). There are indications, however, that wire strings (with low tension, similar to harpsichord or cittern strings) were used on the guitar even earlier. The title page of Corbetta's *De gli scherzi armonici* (1639) shows two guitars.[68] The instrument on the right has strings that run over the bridge and are fixed at the bottom, which could indicate wire stringing (see fig. 3.1). In the inventory (1652) of the deceased luthier Lorenzo Filzer from Rome, "dodici chitarre con corde de cetra"—twelve guitars with cittern strings—are mentioned.[69] It should be remembered that in the first half of the seventeenth century, there were more plucked instruments with wire strings, such as the cittern and pandora.

Chitarrina or *chitarrino* may have been used as a name for different instruments. The characteristics of rare instruments that hardly have any repertoire of their own are not always well-defined. The diminutive chitarrina, used by Agazzari, could be another name for the *chitarra italiana* or *chitarra napoletana*, a small four-course lute-shaped instrument that is depicted in several sources, without any known extant solo repertoire of its own. In the anonymous collection *Conserto vago* (published in Rome in 1645) there is a part for a chitarrino *a quatro corde alla napolitana*—probably lute-shaped, for plucked textures. Its tuning, with a fifth between the third and fourth courses, is fundamentally different from that of the chitarra spagnuola. On the other hand, in Pietro Millioni's *Corona del primo, secondo e terzo libro d'intavolatura di chitarra spagnola* (1631), a four-course guitar is mentioned, the "chitarrino, overo chitarra italiana," tuned like the first four courses of the common chitarra spagnuola. To be able to

Figure 3.1. Detail of the title page of Francesco Corbetta's *De gli scherzi armonici* (1639).

play the chords of alfabeto (from the tablature examples at the alfabeto chart) on this four-course instrument, one has to leave out the figures of the fifth course.[70] By its tuning, the chitarrino napolitana from *Conserto vago* does not link up with the alfabeto tradition, as Millioni's chitarrino italiana certainly does. If Agazzari had a chitarrino napolitana in mind, hand-plucked or played with a plectrum, then there is more reason to suppose that melodic improvisations were played on it, as there were on the violin and pandora, which he mentions in the same breath. If, on the other hand, he was referring to the five-course guitar proper, the chitarra spagnuola, or to Millioni's four-course version, then perhaps a better explanation would be that Agazzari considered the chords of the guitar simply as ornamental embellishment, comparable to the function of the added alfabeto in Biagio Marini's opus 22. And if he did not intend to say that the instruments always played together, perhaps he was only summing up all possible accompaniment instruments. From what is known of continuo groups, it appears that such combinations were the exception rather than the rule. Some ensembles are mentioned often, while others must have been rare. Certain instruments (pandora, cittern, and guitar) were predominantly associated with popular music; but this does not mean that they could never have been used in another, more official musical context.

Chapter Four

Solo Music

Spain's Unwritten Repertoire

In Italy the five-course guitar was invariably called *chitarra spagnuola*, and Girolamo Montesardo, who was the first to publish a guitar book there, speaks of playing and singing "in the Spanish style." It is appropriate, therefore, to start this chapter with a brief survey of the instrument's position in the Spanish musical landscape.

In the sixteenth century, music for the vihuela and the four-course guitar consisted for the most part of polyphonic *fantasías* and intavolations of vocal polyphony, dances taking a more modest place. This repertoire can be roughly compared to that of the lute from the same period. Around the turn of the century, though, the vihuela had lost ground, the last book, *El Parnasso* by Esteban Daza (or Daça), having been printed in 1576. At about the same time, the five-course *guitarra española* began its rise across Europe. And so it is likely that in other countries the guitar was seen as intrinsically Spanish, even though there were no sources of guitar music printed in that country for the greater part of the seventeenth century. This does not mean that a Spanish repertoire did not exist. There is, for example, the *Metodo mui facilissimo para aprender a tañer la guitarra* (1626) by Luis de Briçeño, published in Paris, but of a truly Spanish character. Briçeño used the guitar as a chordal instrument in accompaniment, but also in very simple dance solos.[1] The many references to the Spanish background of the ciaccona and other dances, such as the folia and villano, are an indication that there was more music for the guitar than has survived on paper. Spanish songs are also contained in the numerous collections of arias with alfabeto, edited in Italy in the years after 1600. From all available information it appears that at that time playing *alla spagnuola* was, in fact, chord strumming.

Suárez de Figueroa, in his *Plaza universal de todas ciencias y profesiones* (published in Madrid in 1615) speaks of Vicente Espinel, "autor de las tocatas, y cantares de sala," from which we can learn that Espinel composed *tocatas*, instrumental solo pieces.[2] It is impossible to tell whether these were works for the guitar or for the organ, which Espinel also played. In his *Instrucción de música* (1674) Gaspar Sanz paints the history of the guitar in Spain, which includes "doctor Carlos" (Joan Carles Amat), Vicente Espinel, and "Nicolao Doici" (Doizi de Velasco); no other composers' names are mentioned. With the possible exception of a unique pirated edition of Corbetta's book of 1648, there were no guitar books published in Spain between 1596 (*Guitarra Española* by Carles Amat) and 1674, nor are there any manuscripts extant with solo compositions in tablature predating Gaspar Sanz's *Instrucción*. Yet, we cannot but assume that the guitar continued to be played in the intervening eighty years. In the absence of tablatures, one can imagine aural transmission, for which chord strumming provided the basis, as it is unlikely that polyphonic music was transferred without tablature notation.

Spanish guitar music from the last quarter of the seventeenth century is predominantly written in punteado style—plucked textures, notated in Italian tablature. Obviously, plucking was reintroduced succesfully at some point. It is worth noting that in the continuo parts of the *tonos humanos* by José Marín (one of the rare sources of songs with a fully realized guitar accompaniment), there are no strums at all. A change must have taken place from rasgueado to punteado, as it did in Italy from battuto to pizzicato, or to be more precise: battuto-pizzicato. Was there a repertoire, now lost, from the first half of the century, consisting of *diferencias* on well-known ostinato bass patterns? Louise Stein speaks of a "long-standing, continuing practice of instrumental *glosas* (glosses), both improvised and composed."[3] Although it is tempting to hypothesize that a repertoire of melodic variations survived from the time of Luys de Narváez and Alonso Mudarra (who were the first to publish diferencias), because variations from the late seventeenth century were composed along the same lines, it is problematic that for over half a century there are no sources at all of punteado music (the counterpart of the "lute style" of Foscarini), which could support this idea.

Endless rows of variations on harmonic patterns are typical for Iberian instrumental music whether in the sixteenth century, or in flamenco today. We first encounter them in 1538, in Narváez's *Diferencias sobre Conde claros* and *Guardame las vacas*. Variations on "Las Vacas" still appear two hundred years later, in a manuscript with guitar music by Santiago de Murcia (the *Codex Saldivar IV*). In this sense, the five-course guitar is heir to the vihuela.

During the first half of the seventeenth century, the influence of Italian and French music on Spanish guitarists was probably very limited. Yet, it remains a possibility that some played Italian solo repertoire, as can be concluded from a hispanified pirated edition of Corbetta's *Varii scherzi di sonate* of 1648.[4] In this book there are insertions of Spanish variation works in punteado style, like marionas and pavanas, which may be the earliest of their kind, markedly contrasting with the original compositions by Corbetta (preludes, corenti Francese and almandas in the new French fashion), which are all in battuto-pizzicato.[5]

In 1639 Alessandro Piccinini's *Chiaccona Mariona alla vera Spagnola* for lute (ex. 4.1) was published in Bologna. Certain parts are almost identical to the

Example 4.1. Alessandro Piccinini (1639), p. 49, *Chiaccona Mariona alla vera Spagnola.*

Ciacona capona con variatione by Foscarini (printed in 1640, but possibly composed earlier). The piece opens with the very characteristic chord progression in C major that we also find in many guitar ciacconas by, for example, Bartolotti (1640), Carbonchi (1640), Corbetta (1648 and 1671), Granata (ca. 1650) and Pellegrini (1650), as well as in a large number of anonymous manuscripts. Although Piccinini's version for the lute may have been in print first, it can be supposed that Piccinini took as his point of departure what he had heard on the guitar.[6] Piccinini had a "Spanish connection" through his brother Filippo, who worked at the court in Madrid as a lutenist and composer; and perhaps he knew the true Spanish style from his own experience with the chitarra spagnuola, which was becoming immensely popular in Bologna at the time that his books were printed there.

Battuto Music from Italy

The earliest battuto dance songs (or sung dances) such as ciaccona and folia are harmonic schemes of two or four measures with the simplest alfabeto chords, endlessly repeated. Anyone who could play a few chords could join in. Musical circles offering amateurs many opportunities for melodic variation are characteristic of popular genres past and present. It is no coincidence that popular music in our time is mostly based on repeated harmonic progressions or ostinato bass patterns that sometimes are exactly identical to those from the early seventeenth century.

Girolamo Montesardo's *Nuova inventione d'intavolatura*, the first printed guitar book to emerge from Italy, was published in Florence in 1606. The full title reads: "New invention of tablature to play *balletti* on the Spanish guitar without numbers or notes; by means of which anyone can learn to play without a teacher."[7] Montesardo stressed that it is not necessary to be able to read notes (the mensural notation of the rhythm, usually above the tablature system) or numbers (the numbers of Italian tablature). Although tablature was certainly much used by amateurs on the lute, he made it clear that his "new invention" was even easier to learn.

The letters of alfabeto, in no way connected to tonality or mode, were usually placed on a single (time)line, which initially was not even subdivided into measures (ex. 4.2a) as happened in later times (see ex. 4.3, a ciaccona by

Example 4.2a. Girolamo Montesardo (1606), *La Calata,* and transcription. The stems of the notes in the transcription indicate the direction of the strum.

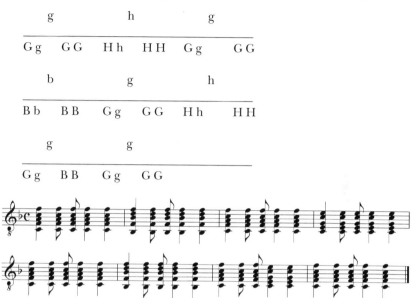

Example 4.2b. Three alfabeto ciacconas. *I-Fn MS Fondo Landau Finaly Mus. 175,* fol. 14v.

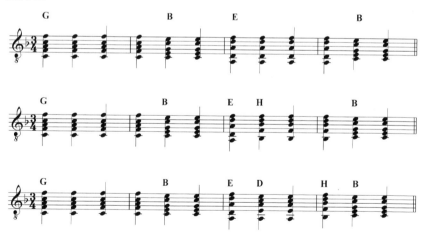

Francesco Corbetta). By using capitals and lowercase letters, Montesardo could indicate the rhythm. The capitals correspond to the quarter notes and the lower-case letters with eighth notes, as can be seen in the transcription. The letters below the line are downstrokes (the direction of the stroke is to the floor, the fingers move from the lower- to the higher-sounding strings), and the letters placed above the line indicate the upstrokes. Thus a genre was created, using block chords only, played in regularly strummed patterns, and in which rhythm and chord changes are the only musical phenomena.

As the example of three different versions of the ciaccona shows (ex. 4.2b), taken from a manuscript (ca. 1610–20) by the hand of Francesco Palumbi, the stable harmonic background of the standard progression of the ciaccona (I–V–vi–V) did allow for internal chordal variation. Comparing this example with the first line of Corbetta's *Chiaccona sopra l'A* (ex. 4.3), it is evident that there, too, the harmonic progression determines the composition, together with the stress on the change of harmony on the second beat of each measure. In the second and third phrases of Corbetta's ciaccona, a melodic line develops while in the fourth phrase, the music returns to the conditions of the beginning, but now with a rhythmic variation (to which he added "in repicco"). At this stage, the idiomatic peculiarities of the instrumental technique set the bounds for the music's development. Despite the simplicity of the composition, this ciaccona represents a next stage in the evolution of guitar music, because now melodic and rhythmic elements were added to the stock chord progressions of popular dances.

In the approximately thirty-five collections of alfabeto solos that were published between 1606 and 1640 we always find the same dance types, the *balletti*, as they were called by Montesardo (folia, Ruggiero, bergamasca, romanesca, pavaniglia, villan de Spagna, ballo del gran duca, and the like). The ciaccona and passacaglia, however, soon to become extremely popular, are a different case. After about 1630 these musical forms were used in harmonic experiments and variations in battuto-pizzicato style, such as we find in Foscarini's *Terzo libro*.[8] Previously, the use of alternative (more dissonant) harmonies had been hindered by the use of alfabeto. To write in a harmonic idiom other than triadic, we need tablature or new alfabeto chords, which is probably why Foscarini included an *alfabeto dissonante*. We shall return to the subject of dissonance in chapter 7.

The Limitations of Alfabeto Notation: Rhythm, Harmony, and Counterpoint

In alfabeto music from the first decades of the seventeenth century, we find only very little rhythmic variation. Around 1620, the rhythm of the strumming was notated in the form of dashes, indicating the direction of the stroke, and placed on a timeline (exx. 4.2b and 4.3). Later, these dashes were placed in a five-line tablature system, still without bar lines (compare ex. 4.7a). To understand the rhythm, one has to be familiar with the repertoire in question,

Example 4.3. Francesco Corbetta (1639), p. 13, *Chiaccona sopra l'A.* In the *repicci* the sixteenth notes with the longer stems were probably played with the thumb.

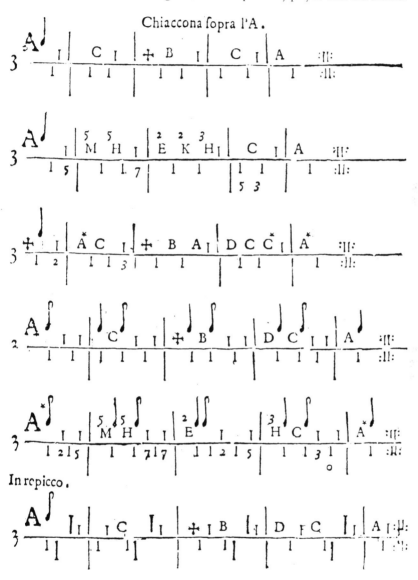

(continued)

Example 4.3.—*(concluded)*

because there were general principles—not too well-defined and not always easy to deduce—with respect to grouping upstrokes and downstrokes. Downstrokes usually fall on a heavy beat and upstrokes on the lighter. In the field of rhythm, notational practices occur that were probably used solely in guitar music. To increase the length of a note, Foscarini used the augmentation dot, not in the normal sense (adding half of the original value to a note), but just to indicate that the note is "longer." With two dots, the note becomes "much longer." Foscarini explains: "If there is a dot placed over or under the letter [of alfabeto], you must give the beat in question a bit more time than the others. And when there are two dots, the beat has to be proportionally longer, in order to make the stroke with one dot a *semiminima* (a quarter note), & the one with two dots a *minima* (a half note)."[9]

It is not surprising that in the early books with mixed battuto-pizzicato music by Foscarini (ca. 1630) and Granata (1646), rhythmic division was not notated in a very consistent way. This is not a value judgement on the aesthetic qualities of the music itself. A similar liberty (or inexperience) can be found in guitar tablatures of twentieth-century popular music. Now, too, the notation of the rhythm is often omitted; tablature is understood more as a representation of successive actions, and the notation of the rhythm as an aspect of music theory.[10]

In several treatises on playing technique there is ample discussion of ornamental strums, like the *trillo* and *repicco*, to obtain variation, by doubling the strokes (in eighth notes) or by multiplying fourfold (to sixteenth notes).[11] In most editions of songs and dances, however, these *repicci* are not indicated. Because alfabeto was used in the first place as a notation for the left hand, we have to face the fact that information for the right hand is often lacking. As a consequence, we cannot even rule out the possibility that chords were not always strummed. References to arpeggio from the middle part of the century, by Foscarini, Bartolotti, Valdambrini, Pellegrini, and Corbetta, show a connection between arpeggio and alfabeto.[12]

The transformation of the harmonic patterns of passacaglia, ciaccona, and folia to solo works forms the basis on which, after about 1630, an advanced battuto repertoire was founded. These harmonic schemes were immensely popular and served as a starting point for new invention. The works of Foscarini and Corbetta (the compositions in the latter's book of 1639 in particular, see ex. 4.3) give an insight into how the art of variation was actually practiced. Bringing together the melody with the accompaniment—still performed exclusively in battuto—is a first step on the way to creating a truly independent repertoire. Richard Hudson, who thoroughly researched the origins of guitar dances, considers the addition of extra harmonies to the standard progressions of the ciaccona and folia as chordal variation. Today these extra chords are sometimes labelled "satellite chords." Their aim appears to be twofold: they can enrich the harmony by variation, as Hudson maintains, but their main function in the "advanced alfabeto" repertoire of 1630–40 probably was to facilitate left-hand fingering, enabling one to play (single-handed) both the melody and the chords.

With chordal variation, different positions of the same harmony are used (as in ex. 4.4 on guitar 2 and 3), and alternative chords introduced (e.g., ii instead of IV or vi instead of I). It seems that in the first guitar part of Foscarini's spagnoletta for three guitars the harmonies are chosen primarily for technical reasons, so that the musician is able to play the complete melody (the top notes of the chords). The number of inversions to choose from remains limited, because by nature battuto chord patterns have to make use of adjacent strings.

This spagnoletta is for an ensemble of three guitars tuned at different pitches.[13] The first guitar (d, g, c', e', a') is tuned a fourth higher than the second, which probably is in the usual tuning A, d, g, b, e'. The third guitar would be one tone lower (G, c, f, a, d'). The *prima*, the first guitar, has a battuto line in alfabeto with additional numbers, for extra melody notes; the others play standard alfabeto chords only. Foscarini called these compositions "sonate semplice," but probably this only takes the simple musical content into account, disregarding the difficulty of the left-hand technique.[14]

If we perform these seemingly innocent chord rows as a guitar trio, fascinating harmonic constructions arise. On the third beat of the fourth (full) measure, the first guitar has the triad F + A + C against the G + B♭ + D of the second and third guitars. The effect recalls the *acciaccatura* clusters in the keyboard music of Domenico Scarlatti.[15] In the next measure the second guitar

Example 4.4. Giovanni Paolo Foscarini (ca. 1630), p. 8, *Spagnoletta* for three guitars. The stems of the notes in the transcription indicate the direction of the strum.

most likely would have played the C-minor chord with an added D (the L chord from Foscarini's own alfabeto chart). At the same time, the first guitar plays a G-minor chord, confirming the C-minor harmony with a seventh and a ninth. This raises the question if such a harmonic simultaneity was intentional, although it is not the kind of dissonance that Foscarini would shrink from. Specifically in his works for guitar in *cordatura differente* (audio exx. 11–13), on page 99 of *Li cinque libri*, a number of ninth chords appear.[16] The use of guitars of different sizes was pushed to the extreme by Antonio Carbonchi, who in his *Dodici chitarre spostate* (1643) published compositions for twelve guitars, all tuned differently, so that every player had to play different alfabeto chords. Although this seems a rather naïve way to try to convince the reader that the guitar is capable of playing in every possible key, it also reflects the wish to explore the guitar's full fingerboard by shifting complete chord shapes up or down. Starting with Montesardo's *Nuova inventione* of 1606, pieces in unusual keys appear in the guitar repertoire. Bartolotti, for instance, included twenty-four passacaglias in his *Primo libro*, one in every "key." The use of equal temperament, achieved by a regular placement of the frets, would enable the use of every possible triadic harmony, even the remotest, such as F♯ or C♯.[17]

In the 1630s, when guitarists began to expand the alfabeto style with melodic elements, surprising chord progressions turned up in solo dances, and established rules of counterpoint were often boldly disregarded. In Corbetta's first book there are many parallel shifts (as in ex. 4.5). Apparently, the theoretical premise of interdependence of the treble melody and the bass did not play much of a role in guitar music, and many parallel fifths and octaves are tolerated. It is significant that in his works in lute style, from the same 1639 book, such chord progressions are absent. There Corbetta provides a consistent bass line in counterpoint to the upper voice. Obviously, he distinguished between

Example 4.5. Francesco Corbetta (1639), p. 73, *Balletto.*

the application of the rules in battuto and in pizzicato. Similar battuto passages, with parallel chord shifts, can still be found in Corbetta's later works, as we can see in a sarabande from 1671 (ex. 4.6). Here they are incorporated into more refined music; Corbetta apparently could still value this typically guitaristic effect, as he did not shrink from using it frequently. In example 4.6a, the D-major chord shape is shifted up to the seventh fret.[18] In example 4.6b things start the same, but then the melody moves downward and Corbetta changes to pizzicato, which enables him to write a proper bass line.

Example 4.6. Francesco Corbetta (1671), p. 4, *Sarabande.* (a) mm. 19–20; (b) mm. 9–10.

(a)

(b)

The Genesis of Battuto-Pizzicato

In the introduction to *Il primo, secondo e terzo libro*, Giovanni Paolo Foscarini explains that he has included works in lute style, here called *pizzicate*, merely to embellish his work.[19] In this same book we find the first printed works in the mixed battuto-pizzicato style, such as the *Balletto del fedel amante* (ex. 4.7). Foscarini distinguishes between advanced battuto style—here notated in a later, more developed alfabeto on a tablature system (ex. 4.7a)—and plucked textures in tablature (ex. 4.7b).

In the these examples, battuto and pizzicato sections are strictly separate. The first example is played battuto, even if the strokes are on one course only (see the last c″ in the third measure, where it would be impossible to hold the

Example 4.7a. Giovanni Paolo Foscarini (c. 1630), p. 24, *Balletto del fedel amante*, mm. 9–12.

Example 4.7b. Giovanni Paolo Foscarini (c. 1630), p. 24, *Balletto del fedel amante*, mm. 15–18.

Example 4.7c. Giovanni Paolo Foscarini (c. 1630), p. 24, *Balletto del fedel amante*, transcription.

preceding G-major chord). The second example is all in pizzicato. The melody is the same in both examples, so we could see this as a pizzicato variation; however, the melodic and harmonic development is so similar that we should rather consider it as the same music, performed with different instrumental techniques. It is like a Rosetta stone, on which the same message is written in different scripts.

Foscarini's balletto, not exclusively in lute style, should not be considered a "sonata, included for the embellishment of the work." In this composition there are also sections that belong to the domain of the guitar (being in battuto style). It is one of the first works in which both styles are represented, albeit still separate from each other. In other pieces, like the "Capriccio sopra la ciaccona" on page twenty-eight (audio ex. 1), Foscarini changes almost imperceptibly from battuto (in alfabeto) to pizzicato (in tablature). The stroke signs disappear and the harmonies are no longer placed on adjacent courses only, which is why they have to be plucked. Thus we witness a development in which Foscarini, almost in spite of himself, switched to writing music in the mixed style. This ambiguity is preserved in his fourth and fifth books, added to the edition in 1632 and 1640, where there is a continuous succession of battuto sections (with stroke signs on the first line of the tablature system) and pizzicato textures, mostly polyphonic, from which battuto signs are absent.

Francesco Corbetta, born in Pavia around 1615, was involved in the different stages of these developments from the outset of his long career. In the *Scherzi armonici* (1639), we find eight compositions in lute style, in which there are only a modest number of strummed chords. These pieces bear some resemblance to the dances from Alessandro Piccinini's *Intavolatura di liuto* (published posthumously by the same printer, Giacomo Monti, in Bologna, and also in 1639), and they are very different from the other seventy-odd "advanced alfabeto" pieces from the same book. It is likely that Corbetta mixed in lute circles and that he had some experience with that instrument himself. This would put a different complexion on his preface to *La guitarre royalle* (Paris, 1671) from thirty years later, in which he states not to know a single chord on the lute.[20] It would be a misunderstanding to suppose that the works in battuto style from *De gli scherzi armonici* (1639) are any easier to play than the ones in lute style. Many of the dances, notated in "advanced alfabeto" (see ex. 4.5), pose considerable problems for the left hand. Compositions like these, with many strummed chords and continuous position shifts, are certainly not a step backward in terms of technical difficulty, compared to music in lute style.

Music in lute style was not necessarily considered to be better (or more beautiful) than that in the mixed style. This probably has to do with the specific advantages offered by battuto, such as the rhythmic strumming of the *repicco* (see ex. 4.3), or rapid chord change. The battuto-pizzicato music from Corbetta's Italian books (1639, 1643, and 1648) is marked by a great freedom with regard to counterpoint. The number of voices varies constantly, from one to four. Battuto chords include a melody (usually at the top) and an accompaniment with block harmonies, and it often is unclear which one of the notes (if any) should be regarded as the bass (like in ex. 4.6a). In other situations, even within the same compositions, polyphonic textures arise—in pizzicato—in two- or three-part cadences.

In the books of Foscarini, Pellegrini, Granata, and Bartolotti there are toccatas and preludes with a distinct pizzicato character. Most of Corbetta's preludes are in pizzicato as well, but the dances in his *Guitarre royalle* collections are all in mixed battuto-pizzicato style, and we must assume that he had an aesthetic preference for it. It probably was the style in which he could express himself best, coming from a purely guitaristic background.

Foreign Influences

Foscarini's third book (ca. 1630) is organized in larger groups of pieces in one key (toccatas, passacaglias, and dances). Within these "suites" we find works in pizzicato, like the toccata shown in example 4.8 (audio ex. 5), while others are in plain battuto, or in mixed style. Without doubt, Foscarini wished to present in his book a multitude of genres from different countries (Italy, Spain, and France). In his preface he speaks of his "Passacagli spagnoli passeggiati," and he includes a number of *corrente francese* (audio exx. 6 and 12). On the other hand, some of the pieces bear a strong resemblance to late sixteenth-century Italian lute music, like the set of variations on the "Pavaniglia," on page 39. His toccatas (see ex. 4.8), finally, show that he was familiar with the style of the newer music by composers like Kapsberger and Frescobaldi.

In Italy the lute as a solo instrument gradually lost ground. The multicourse lutes from around 1600, linked to a predominantly polyphonic repertoire of composers such as Giovanni Antonio Terzi (1593 and 1599), Simone Molinaro (1599), and Alessandro Piccinini (1623 and 1639), turned out to be incompatible with the taste for affective melodies, as they were now written for (bowed) string or wind instruments. The then emerging genre of the sonata with basso continuo is defined by a virtuosic and expressive style of playing. The theorbo and the guitar managed to survive, mainly because of the great demand for accompanying singers and instrumental soloists. The theorbo could immediately find its place in basso continuo, while the guitar became used in popular song. Naturally, players of these instruments started to compose their own (highly idiomatic) solo works. While Girolamo Kapsberger created an outstanding innovative œuvre for the theorbo, consisting of toccatas and dances reminiscent of the keyboard music of Frescobaldi, the strummed guitar initially could not achieve the scope of the polyphonic style of other solo instruments (keyboard and plucked). This may have slowed down the creation of a serious solo repertoire.

Example 4.8. Giovanni Paolo Foscarini (c. 1630), p. 73, *Toccata.*

It was probably on Italy's musical periphery that players of the lute (as opposed to the theorbo) and of the guitar came into contact with another compositional approach. This is apparent in the music of Michelagnolo Galilei—the son of Vincenzo Galilei and brother of the famous astronomer (and also lutenist) Galileo—who worked abroad for a long time, first in Poland and later in Bavaria, at the ducal court in Munich. In his *Primo libro d'intavolatura di liuto* (Munich, 1620), one of the last printed books for the lute by an Italian composer, and written in French tablature, we find the most modern compositional styles of the time. According to Dinko Fabris this is particularly evident in the *durezze*, and the dissonances in the Italian manner of Kapsberger, the use of the *stile brisé* and the exploration of textural effects in the French style, next to a more conservative contrapuntal style as found in Lorenzino or Piccinini.[21]

The well-traveled lutenist and guitarist Foscarini also turned to the more esoteric French style. Early in his long career Foscarini acquired fame by his lute playing. He prided himself on being "known by many Princes, in Italy and abroad, and in particular in Flanders by his Highness the Archduke Albert."[22] He could have met leading French lutenists during his travels on the other side of the Alps. Celebrated composers such as René Mesangeau and Ennemond (or Denis) Gaultier may have served him as models.[23] The *Corrente francese con le sue parti doppie* on page 42 of Foscarini's third book (ca. 1630) is a transcription of a courante for the lute by one of the Gaultiers.[24] In this book we find a number of works in the French style, completely in pizzicato, which reveal the influence of the lute. Already before 1621 Foscarini performed (most likely on the lute) at the court of Albert and Isabelle in Brussels, the capital of the Spanish Netherlands.[25] From his correspondence with Constantijn Huygens, it appears that he was known as a musician in France in the 1640s, which invites speculation that he had been in Paris before 1647 (where and when he published his treatise *Dell'armonia del mondo*). With the decline of the lute in Italy and the increasing popularity of the guitar, it was only reasonable for him to take advantage of all his experience and create a new repertoire for the many amateurs of high rank (some of whom may have played the lute, as well), to whom his pieces are dedicated.

In his *Terzo libro* Foscarini introduced the mixed battuto-pizzicato style. In its less formalized musical framework, allowing a freer treatment of polyphony and voice leading, the inherent characteristics of the guitar could be exploited with succes: the modest volume of sound, a tendency to an ambiguous presentation of the counterpoint and even a capricious variation of textures (making use of battuto and pizzicato). Foscarini's amalgamation of influences paved the way for Corbetta and Bartolotti. From the moment that the mixed style arose, the portion of newer dance types such as corrente (francese), allemande, and sarabande increased enormously. In all books in mixed style from this period there are corrente in great numbers, as well as the aleman[d]a and zarabanda francese. This change is significant: from that moment forward a repertoire began to emerge, composed specifically for the guitar.

It is obvious that Bartolotti, too, as an experienced lute and theorbo player, was inspired by French lute music. In the "suites" from his *Primo libro* (1640), battuto and pizzicato are blended in a compositional style in which the effect of strummed chords is applied to give expression to more abstract musical gestures, rather than to represent part-based cadences. There is a parallel here with the *stile luthé* (or *stile brisé*, as it is often called), in which parts are played successively rather than simultaneously, spread out as irregularly broken chords, presumably often played with *inégalité* to evade the gravitational pull of what would commonly be felt as metric accents (for example, in the prelude in E minor, audio ex. 21). David Ledbetter observes:

> The "style brisé" was first used as a thoroughgoing principle by Robert Ballard . . . in the varied repeats (*doubles*) of courantes in his lute books of 1611 and 1614, and it subsequently became the distinctive French lute texture. Its aim is twofold: to give subtlety of expression to what would otherwise be an ordinary harmonic progression, and to provide a continuum of sound which the player can mould for expressive ends.[26]

Perhaps Bartolotti knew the works for lute of Pierre Gautier ("Gautier de Rome," who was probably not related to Ennemond and Denis Gaultier), published in Rome in 1638. In the *Oeuvres de Pierre Gautier* there is a *chacone* with extended *campanela* passages and slurred scales, rather unusual for the lute music of the time, and possibly inspired by the experiments of theorbists and guitarists. On the opposite side, examples of the *stile brisé* can be found in guitar music published after 1640. In example 4.9, a section from a prelude by Bartolotti, we can see that the composer made varied and discriminate use of delayed resolutions.

It would be too simple to view these developments exclusively from the perspective of national traditions, concluding that battuto, as opposed to pizzicato,

Example 4.9. Angelo Michele Bartolotti (1655), p. 42, *Prelude.*

typically represented an unassuming Italian or Spanish style. Battuto could be employed for widely divergent objectives. The majestic opening of an allemande, for instance, could be reinforced by the broad, rhythmic strumming of five-part chords,[27] but on other occasions Bartolotti decides to strum three-part harmonies on unaccented beats (in a pizzicato context) that could easily have been plucked. By so doing, he extended the expressive palette of the guitar, not so much by increasing the tonal range or volume, in order to turn it into a melody instrument, but by subtle variation at the microscale.

Another use of battuto can be found in the chord chains (actually three-part counterpoint in close position) that we encounter in works by Foscarini, Bartolotti, Granata, and Corbetta).[28] Here the nimbleness of battuto adds to the linearity of the music, perhaps even more than pizzicato could. Probably strumming is to be done elegantly in this type of repertoire, with refined articulation and good tone, rather than offering a boisterous display of virtuosity, forcing the instrument to raise its voice unpleasantly. According to Foscarini the "sonate, like corrente, balletti and gagliarde in French style should be played quietly, in the appropriate spirit, according to the tempo [of these dances]."[29] French influence is increasingly apparent in Corbetta's books from 1643 and 1648, particularly in the alemandas and correntes, with phrases of irregular length and chains of motivic imitation. The rhythmic shape of the incipits of most of the alemandas from the latter publication bear a close resemblance to those of Ennemond and Denis Gaultier (ex. 4.10).[30]

It is significant that in Bartolotti's *Secondo libro* (ca. 1655) the titles of the dances are consequently spelled in French ("allemande," "courante," "sarabande," and "gigue"). In this book there is a clear differentiation of styles, related to genre. The same procedure is also to be found in later publications by Corbetta and Visée. With Bartolotti's second book, the repertoire for the five-course guitar reaches one of its highest peaks. It represents the mature battuto-pizzicato style, in which both elements are in perfect balance, with refined polyphonic textures, and battuto chords smoothly adapting to the rhythmic flow of the composition. At the same time a different approach can be seen, particularly in the well-shaped pizzicato style of the gigues in example 4.11 (listen to audio ex. 25), which lack battuto almost completely, reminding us of the keyboard music of Froberger, who moved in the same court circles as Bartolotti. The counterpoint is of uncommon quality and the music is extraordinarily complex in terms of guitar technique. This is a gigue in the "classic" sense, with the theme, exposed in imitative counterpoint at the beginning, appearing in "inversion" after the first double bar.

Example 4.10. Rhythmic incipit allemande.

Example 4.11. Angelo Michele Bartolotti (1655), p. 7, *Gigue.*

Bartolotti's preludes (listen to audio ex. 21), predominantly in pizzicato, reflect the style of Italian toccatas for lute or harpsichord, with imitative polyphonic passages, chordal sections, and virtuosic cascading runs with many campanelas. In the *Secondo libro* there is also one lute-like *prélude non mensuré*, with irregular grouping of melodic and harmonic material, notated without barlines or rhythm.[31] Sarabandes (audio ex. 24), with a long history in the guitar repertoire, are mostly in battuto. Passacaglias (audio ex. 26) are usually set up as an alternation of virtuosic passages and chordal sections, spiced with daring harmonies. Finally, Bartolotti's allemandes and courantes (audio exx. 22 and 23) exemplify dances in battuto-pizzicato in which the two playing styles of the guitar are merged most successfully.

We can think of several reasons why the guitar was not used in a similar repertoire in France before the last part of the seventeenth century: in that country the instrument was probably often strung without bourdons (in re-entrant tuning), which makes it largely unfit for performing contrapuntal music in lute style. Besides, its extended repertoire from this era demonstrates that, unlike in Italy, the lute was still held in high esteem as a solo instrument, which may have prevented the guitar (as an attribute of comedians and figures from exotic places) from obtaining a position as a serious instrument for art music. As Trichet concluded in 1640, the guitar was used in particular for singing and fashionable dances, and perfecting your playing was much easier on it than on the lute.[32]

There are only a few early sources of French tablature in existence, with songs and dances, predominantly in battuto. In the three manuscripts (one is dated 1649) of Monsieur Dupille, Commissaire des Guerres (F-Psg Ms Rés 2344, 2349 and 2351), we find typical dances from France such as gavotte, branle, ballet, allemande, courante and sarabande, with no more than rudimentary counterpoint, set up as one single melodic line with some accompanying chords. Dupille even gives complete songs—*airs a pinser*—single melodies, predominantly plucked (see ex. 2.1). In a manuscript of Marie Catherine Ursule Comtesse de Montfort, inscribed Cologne 4 August 1648, there is a comparable repertoire of simple dances in French tablature.[33]

Corbetta, Example and Enigma

In *La guitarre royalle* (1671), one of the first guitar books published in France, Corbetta's music has taken features of lute music from the middle part of the century, of the very particular style of the Gaultiers, Nicolas Hotman, François Dufaut, and Jacques Gallot, a repertoire with a deeply serious tone.[34] Even in the works of harpsichord composers like Jean-Henry d'Anglebert (who made arrangements of lute works) and Jacques Champion de Chambonnières, the influence of the lute is clearly recognizable. In his first book in French tablature Corbetta writes fluent singable lines, as can be seen in the guitar arrangements he made of his own works for three voices and basso continuo, which are dance songs in the tradition of the *airs sérieux* of composers such as Michel Lambert or Jean de Cambefort.[35] The melodies are littered with suspensions—avoiding to arrive directly at the structural notes in the phrase. In some of the movements from Corbetta's suites there are *stile brisé* type of textures, in particular in the doubles of some courantes and sarabandes, while in other more homophonic, danceable pieces there are musical gestures clearly referring to the theatrical style of Lully.

With *La guitarre royalle* and the two books of Robert de Visée (1682 and 1686) the progress of the battuto-pizzicato style came to a standstill. The instrument proved to be ill-equipped for the rich harmonic language (and the apparent predilection for lower tessituras) of late-seventeenth-century French instrumental music, as represented by the stately suites for the viol by composers like Antoine Forqueray and Marin Marais. In that very particular musical atmosphere the theorbo, Visée's other instrument, could thrive, both as a solo instrument and in basso continuo.[36] Besides, it is evident that the guitar could not keep up with the extrovert brilliant new Italian style of the *concerti* of Archangelo Corelli (1653–1713), which was followed throughout Europe. Apparently, the resources of the five-course guitar had been fully explored. The limited melodic powers and the small volume of the tone and the absence of a true bass register made the instrument largely unsuited to the music of the eighteenth century.[37]

Apart from differences in compositional style, Visée's guitar music shows a treatment of the instrument which is very similar to that of Corbetta. The works from Visée's two guitar books are perfect examples of late battuto-pizzicato music. Yet, there seems to be no evidence to confirm that Corbetta was his teacher, as is often supposed today. Robert de Visée was probably born in the late 1650s; but after 1660 Corbetta spent most of his life in England. It is known, however, that Corbetta visited France several times during the 1670s, making it not impossible that Visée met the elderly virtuoso on one or more of those occasions. In his first guitar book, published in the year after Corbetta's death (in 1681), there is an "Allemande, Tombeau de Mr. Francisque."

For Robert de Visée, it seemed opportune to declare about his own style: "I have sought to conform to the taste of connoisseurs in giving my pieces, as far as my humble talent would allow me, the character of the inimitable Monsieur de Lulli's compositions."[38] Thus, two Italians, Lully and Corbetta, served Visée as models. Apart from that, we see in Visée's compositions an unbroken tradition stretching from the French lute repertoire to his works for guitar and theorbo.

In the preface to his second *Guitarre royalle* collection, 1674, Corbetta elucidated his own compositions as follows:

In order to satisfy the liking that I always have had for the guitar, I traveled throughout Europe to see those who played it professionally. And because they asked me to publish some compositions based on their style of playing, I published several books to satisfy them. Two years ago I had a book published [*La guitarre royalle* of 1671], containing various styles of guitar playing. There were pieces for mediocre players in it and others for those who pride themselves on playing well. Now that I have the opportunity of publishing new compositions, I wish to keep to the style that most pleases His Majesty. This style is the most chromatic, the most delicate and the least awkward. I hope that the great monarch, who has honored me from time to time with his commands, will add to my happiness the honor of his approbation and his protection. If you consider them to have some merit, either for themselves alone or because of the custom of the French of always following in the tracks of their great king, I shall be most grateful.[39]

Corbetta indeed included pieces for less-advanced players next to more demanding works. Still, it should be asked if his style can be characterized as "the most delicate and the least awkward," as occasionally the music appears to be extremely dissonant. We will return to this issue in chapter 7. Today it is often assumed that this is music in a simpler style, predominantly strummed, that would be eminently playable by the king. Few of the pieces in Corbetta's 1674 book, however, are true battuto music, and most are no easier to play than the works from his previous collection.

The unanimous opinion of his contemporaries—and in particular of those who had the opportunity to hear him play—was that Corbetta was a great instrumentalist. The fact that his compositions are included in many contemporary manuscripts underlines the importance that was attached to his music. Corbetta was the seventeenth century's greatest promoter of the guitar, and there is little doubt that he was the catalyst for the guitaromania of the 1660s and 1670s, and that without the influence of his personality the guitar would not have experienced a revival of this scope in Paris and London. At the same time it is questionable whether the tablatures from his masterwork *La guitarre royalle* were fully comprehensible to other players of his time.[40]

In our age, the uncommon level of dissonance of these tablatures has given rise to widely divergent views. Richard Pinnell points at the occurrence of non-harmonic tones that are difficult to explain.[41] Corbetta's harmony reminds some listeners of the music of Darius Milhaud.[42] It seems unlikely, however, that a style "la moins embarrasante . . . , la plus delicate" will have been characterized by a harmony so at variance with the prevailing tastes of the time. In today's literature, Corbetta's style is only rarely subjected to analysis, which is curious, because in his tablatures there are so many unusual, harsh dissonances. And that is perhaps the main reason his music is almost completely ignored nowadays. James Tyler refrains from giving any value judgement with regard to the contents of Corbetta's book of 1671: "The music it contains is entirely in the French style" is a very superficial pronouncement, standing in striking contrast to his enthusiasm for Corbetta's earlier works, which are in a simpler and less dissonant idiom.[43] One would expect a thorough analysis of the book that is considered to be Corbetta's principal work. Richard Pinnell is more explicit in his opinion of *La guitarre royalle*, saying that "more than any other book or manuscript, his collection of 1671 remained the apotheosis of the five-course guitar and his style was the epitome of the baroque."[44]

There are several manuscripts in which pieces from *La guitarre royalle* are copied, and some of Corbetta's most extreme harmonies have been changed.[45] From how the tablatures are altered, it appears that some of Corbetta's contemporaries perhaps played differently from what his tablatures say. This subject has not received much attention in our time. Richard Pinnell suggests why considerably fewer works were copied from the *La guitarre royalle* than from Corbetta's other books: "Gallot demonstrates a knowledge of all of Corbetta's printed books and a certain intimacy with three of them. Gallot's favorites are those from 1643, 1648 and 1674. Occasional excerpts from Corbetta's book of 1671 . . . show that Gallot knew the book, but either could not play the music, or simply did not care for it."[46] It is just as likely that the scribe of the Gallot manuscript (or the scribe of a source it was copied from) did not know how to make sense of the harmonies of some of the tablatures from *La guitarre royalle*. Most of the alternative versions of Corbetta's compositions that we find in the Gallot manuscript are no easier to play, and the alterations are often rather awkward.[47]

Although Richard Pinnell has given a first impulse to the discussion about the nonharmonic tones, the subject has not yet received much attention.[48] A thorough investigation is indispensable for a sound analysis of Corbetta's music, to map out the problem and to formulate possible answers. As will be argued in chapter 7, Corbetta may have used tablature letters as a means to indicate left-hand fingering (in particular to show that a barre should be placed), not to actually represent the notes that should sound. Corbetta was not the only guitarist to write such unusual "harmonies"; this barre-notation virus affected the tablatures of a few others, too.[49] It is not likely that there was full agreement on how the music should be performed. When Corbetta played his own music, however, the result would certainly have convinced the ear.

Opinions of the merit of works by Corbetta's French contemporaries differ widely. The problem is that the repertoire under discussion, by the likes of Antoine Carré, François Martin, Remy Médard, and Henry Grenerin, is hardly ever performed today. For an appraisal of the extensive repertoire of the five-course guitar, it is necessary that the music be played. Only then can we form an opinion of the quality of the works, so that order can be created in the corpus.[50]

Chapter Five

Counterpoint

Different Positions

The application of battuto and pizzicato has great impact on how the different parts of the music are represented. As we have seen in the examples of alfabeto accompaniment, the positions of the lowest notes of the chords often do not match the bass, as provided in staff notation by the composer. The result is that many harmonies are in a less favorable position ($^6_4$ or $^6_3$), even at cadence points and endings. This apparent indifference to theoretical issues has been a cause for contempt in both our time and the seventeenth century; however, from the way the subject is discussed in historical sources and how the music is intabulated, we must conclude that there was an awareness of this imperfection. It is obvious that some composers showed more respect for the rules than others, and therefore we should judge each case on its own merits.

In our age, the topic has given rise to theoretical speculations. James Tyler has brought up the acoustic properties of a guitar in re-entrant tuning (without the bourdons A and d, on the fifth and fourth courses), to explain the widespread disregard for the rules of counterpoint, arguing that the actual position of the harmony is hard to perceive when we play battuto on a guitar without low octave strings: "The guitar was commonly (if not exclusively) tuned in a totally re-entrant manner—*aa, d'd' gg, bb, e'[e']*—that is, without any true bass strings. When chords are sounded, this peculiar tuning arrangement, with the lowest pitch the same as that of a violin, produces no strongly audible inversions. The chords are heard as units of pure block harmony."[1] Tyler presupposes that there was a general preference for re-entrant tuning in the first part of the seventeenth century, suggesting that this stringing arrangement was favored because it would facilitate a style of accompaniment where all chords can sound and function as inversion-free "harmonic sonorities," regardless of the actual order of the notes. Before turning to questions about acoustic phenomena, it has to be stressed that it is questionable whether re-entrant tuning was at all widely used at that time. The first unequivocal (and rather late) indications for this method of stringing do not come from Italy but from France.[2] Moreover, in most early printed sources of battuto music (all from Spain and Italy) instructions appear for the tuning with bourdons.[3] As far as the chronology of primary sources is concerned, there is little reason to suppose that the rise of alfabeto coincided with an advance of re-entrant tuning.

Tyler goes on to maintain that the acoustic effects of strumming on the representation of harmony are not confined to re-entrant tuning alone; any inversions would be virtually inaudible even on a baroque guitar strung *with* bourdons.[4] With regard to the presentation of polyphony in the mixed battuto-pizzicato style, Monica Hall argues in a similar vein: "When we listen to music we hear not only the root of each note but the whole range of overtones which gives the instrument its individual timbre. This enables us to hear what is implied rather than what appears literally on the page . . . ultimately the different ways of stringing merely highlight different voice leading. They do not materially alter the musical content."[5] Thus, in recent years the view has gained ground that harmonies in less favorable positions should not be seen as a problem at all; because of the very particular acoustic properties of the five-course guitar, there would be no need to avoid unsuitable inversions, on the assumption that the mind will fill in the missing information. The implication of this claim is far-reaching: although the different methods of stringing occasionally lead to uncommon inversions of the counterpoint, the effect is of limited importance because the ear is still able to distinguish the intentions of the composer.

Perhaps we should consider other explanations. What we observe is inevitably influenced by the parameters of the performance, the features of the instrument, and the qualities of the strings. The idea that we would not notice clearly which tone is the lowest, even on a guitar with bourdons, is subjective, not necessarily valid for other listeners or players. It is a topic that was not comprehensively reviewed in seventeenth-century sources. Pizzicato and battuto are different in one important respect: when playing downstrokes with the fingers (strumming in the direction of the floor), the strings are touched with the outside of the nail, which adds a certain amount of noise to the sound.[6] It goes without saying that it makes a great difference how the strokes are played, and with a carefully differentiated battuto technique, some performers play in such a way that the bass line can be followed clearly, while others mask the position of the chord by producing an airier and much vaguer sound. Similar differences (intentional or not) in the techniques of seventeenth-century players may have been part of the reason that a variety of different continuo practices came into existence.

For contrapuntal pizzicato textures, the lower courses, plucked with the thumb, are sounded for the "bass" notes. On a guitar in re-entrant tuning, these notes sound an octave higher than they would with true bass strings. It seems far-fetched to suppose that the resulting voice crossings will be corrected in the mind of the untrained listener (or even in the mind of someone with a background in music), since this would require the ability to imagine, while listening, the bass to be an octave lower than it actually sounds. We will return to this issue later on in this chapter.

The Bass in Battuto

The writings of seventeenth-century guitarists can give us insight into the efforts that were made to follow general theoretical principles. Battuto notation does not always provide information about the exact number of courses that should be included in strumming. In the first printed book with music in battuto-pizzicato style, Foscarini's *Libro terzo* from about 1630, there are many battuto chords including fewer than five courses, which most likely reflects the usage of the moment. This innovative approach to strummed textures, which at least is new in how it is notated, made it possible to make allowance for the most favorable position of the chord with regard to the bass. The vast repertoire in battuto-pizzicato style that followed gives a very mixed picture of how composers dealt with inversions.

Nicolao Doizi de Velasco, Gaspar Sanz, and François Campion all objected to the use of inappropriate inversions (mostly $\frac{6}{4}$) in certain situations. The issue inspired theoretical observations during the heyday of the five-course guitar, and even as late as 1757 the philosopher Jean-Jacques Rousseau, who wrote the entry for "Guittarre" in Diderot's *Encyclopédie*, could comment:

> Overwound bourdons have two deficiencies. One is that they cut into the frets; the other, which is greater, is that they dominate the other strings and override the final note of the cadence with their resonance especially in strummed passages. There are some chords where they are useful because they supply the root of the chord, but as this does not happen very often, it is better to have plain bourdons at least when playing in lute style.[7]

Apparently Rousseau considered the tuning with bourdons suitable for playing music in "lute style" on the guitar. His argument about the position of the bass in strummed chords makes one doubt if he was familiar at all with the more differentiated battuto techniques applied by the leading guitarists of the seventeenth century, when the practice to avoid unwanted notes on the lower courses was widespread. Rousseau's preference for bass strings of plain gut presumably was motivated by the wish to obtain a milder timbre and a better instrumental balance. It would be interesting to know how Rousseau came by his knowledge about guitar playing, and if he was in contact with certain players.

Sanz, Doizi de Velasco

Gaspar Sanz wrote extensively about the guitar as an instrument of basso continuo, and he expressed his preference for the tuning with bourdons for accompaniment. Sanz noticed that when we strum, sometimes the wrong note appears in the bass: "With a bourdon, if you play the letter or chord of E, which is D lasolre [i.e., a D-minor chord], the open fifth course sounds a fourth below the root of the chord and confuses the proper bass, giving the music some imperfection, as the rules of counterpoint demonstrate."[8] It seems he supposed that all courses should always be included when playing battuto. This can be partly explained by his Spanish background—most of his solo music is in punteado style, and he may have had little experience with the more nuanced Italian battuto-pizzicato style. Apart from that, the undesirable position of the bass in strummed chords was no reason for him to renounce the bourdon tuning for basso continuo. This is quite understandable if we look at the example of his style of accompaniment, which is completely void of battuto—and therefore without any displaced bass notes, at least when played on a guitar strung with bourdons.[9]

Long before the publication of Sanz's *Instrucción*, a solution was formulated for the problem of the position of the bass. In his *Nuevo modo de cifra para tañer la guitarra* (ca. 1640), published in Naples, Nicolao Doizi de Velasco describes how to accompany a bass line correctly, noting unavoidable $\frac{6}{4}$ chords, though he says these can be "made good" when the chords are strummed.

> When one wishes to play counterpoint, the notes [of the guitar] are not so few that they do not exceed seventeen, a range sufficient enough to encompass any counterpoint. For this reason it seems to me better to string the guitar with bourdons on the fourth and fifth courses, rather than without, because it is then more sonorous and similar in range to that of natural voices. Whichever way it is strung, some chords will have fourths between the lowest voices [i.e., will be six-four chords]. These can be made good when playing rasgueado.[10]

In example 5.1 we can see how Doizi de Velasco solves the problem of the $\frac{6}{4}$ position of strummed chords. In the second chord of the first measure there is a barre in third position (the index finger stopping all five courses). Doizi uses an x to indicate that the fifth course should not be played. The second chord of this measure then, in root position, is better (*mejor*) than the first, a $\frac{6}{3}$ chord. In the first chord in the third measure, there is a $\frac{6}{3}$ on the note g (*con 6. ma. y 3. ma.*) with a major sixth and a major third, resulting in the chord g + b + e'. Alongside we see two x's, on the fourth and the fifth courses, meaning that one should only play the first three open courses, which indeed makes the chord intended.

Example 5.1. Nicolao Doizi de Velasco (1640), p. 37, chord diagram.

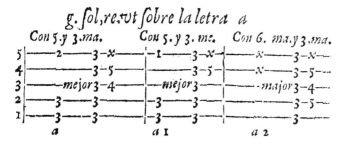

On page 51 we find a D-minor chord in $\frac{6}{4}$ position. It is the alfabeto E, of which Sanz supposed it would be in $\frac{6}{4}$ position, if played battuto. Doizi includes an *x* on the fifth course, to make it a root position chord.[11] In modern guitar-chord charts, too, strings that have to be avoided are sometimes indicated with an *x*.

Bartolotti's Lettere Tagliate, New Chords for Alfabeto

In his *Libro primo* (Florence, 1640) Bartolotti introduced special alfabeto letters, the *lettere tagliate* ("cut letters," in the sense of truncated), to show that chords should be strummed over four courses only instead of five (see ex. 5.2). Gary Boye comments:

> While the multiple use of octave stringing can help the performer by bringing out individual lines, it must be noted that in chordal strumming both strings of the pair will naturally be sounded, sometimes resulting in odd inversions if *bourdons* are being used. Angiol Michele Bartolotti's books from 1640 and 1655 provide a solution to this problem. Several chords are given in his alfabeto with slashes through their letter symbols, called lettere tagliate, indicating that the fifth course should not be played. This results in chords sounding in root rather than in 6-4 position.[12]

Monica Hall argues that the function of Bartolotti's lettere tagliate is not to avoid $\frac{6}{4}$ inversions but to facilitate the introduction of passing notes between the chords, and to satisfy similar practical requirements.[13] While Bartolotti may indeed often have chosen fingerings that require a tagliate chord in order to be able to execute passing notes or suspensions, in many other situations the tagliate shape offers no advantage for fingering at all, and because the result at all times is a root position chord, the most likely explanation remains that

Example 5.2. Bartolotti (1640), Alfabeto chart. The last three chords are
lettere tagliate.

Bartolotti strove for better control over the bass. Nevertheless, it is probable that
the composer then took advantage of this opportunity to write passing notes and
ornaments for some of the chords that he had decided to give as tagliate. This
would explain why certain chords are surrounded by embellishment (whose execution is indeed facilitated by a practical fingering) while others are not.

Bartolotti's *Secondo libro* (ca. 1655) contains alfabeto chords C, E, M and M⁺
(D-major and D-minor chords and their barre transpositions) with the notation for strumming, a note head within the stave, placed on the fourth course,
as in example 5.3—a novel way of showing that the fifth course should not be
struck, with the consequence that these chords are in $\frac{5}{3}$ (root) position, instead
of $\frac{6}{4}$. This must be considered an advance on earlier alfabeto practice and as
a refinement of the system of lettere tagliate. In his first book Bartolotti had
given tagliate versions only of chords G, P, and F (F major, F minor, and E
major), as can be seen in example 5.2.

Alfabeto chords C and E (D major and D minor) do not have any indication
of fingering on the fifth course. Bartolotti probably found it unnecessary—or
even impossible, given his method of notating alfabeto with information for
the left hand—to provide information about the open strings in the chord,
and so he had no way of describing C or E tagliate; but there is a clue that he
may have regarded M and M+ as barre transpositions of C and E. Note that the
chords in examples 5.3 and 5.4 are to be strummed from the fourth course
only, as the position of the strum sign shows. Significantly, in his *Secondo libro*,
alfabeto chords with the fundamental note on the fifth course (B, D, H, I, K,
L, R, and &) are always indicated with a strum covering all five courses, and
therefore in root position.

Of course, if one argues that four-part lettere tagliate chords were *not* a
means of avoiding unwanted $\frac{6}{4}$ inversions on a guitar strung with bourdons,
then one has to allow for the possibility that Bartolotti may have used re-
entrant tuning or even French tuning.[14]

There is no reason why Bartolotti's treatment of the bass in strummed
chords should have been confined to solo repertoire only. As one of the most
celebrated theorbo players of his time, he must have preferred a proper treatment of the bass when playing continuo.[15]

The "open" chords A and O (and N, as a transposition of A, with a barre)
need to be discussed separately (see table 5.1). From the moment that alfabeto

Example 5.3. Angelo Michele Bartolotti (ca. 1655), p. 6, *Courante*, mm. 26–27.

Example 5.4. Angelo Michele Bartolotti (ca. 1655), p. 95, *Allemande*, m. 11. The stems of the notes in the transcription indicate the direction of the strum.

was introduced, G major and G minor were among the most common chords. On a guitar with bourdons they are both in $\frac{6}{3}$ inversion. The main reason that G major and G minor seldom appear in root position is that the g of the third course is the lowest G of the guitar. While the third of the chord (the B of a major chord or the B♭ of a minor chord) would be on the fifth course, A and O are the only possible complete triadic harmonies of G in first position, making use of all courses and including unstopped strings.[16]

Another notable exception is F major. Instead of writing alfabeto G, several composers have written this chord out (as well as its transpositions in higher positions) in tablature, without stopping the fifth course, so that it would be identical with the alfabeto G tagliate from Bartolotti's chord chart (compare ex. 5.2). Perhaps one reason is that it would be easier to play, but in any case the result is that the chord appears in an advantageous root position. F major is one of the alfabeto chords we cannot do without, even in the simplest arias. In his *Secondo libro*, Bartolotti usually gives this chord in tablature, on four courses, probably to make it clear that the fifth course should not be played.[17]

Table 5.1. Chord inversion in Bartolotti's guitar books

B, D, I, and L	"Open" chords (chords including open strings) in root position.
A and O	Open chords in $\frac{6}{3}$.
N	Barre chord in $\frac{6}{3}$.
H, K, R, and &.	Barre chords. As all have the fundamental note on the fifth course, they are all in root position.
G and P	Barre chords in $\frac{6}{4}$. As lettere tagliate (G and P), they are in root position.
F and +	Open chords in $\frac{6}{4}$. F tagliate (in root position) compares to G tagliate.
C and E	$\frac{6}{4}$ chords. These chords can be played in root position if we treat them as "tagliate" (compare exx. 5.3 and 5.4), by leaving out the fifth course.
M and M+	Ditto.

Note. A tuning with bourdons (aA, d′d, gg, bb, e′) is presumed.

We will conclude with E minor (symbol +), the very first chord of alfabeto. It represents Christ's cross (Spanish: *La Cruz*), a symbol that cannot be cut. This would explain, at least partly, why the chord does not exist as tagliate.

Both systems (the lettere tagliate and the indication for strumming with note-heads in the tablature staff) were probably of Bartolotti's own invention; and before editing his books, the composer obviously did not yet have much experience using these notations. In the *Secondo libro* there are many places where the stroke signs are over five courses where they should be over four or three, to avoid unintended dissonances.

Pizzicato and Chord Position

The use of pizzicato enables one to decide which courses to include and which not, and many composers have written plucked textures with the bass in proper position.[18] Normally, crossings of the bass and the upper voices are avoided. In the *Corrente al serenissimo sig. Prencipe Leopoldo di Toscana*, from Granata's first book (ex. 5.5), the very first chord (C major), played pizzicato, would be in an unfavorable $\frac{6}{4}$ inversion if performed on a guitar in re-entrant tuning. Similarly, the lute-like part-writing in the *Sarabanda detta la Pepoli* from Corbetta's 1639

Example 5.5. Giovanni Battista Granata (1646), p. 13, "Corrente."

C O R R E N T E
AL SERENISSIMO SIG. PRENCIPE
L E O P O L D O   D I   T O S C A N A.

book (ex. 5.6) would be oddly inverted in several places, for example, measure 4. Bartolotti, in the E minor courante from the *Secondo libro*, is very conscientious with respect to bass position, as much in pizzicato as in battuto chords (ex. 5.7). In all these examples, the bass line would gain from the low octave strings of conventional Italian tuning.[19]

In re-entrant tuning, the tuning that Gaspar Sanz advocated for his solo works, voice crossings can hardly be avoided. In the first measures of his well-known Pavanas (ex. 5.8) we see how the bass, played with the thumb on the fourth and fifth courses, disappears in the harmony (the bass is here transcribed with the note stems down). It even rises above the treble voice in measure 3. If we were to play it on a guitar in bourdon tuning, there would be a proper bass, an octave lower. Sanz's musical output is marked by a very limited number of keys, as many of his works are in D major, D minor, G major, or A minor, with an abundance of open basses (A, D, and G), and somewhat predictable melodies. On the other hand, his compositions have the immediate charm of a repertoire inspired by the traditional folklore of the Iberian Peninsula. The style of his works, however, is not modern, compared to guitar music from Italy. In the decades before, Corbetta, Granata, and Bartolotti had created a more cultivated repertoire, in terms of melodic invention, polyphony, and harmonic variation. It is questionable, therefore, whether Sanz's comments on theoretical matters reflect the ideas of other composers; nevertheless, his observations give highly valuable insights into the guitar world of his time.

The peculiar voice crossings in this Pavanas make one doubt that Sanz had re-entrant tuning in mind for all his works, especially as he included his basso continuo examples amid his solo works, and not in a separate section of his book.[20] His instructions make it clear that he considered bourdons a prerequisite for accompaniment,[21] and raise the question whether, occasionally, he might have used the tuning with bourdons for the surrounding solo pieces, as well.

On the other hand, in his book there are many little dances with simple two-part pizzicato writing, in which voice crossings are largely unproblematic.[22]

Example 5.6. Francesco Corbetta (1639), p. 61, "Sarabanda detta la Pepoli."
The family name of Corbetta's patron Odoardo Pepoli is spelled in alfabeto
letters: PEPOLI.

Perhaps Sanz had these compositions in mind when he expressed his preference for re-entrant tuning, saying that he has had much experience with stringing "with thin strings only."[23] In spite of that, others may have played his music
on guitars with bourdons, which, according to Sanz, was the usual method of
stringing in Spain. On the title page of his *Instrucción de musica* (1674), Sanz
speaks of a "variedad de sones, y dances de rasgueado, y punteado, al estilo
Español, Italiano, Francès y Inglès." The dances of Spanish provenance (mariona, villano, dance de las hachas, españoleta, jacaras, canarios, matachin and
the like) are predominantly written in a "modern" Spanish punteado style, for
which re-entrant tuning would be appropriate, or at least unproblematic.

The different effects of playing battuto or pizzicato on voice leading were
probably well understood in the seventeenth century. In the preface to his
Livre de guitarre (1682), Robert de Visée remarks: "I beg those who understand

Example 5.7. Angelo Michele Bartolotti (c. 1655), p. 6, Courante, mm. 26–38.

Example 5.8. Gaspar Sanz (1674), tomo 2, p. 10, Pavanas, with two transcriptions of mm. 1–4, without and with bourdons.

the art of composition well and are unfamiliar with the guitar not to be scandalized if they find that I sometimes break the rules. The instrument calls for it and it is necessary above all to satisfy the ear."[24] From the time of Foscarini, half a century earlier, when the mixed battuto-pizzicato style came into being, battuto was always considered characteristic for the instrument and many composers seem to have treated it differently from pizzicato, consciously disregarding theoretical objections. In Visée's *plucked* textures, bothersome voice crossings of the bass and the other voices are largely absent. Only when chords are strummed do odd inversions occur, even in final cadences. It is not the restricted tonal range of the instrument that causes unfavorable chord positions, but the (deliberate) use of battuto. It is not known if Visée, who as a theorbo player must have been very familiar with the rules of counterpoint, ever used the guitar for playing basso continuo. His French tuning, without a bourdon on the fifth course, probably did not provide him with the necessary resources in the bass register.

Robert Strizich describes battuto as "vertical" and pizzicato as "horizontal."[25] According to Strizich, the interest in "la correttezza" was hindered by the use of battuto. Although there is a clear distinction in how the techniques are applied—indeed, with strummed chords there often is not much attention for voice leading—this classification does not do full justice to the function of battuto in music in mixed style. Normally the upper note of a battuto chord fits in the treble line of the surrounding (pizzicato) texture. In the works of Bartolotti, Grenerin, and Corbetta there are many situations in which the progression of the bass is taken into account, as well (see ex. 5.7). It is probably more rewarding to consider the guitarist's persistence with respect to battuto to be a continuation of a tradition, with appreciation of the innate characteristics of the instrument.

The treble melody can be easily combined with the harmony by making use of battuto chords; and without too much effort, a pronounced rhythm can be realized on the guitar. In this respect, the strummed style of the guitar is different from the plucked polyphony of the lute. By mixing battuto chords into plucked textures, some of the benefits of both styles can be preserved. At the start of Visée's Allemande in G minor (ex. 5.9), the first motif is played battuto. On a lute, such an opening would probably be in a single voice; with a strum on the guitar, it is possible to plunge into the matter at once. It is likely that even harpsichordists imitated this effect. In the contemporary literature the consequence of the two different playing styles for chord position is seldom recognized. Yet it could provide a satisfactory explanation for the frequent appearance in the works of Robert de Visée of odd inversions in the strummed sections that are in marked contrast to the perfectly shaped polyphony of the plucked sections.

In the G-minor allemande we can see that as long as it is plucked, the bass stays below the treble melody, even when it is on the fifth course (Visée used the French tuning, with only high strings on the fifth course). In the third (full) measure the composer has made a clever use of the high note of the fifth course in the treble melody (the a belongs to the anacrusis a–d'–c'). It is a form of campanela writing, earlier applied by Bartolotti, Granata, and Corbetta.[26] Generally, Visée's treatment of counterpoint is more precise than that of Corbetta, whose contrapuntal textures can be quite ambiguous.

Example 5.9. Robert de Visée (1686), p. 18, *Allemande*, mm. 1–4. (a) tablature; (b) guitar transcription; (c) the same piece notated "en musique" (on two staves), for treble and bass instrument. In mm. 3 and 4 of the guitar transcription (b), the notes of the fifth course, played with the thumb, are indicated by a long stem downward.

Some composers made use of the instrument's peculiarities in an unorthodox fashion; Corbetta, for instance, was a master in writing covered voice leadings, which probably could be performed satisfactorily only by the most accomplished players of his time. In example 5.10 we see two versions of a Sarabanda, both taken from *La guitarre royalle*. The melody of the vocal version is spread over four courses of the guitar (indicated in the version for guitar solo). It requires a well-developed imagination for the performer to bring out the various voices clearly. It is certainly problematic to reconstruct voice leading in pieces for which no alternative vocal arrangement exists. In a musical analysis, we are often confronted with ambiguities for which there seem to be no ready answers.

A situation like this can best be understood as a peculiarity of the guitar repertoire, arising from an unconventional, playful approach to the idiosyncrasies of the instrument. Thus, sometimes tones are played in a "wrong" octave, and not always out of technical necessity.

Basso Continuo as Playground for Exemplary Counterpoint

In Corbetta's instructions for accompaniment, included in his books from 1643, 1648, and 1671, we find examples of 4–3 suspensions and I⁶–IV progressions. In example 5.11 there is a suspended chord (4–3) on the bass note D, played

Example 5.10. Francesco Corbetta (1671), p. 93. "Sarabande Tombeau de Madame." (a) Vocal version, mm. 1–4; (b) version for guitar; (c) guitar transcription. The version for guitar solo is a fourth higher than the part song.

pizzicato, followed by a G major chord in $_3^6$ position (alfabeto A, which has the B on the fifth course as the lowest note), at least when played on a guitar with bourdons.[27] In Corbetta's basso continuo examples, pizzicato chords are often followed by an alfabeto chord. Evidently, many of these alfabeto chords will not be in the inversion that is implied by the bass in staff notation. Apparently, he thought that it would be acceptable to use the $_3^6$ chord (alfabeto A) in place of a root-position chord. Corbetta's method is an "advanced" form of alfabeto; plucked chords in proper position, are mixed with strummed harmonies, and often there is no identifiable connection between the bass notes. For the accompaniment of solo songs, this was probably regarded as permissible; but in a repertoire of greater complexity, with more active bass lines, or in the polyphony of instrumental ensemble works, such as canzonas or sonatas, this approach would fall short.

In their treatment of battuto chords, the differing methods of the composers become apparent. In example 5.12, a realization of a figured bass by Henry Grenerin, the guitar performs the complete bass line, as written in staff notation in the open score. Supposing that the bass should in principle be the lowest note, bourdons would certainly be needed. Grenerin adheres to the proper placement of the bass almost without exception—even if chords are strummed. Apart from using the standard chords from alfabeto, Grenerin writes many chords with only three or four courses. Also, there are battuto chords where the first course is left out (as in the third measure of ex. 5.12).[28] The notation of Grenerin's guitar continuo is probably the most accurate in the entire

Example 5.11. Francesco Corbetta (1648), p. 83, cadence.

Example 5.12. Henry Grenerin (1680), p. 76, Simphonie, mm. 4–7.

battuto-pizzicato repertoire, indicating which open courses to include—and which not to—even in battuto chords.

Robert Strizich notes that Grenerin avoids chords with notes that sound lower than the continuo bass, even when the bass is on the third course.[29] With a fifth course sounding in the high octave, a plucked C-major chord like that on the last quaver of the first measure of example 5.12 would, however, be in $^6_4$ position.

Right away in the first printed examples of realized basso continuo, Foscarini's *Cinque libri* (ca. 1640), the harmony is related to the bass by means of figures representing the structure of the chord. In his "Modo di sonare le dissonanze e consonanze sopra le noti" (ex. 5.13) he indicates some harmonies—*dissonanze e consonanze*—that should be played *above* the notes of the bass. Because Foscarini played on a guitar with bourdons, this indeed always gives the desired result.

Here, too, battuto and pizzicato have different effects. In the plucked chords in the first six measures of the example, the lowest notes correspond to the bass in staff notation. In contrast, the strummed G-major chord in the last measure is in $\frac{6}{4}$ position with D as the lowest note. The same applies to Foscarini's solo works: in his compositions in battuto style (unlike in his works in pizzicato), there is often no clear bass line. Example 5.14 demonstrates that, if the bass is in small note values (sixteenth notes), Foscarini chooses to play

Example 5.13. Giovanni Paolo Foscarini (ca. 1640), p. 135, basso continuo example.

Example 5.14. Giovanni Paolo Foscarini (ca. 1640), p. 135, realization of basso continuo. The last three measures of the excerpt have bass lines in shorter values.

only the bass, without chords. A similar approach can be found again half a century later in Nicola Matteis's basso continuo manual. Both Foscarini and Matteis found practical ways to do justice to the bass line, overriding the imperfections of the guitar. Their method is very different from early alfabeto practice, when battuto chords were commonly used as an alternative to a "correct" realization of basso continuo on theorbo or harpsichord. Foscarini was one of the first to apply an alternation of battuto chords (on longer bass notes, if the bass allowed for that) and thinner textures when the bass moves more quickly (see the last three measures of ex. 5.14).

In Foscarini's *Cinque libri*, there are compositions in lute style next to battuto and battuto-pizzicato music, and his basso continuo examples are similarly diversified. Italian composers tended to realize their continuo in mixed battuto-pizzicato style, while the Spaniards Gaspar Sanz and Santiago de Murcia did not use strummed chords at all—in striking contradiction to the widespread modern concept of the "typical Spanish" rasgueado style. Although Gaspar Sanz recommended a tuning with two bourdons for accompaniment, the lowest notes from his tablature correspond to the bass of the continuo in staff notation (ex. 5.15).[30]

The books of Henry Grenerin and Nicola Matteis were both published in 1680, and it is interesting to compare them. In his examples of basso continuo, Grenerin meticulously follows the figured bass; but in his solo works, he simply writes many $\frac{6}{4}$ chords. In the latter we see an obsolete battuto-pizzicato style, with little subtlety and variation, compared to the music of Corbetta or Visée. Grenerin's diverse methods of working in solo music and basso continuo— both in the same book—tell much of the worth he assigned to following the rules in the two different genres.

We find a similar approach with Nicola Matteis. He begins his tutor with a number of simple battuto-pizzicato solos, very much like the ones by Grenerin. However, while the latter always took into account the position of the bass in continuo, the examples by Matteis are worked out in various ways. For a better understanding of Matteis's style, we have to compare examples 5.16 and 5.17. The first example—one of the "easy basses for a beginner to learn to play his

Example 5.15. Gaspar Sanz (1674), tomo 1, p. 15, detail of a basso continuo example.

Example 5.16. Nicola Matteis (1680). p. 23, basso continuo example. Where the lowest tones do not match the basso continuo, there are simple battuto chords in standard patterns known from alfabeto. The stems of the notes in the transcription indicate the direction of the strum.

Example 5.17. Nicola Matteis (1680), p. 34, basso continuo example.

part"[31]—is in a somewhat crude battuto style, almost completely without pizzicato. The chords are the usual alfabeto patterns (now notated in tablature), and often the lowest notes clash with the bass in staff notation.

By contrast, other pieces, such as that in as example 5.17, are carefully composed, almost like examples of keyboard music. There are many exercises in Matteis's book in which the bass line is followed with great care, as a consequence of a predominant use of pizzicato technique. Many of the harmonies in example 5.17 are different from those found in standard alfabeto.[32] The music is written in a refined universal style that could as well have served for the lute or harpsichord. With his exercises Matteis underlines that there are various ways to realize an accompaniment. The examples in battuto are probably intended to accompany simple songs or dances, while the well-developed pizzicato examples were meant to serve for more refined compositions. His book's central concern is the application of music theory to the guitar (with an appreciation of its "true nature"), and it would be illogical to suggest that Matteis was indifferent to the issue of the position of the bass. Matteis clearly distinguishes between battuto and pizzicato (in accord with Visée), and the great majority of his *plucked* chords have the bass in its proper position—provided that bourdons are used on both the fourth and the fifth courses.[33]

In the second example, he demands no less of the instrument than Corbetta or Visée did in their solo works. Moreover, one can rightly question whether these are only basso continuo exercises or if they are meant to show how to compose for the guitar according to the rules; it is remarkable that the treble melodies to which his examples should belong are always absent. In the seventeenth century it was not unusual to include composition lessons in a treatise on basso continuo.

The limited range of the bass register of the guitar cries out for pragmatic solutions. In the *Addition au traité d'accompagnement* by François Campion (Paris, 1730) we read:

> It is unnecessary on this instrument to be preoccupied too much by the jumping of the bass from the low to the high register. It is sufficient that in reality the note is there. We even see that on the harpsichord, on which low and high notes are both possible, the accompanists, for reasons of pleasure or by indifference, change one octave for the other . . . such indifference has become acceptable to the ears.[34]

His description fits the style of the continuo of Henry Grenerin like a glove: although there are occasional jumps from one octave to the other, the bass is always the lowest note (independent of battuto or pizzicato). In our time it has been supposed that the bass line would have been provided by a viol or a theorbo. Even though there is a wealth of vocal music with guitar accompaniment, there is very little historical evidence for that, and we can safely assume that on most occasions the guitar executed this task on its own.[35] The tuning with two bourdons enables the guitarist to realize a complete continuo, as we can see in the works of Grenerin and Matteis, and Campion considered the guitar as a fully mature instrument for basso continuo. Although the instrument has its limitations, Campion also saw clear benefits:

> However, one is not prejudiced against the guitar without reason. I acknowledge, along with everyone else, that it is not as strong of harmony as the harpsichord or the theorbo. I believe, nevertheless, that it is sufficient for accompanying one voice. At least this is the verdict given by those who have heard me play. As to the harmonies, I do not know of any impossibilities. It has, compared to the others, ease of transport and playing and, in contrast with the theorbo, *accompaniment parts which are not inverted* and are consequently very harmonious.[36]

This last observation is crystal clear: while the guitar did not have a re-entrant tuning, in contrast to the theorbo, no inverted chords were produced. In spite of this, in his article "François Campion's Secret of Accompaniment for Theorbo, Guitar and Lute" (1981), Kevin Mason takes the view: "Campion fails to mention that the guitar has its own peculiar inversion problem caused by the fact that the fifth course of the guitar is tuned a fifth higher than the fourth course. Since the lowest note that the guitar can play is bass clef d, what does one do when the written bass line goes even lower? The only option is to play as if the fifth course were tuned an octave lower."[37] This same idea resonates in several publications from the early 1980s, such as James Tyler's *The Early Guitar* (1980) and in the two articles by Robert Strizich from 1981 mentioned above.

The Basso Continuo Treatises

The design of most basso continuo instructions is confusing. Often it seems as if theoretical considerations are put aside completely; however, since we are comparing publications originating from different times and places, we should consider that various different traditions may have existed. On closer examination there is a certain coherence in these sources. Foscarini (ca. 1640), Corbetta (1643, 1648, and 1671), Granata (1659), Sanz (1674), and Matteis (1680) all begin their instructions with a general introduction to the ancient alfabeto, to be learned by heart by the accompanist. Then the so-called scale triads follow (see ex. 3.3). In Corbetta's *La guitarre royalle* (1671), for example, there are the by-then archaic scales of B quadro and B molle, derived from the alfabeto practice of the early seventeenth century, provided as a simple rule of thumb for finding the chords to a given bass note without concern for inversions.

Next in most tutors are the figured-bass exercises—short harmonic formulas, easily applicable, showing suspensions and how they resolve, in which pizzicato and battuto are mixed (see ex. 5.11). Normally, the pizzicato chords are "correct" with regard to the position of the bass, while in battuto the inversion of the chord seems to be irrelevant. In Grenerin, however, even strummed chords are in the desired position (see ex. 5.12) because many chords are played over fewer than five courses.

The extant treatises represent every stage of guitar accompaniment, from the most elementary alfabeto to a genuinely contrapuntal approach. Composers such as Corbetta and Matteis switch without comment or compunction from one style to the other. In their exercises we can often find the remains of the old battuto practice. Others, like Sanz and Grenerin, adhere more strictly to textures with a proper bass line. Sanz and de Murcia give examples of basso continuo without any battuto chords, a practice reflected in the realized continuo tablatures in the collection of songs by José Marin, and in the accompaniment to arias from Jacob Kremberg's *Musikalische Gemüthsergötzung* (Dresden, 1689), completely in lute style.

Although the accompaniments of the polyphonic songs from Corbetta's *La guitarre royalle* should probably not be taken as representative of the' continuo practice from the last part of the seventeenth century, they are still often referred to as classic examples. Battuto style predominates and it seems that Corbetta did not attach great importance to the position of the bass. But he may have chosen to realize the continuo in the way he did for reasons of audibility, as for instance in the "Allemande aymée du Roy," a three-part vocal setting (ex. 5.18). In some places, like the second (full) measure, the guitar follows the bass carefully; but more often than not, strummed block-harmonies prevail. Of course, the bass line in the score is almost completely covered by the lowest vocal part. From the accompaniments of some of the other songs, it becomes apparent that Corbetta's continuo style was richly varied and perhaps comes closest to that of Matteis. Sometimes his approach is rather plain, while elsewhere it is quite sophisticated, as in certain places in the chanson "Chi vuol la liberta" (ex. 5.19), where the guitar performs the complete bass, with all the figures.

With the older alfabeto practice in mind, the strummed sections from example 5.18 can best be considered as producing "harmonic sonorities" to be compared to the alfabeto chords in Biagio Marini's *sonate da camera* from his opus 22.[38] Regrettably, Corbetta did not leave any examples of accompaniment to solo song, which may well have been different with regard to the density of the texture. Corbetta generally uses more battuto than Matteis or Grenerin. The latter provided examples of realized continuo in a perfect battuto-pizzicato style, showing the full capabilities of the guitar as a continuo instrument.

Example 5.18. Francesco Corbetta (1671), p. 83, "Allemande aymée du Roy," mm. 1–4, and a transcription of the guitar part.

Example 5.19. Francesco Corbetta (1671), p. 89, "Chi vuol la liberta" (*Allemande Cherie du Duc d'Yorck*), mm. 6–7, and a transcription of the guitar part.

Chapter Six

Stringing Matters

Campanelas Rediscovered

The guitar music of Robert de Visée was rediscovered halfway the nineteenth century. In Napoleon Coste's *Methode* (ca. 1851) and the *Livre d'or* (1880) there are transcriptions of several of Visée's compositions. This music became more widely known through a gramophone recording by Andres Segovia from 1944, and an entire generation of guitarists grew up with Karl Scheit's twentieth-century transcriptions of suites from Visée's *Livre de pièces pour la guittarre* (1686). Transcribing from tablature presupposes a theory about how the instrument was strung, and in his editions from the 1960s and '70s Scheit assumes that the five-course guitar had both the fourth and the fifth courses strung in octaves.[1] In the transcriptions these two courses are sometimes used as part of the treble melody (as campanelas—although Scheit did not use this term) and for the rest in the lower octave, as a bass (ex. 6.1).[2]

For the revival of the baroque guitar, the publication of Sylvia Murphy's article on tuning in *The Galpin Society Journal* of 1970 has been crucial.[3] This article reviewed a number of important sources, and it has been referenced by many authors since. Murphy presented the three tunings probably most commonly in use: (a) tuning with one bourdon each on the fourth and fifth courses ("Italian tuning"); (b) re-entrant tuning (with no bourdons); and (c) "French tuning," with one bourdon on the fourth course.[4] She was one of the first writers to note the effect of campanelas (scale passages in which alternate notes are played on different courses, giving an effect like a peal of bells as successive notes ring on at the same time), specifically in connection with re-entrant tuning, and illustrates this with an example of music from the well-known Pavanas by Gaspar Sanz. These idiomatic passages could apparently be performed convincingly only on a guitar without bourdons.[5]

In the last part of the twentieth century, several views have crystallized on the tuning of the guitar and the performance of this repertoire. The more music of the seventeenth century was played, the clearer it became that there have been many composers who used the fourth and fifth courses as trebles. In his 1971 handbook Bruno Tonazzi remarks: "We are convinced that . . . there

Example 6.1. (a) Tuning with two bourdons ("Italian tuning"); (b) re-entrant tuning (Valdambrini, Sanz); (c) "French tuning" (Visée).

a)   b)   c)

are passages that are *deliberately* composed of notes that proceed stepwise and where every note is produced by another string. The guitarists of that time had the intention to obtain sounds that are very much legato and mingled, with a suggestive refinement of tone color. This effect can, with other means and with certain adaptations, be reproduced on a modern guitar."[6] Murphy does not mention the possibility of putting the high octaves on the bass side of the fourth and fifth courses (aA, d'd instead of Aa, dd'), and neither does Tonazzi. Therefore, when plucked with the thumb, campanela passages can be rendered quite effectively, as noted by Donald Gill in an article in *Early Music* in 1975.[7] This possibility notwithstanding, Gill proposed a theory to deal with what he saw as the unfavorable aspects of tuning with bourdons (due to the supposedly inferior acoustic qualities of the fifth course bourdon), which claims that around 1600 the guitar was normally strung with them, not only for strumming and accompanying, but for music in lute style, too.

> Writing *punteado* music, plucked "in the lute way," as was done in the early seventeenth century, merely showed up the deficiencies. Obviously the low fifth was often left off, so producing stringing arrangement 3 [French tuning]. An idiomatic style of playing developed which used the high fifths as one of the treble courses, with alternating thumb and finger plucking as with the modern banjo, interspersed with plucked and strummed chords. . . . In this tuning the low fourth bourdon tends to obtrude, so it too was left off, resulting in stringing arrangement 4 [re-entrant tuning]. The bass course is then in the middle, with treble strings above and below it and the alternating thumb and finger treble runs became more extended ("Campanella" play).[8]

This theory resonated in James Tyler's influential handbook, *The Early Guitar* (1980). In his bibliographical list of musical sources, Tyler recommends using the French tuning for works in the mixed battuto-pizzicato style of most Italian composers, probably because removing the bourdon of the fourth course as well would result in an undesirable reduction of the instrument's range—overlooking the fact that the French tuning, with only one bourdon, is never clearly described in Italian sources.

In the latter part of the twentieth century the focus of interest was largely on music from after 1670, the works of Gaspar Sanz, Robert de Visée, and Santiago de Murcia. Italian repertoire, however, including a large number of printed books of solo music, remained relatively obscure. An additional problem was that many of these sources were not easy to access. In 1970 research of the extensive solo repertoire from Italy had just begun. As Richard d'Arcambal Jensen states in his unpublished thesis of 1980, he had been able to locate five more Italian books with information on tuning not mentioned by Sylvia Murphy in 1970.[9] Jensen observes that to draw conclusions, scholars use two different types of information:

> The reader cannot help but notice the dearth of sources documenting Italian tuning practices. . . . [I] uncovered an additional five sources which seem to suggest that the so-called Italian tuning is most appropriate for the majority of guitar music published in seventeenth-century Italy. Most of the tuning directions found in Italian guitar tutors . . . fail to reveal the disposition of the bass courses. To solve this riddle, scholars have turned to two contrasting types of evidence: historical and internal. The advantage of historical evidence is that it is far more conclusive than evidence gathered through musical analysis; unfortunately, composers very rarely specified the tuning required for their music. Internal evidence is found by observing the function of the third, fourth and fifth courses. If the third acts as a bass and the fourth and fifth carry the melody, then it may be assumed that the guitar is tuned in a re-entrant tuning. If on the other hand, the melody lies on the first three courses, then it may be assumed that the most appropriate tuning requires octaves on the fourth and fifth course.[10]

Both Murphy and Jensen thought that the disposition of the bass courses—whether bourdons were present or not—could not simply be deduced from the available historical information: tuning charts or verbal instructions. An overarching theory about the development of guitar stringing was lacking, and information from the sources seemed contradictory, leading Murphy to conclude that "many . . . works for the guitar were published in the seventeenth century, but few give precise instructions for its stringing."[11] Jensen suggested that secondary evidence was needed, gathered through musical analysis. Like Tyler, he supposed that a new way of composing arose around 1650, not clarifying, however, what repertoire he had in mind when he wrote that "the third acts as a bass and the fourth and fifth carry the melody."[12]

Guitar music from the middle of the seventeenth century is packed with idiomatic effects, often employing the fourth and fifth courses as trebles, which strongly suggests the presence of high strings on those courses. Concurrently with the growing interest in the baroque guitar in the 1970s and 80s, the idea that this repertoire would require re-entrant (or else French) tuning became broadly accepted. Attention was directed mainly toward the music of Gaspar Sanz and Robert de Visée, whose suites are without doubt a high point of the repertoire. French tuning became the prevailing fashion, and in those years most players strung their instruments the French way. The completely re-entrant tuning, on the other hand, was only seldom used, despite the fact that Gaspar Sanz (whose works were perhaps played the most) had a liking for this tuning. The very limited scope of the tuning without bourdons, making it ill-fitted to play the works of most other composers, may have been the cause of a general preference for the French tuning with one bourdon.

With regard to Spanish music a new style of performance came up, with extensive improvisation in a folkloristic style (almost like flamenco *falsetas*) and instrumentation in multi-guitar groups, sometimes making use of bass instruments and percussion. The simple tablatures of Sanz and Ribayaz were considered as incomplete, and the idea occurred to some that this music was in a kind of lead-sheet notation, in which no more than the framework of the composition is given. The capacity of the player to dress up the music was supposed to define the artistic value of the performance. The view was widely held that there must have existed a rich tradition of intricate, virtuosic strumming, which was not written down on paper.[13]

At the time of this modern revival, Italian repertoire from the fecund middle of the seventeenth century was almost completely neglected. Perhaps the battuto-pizzicato style differs too much from the customary (plucked) guitar and lute technique. Without a nuanced approach of strumming doing justice to the melody and the rhythmic continuity, however, the music seems to fall apart and to inhabit two irreconcilable musical hemispheres. Because this repertoire was and is seldom played, little attention was paid to the conventional Italian tuning with two bourdons. And so it almost looked as if the solo repertoire for the five-course guitar did not predate 1670.

Today it is generally assumed that in France before that time the completely re-entrant tuning without bourdons was most frequently used, based mainly on a few sources from the first half of the century, like the representation of re-entrant tuning in staff notation in Marin Mersenne's *Harmonie universelle*.[14] This same tuning was described in the *Metodo mui facilissimo para aprender a tañer la guitarra* by the Spaniard Luis de Briçeño, published in Paris in 1626. The French tuning, which can be seen as a modification of the re-entrant tuning, is generally assumed to have gained ground only later. After 1670, Francesco Corbetta, Antoine Carré, and Robert de Visée gave the advice to add an octave to the fourth course, and this seems fully to support the modern reconstruction of the sequence of events.

About the situation in Italy and Spain there is more doubt. In a number of sources from different times and places (Amat, Montesardo, Sanseverino, Sanz, Ribayaz, Guerau, Stradivari, and others), the bourdon tuning is only implied, and we must assume that this way of stringing was much in use. A few other sources confirm, however, that re-entrant tuning did exist in Italy as well. In Athanasius Kircher's *Musurgia universalis*, a theoretical work, the five-course guitar is depicted accompanied by an example, of the tuning in staff notation that leaves little room for doubt (fig. 6.1).[15] It turned out to be not so simple to determine which tuning was preferred by each composer, and on this subject opinions still differ widely today.

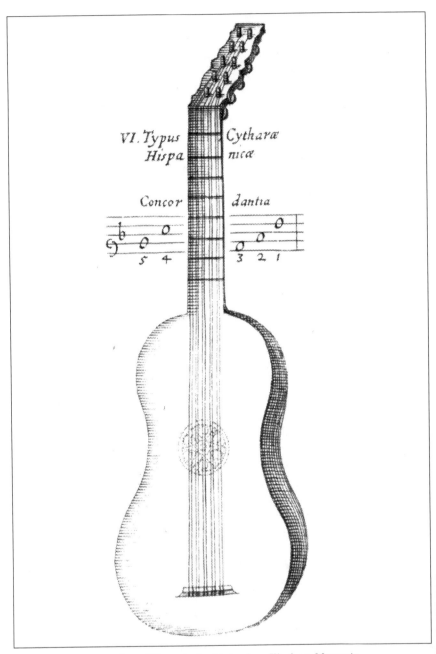

Figure 6.1. "Typus cythara Hispanica" with tuning. Kircher, *Musurgia universalis* (1650).

In 1997, Gary Boye entered the debate with another point of view, assuming that in the works of some composers the fourth and fifth courses actually had a double use, which undermined the idea that the occurrence of campanelas meant no bourdons. Boye presents the idea of two different traditions, one group of players (from the north) who used bourdons, while the others (including Valdambrini, and the "Maestros in Rome," as they were referred to by Sanz) did not: "The bulk of the Bolognese repertory generally gives the lower two courses of the instrument a dual role: as a bass note and, when played only on the uppermost string, as part of the melody. While the music can certainly be performed without the fifth-course *bourdon*, there is no systematic avoidance of its use and the performer gains much by having the lower range of the instrument available."[16] From a few sources from the second half of the seventeenth century, such as the instructions for stringing the *chitarra tiorbata* (in the Stradivari Museum in Cremona) and Ruiz de Ribayaz's instructions (1677), it is apparent that the high octave string is on the bass side of the course and would therefore sound first if played with the thumb. Evidence for the same practice is found in the writings of Rousseau (1757) and Corrette (1761). Earlier sources, however, do not generally make it clear on which side of the course the high octave was placed. It is even possible that the order of the high and the low strings was interchangeable. In figures 6.2b and 6.2c, details from an anonymous seventeenth-century painting show a thin and a thick string on the fifth course. All the other strings seem of indeterminate thickness, which can be explained in different ways. It could mean that the artist has especially highlighted the most eye-catching string. It is impossible to tell if the two strings of the fourth course were of the same gauge or not.[17] In figure 6.3a and b, with details of Della Bella's Cantù (fig. 2.1), there are depicted strings of different gauges on the fifth and fourth courses.

The Tuning Charts

The first place to look for information on the tuning is the prefatory material from guitar books. During the seventeenth century more than sixty collections with solo guitar music were published in Italy; about half of these contain music in the mixed strummed and plucked style, while the others have simpler music in alfabeto. The heyday of the Italian battuto-pizzicato style was in the middle of the century. Although the publication of guitar music continued until 1692, the works of Francesco Asioli (1674 and 1676), Giovanni Bottazzari (1663), and Francesco Coriandoli (1670), as well as the later books of Granata are perhaps of lesser significance; those from an earlier period, by Foscarini, Corbetta, and Bartolotti, represent the summit of the repertoire. Only Roncalli's *Capricci armonici sopra la chitarra spagnola* (1692) stands out as a late work of greater

Figure 6.2a. *Guitar Player.* Anonymous painting (c. 1610–30). Courtesy of the Concertgebouw, Amsterdam.

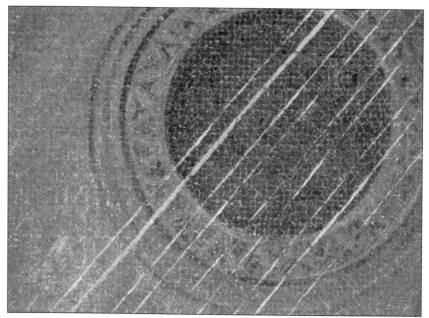

Figure 6.2b. Detail from *Guitar Player*. The arrangement of the fifth course with a thick and a thin string.

Figure 6.2c. Detail from *Guitar Player*. The strings at the nut.

Figure 6.3a. Detail of the *Portrait of Carlo Cantù* (fig. 2.1), showing strings of different gauges on the fifth and fourth courses.

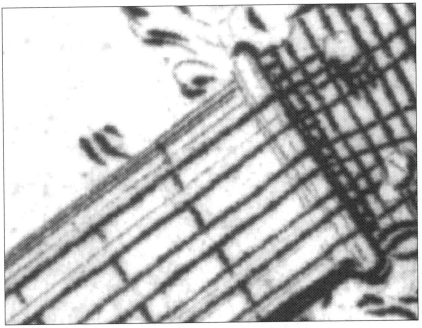

Figure 6.3b. Detail of the *Portrait of Carlo Cantù* (fig. 2.1). The strings at the nut.

merit. Not all the sources are reprinted in our time, creating some problems of access—hence, in part, the current unfamiliarity with Italian repertoire and its requirements.

Most guitar books from the first half of the seventeenth century contain information on tuning and almost all composers who published music in the mixed style between 1630 and 1660 included instructions in one or more of their publications, mostly in the form of a tuning chart in tablature, sometimes accompanied by verbal instructions (see table 6.1).

A chart to check the tuning in octaves is given in a few publications, such as the *secondo esempio* in tablature in Stefano Pesori's *Galeria musicale,* 1648 (ex. 6.2a).[18] Differences of opinion about the meaning of these tuning charts center on whether they represent unisons or simply the identically named notes in unison or at the octave: do the tuning checks compare the strings in octaves, or may there also be unisons involved? In a few books, such as Pesori's *Galeria* and the *Cinque libri* of Foscarini, we find verbal instructions added to the tuning checks mentioning octaves, implying that bass strings were present and that the low strings of the fourth and fifth courses were tuned *in unisono* to the adjacent course.

On lutes with a relatively short scale, bass courses were traditionally provided with a high octave string to enhance the tone.[19] This applied to the five-course guitar as well. Generally, in tuning charts in both lute and guitar books, the presence of these high octave strings is not indicated. A simple chart like Pesori's *primo esempio* is perfectly adequate for representing Italian tuning, but not re-entrant tuning. The low strings of the courses were presumably considered to be the principal strings and the high octaves seen as subordinate. This is also apparent from Benedetto Sanseverino's instructions in *Il primo libro d'intavolatura* (Milan, 1622), where he speaks of "the fifth course, known as the bass." In this book the tuning (G, c, f, a, d′) is shown in the example in staff notation (ex. 6.2b), corresponding to the usual tablature chart, in which only the notes of the low strings of the fourth and fifth courses are represented. He writes:

The guitar has five courses comprising two strings for each course, except the cantino.

The fifth course, known as the bass, has a cantino uppermost, accompanied by a thicker string, which two together make an octave. Tune them to a convenient pitch for the singer,[20] as is usual on other instruments, or tune them to a note which is appropriate for the size of the guitar.

The fourth course likewise has a cantino accompanied by its bass, which two together make an octave like the above. To tune it with the fifth course, make it a fourth higher than the fifth course, stopping it at the second fret of the above-mentioned [fourth course] makes a fifth with the bass, or stopping the fifth fret of the fifth course all together makes a unison.

Table 6.1. Selection of Italian printed books of mixed tablature with tuning information

Giovanni Paolo Foscarini	*Li cinque libri* (Rome, c. 1640), tuning chart and a tuning check that says "ottave."
Francesco Corbetta	*De gli scherzi armonichi* (Bologna, 1639), tuning chart and tuning check. In *Varie capriccii* (Milan, 1643) and *Varii scherzi* (Brussels, 1648) there are tuning charts, but only for different new tunings. Like the usual tuning charts, these charts compare the courses as unisons.
Antonio Carbonchi	*Sonate di chitarra spagnola* (Florence, 1640), tuning chart and check.
Carlo Calvi	*Intavolatura di chitarra* (Bologna, 1646), tuning chart and check.
Stefano Pesori	*Galeria musicale* (Verona, 1648), text on tuning, very similar to Foscarini's; a tuning chart and a tuning check that says "in ottava." *Toccate di chitarriglia* (Venice, c. 1650), tuning chart and check.
Giovanni Battista Granata	*Capricci armonici* (Bologna, 1646), Foscarini's text on tuning (almost verbatim) and a tuning chart. *Nuove suonate* (n.p., c. 1650), one tuning chart for a new tuning. *Soavi concenti* (Bologna, 1659), tuning charts for different new tunings; includes works for the theorboed guitar, which presupposes bourdons at the fourth and fifth courses.
Ferdinando Valdambrini	*Libro primo* (Rome, 1646), tuning chart and a tuning check, that says "ottave." A rare Italian source with tuning chart and check, clearly intended for re-entrant tuning.
Giulio Banfi	*Il Maestro della chitarra* (Milan, 1653), tuning chart and check plus a text on how to tune in "unisoni." This implies bourdons.
Giovanni Bottazzari	*Sonate nuove* (Venice, 1663), several tuning charts for different new tunings.

Example 6.2a. Stefano Pesori, *Galeria musicale* (1648), tuning chart.

Primo Efempio.

Quinta corda
Quarta corda
Terza corda
Seconda corda
E prima corda

Secondo Efempio in Ottaua.

Quinta corda
Quarta corda
Terza corda
Seconda corda
E prima corda

Example 6.2b. Benedetto Sanseverino, *Intavolatura facile* (1620), tuning chart.

Effempio dell'accordatura della Chitarra.

In quarta, In quarta, In terza, In quarta,

The third course has two strings which together sound a single note in unison, tuned a fourth above the fourth course, so that when it is stopped at the second fret it will make an octave with the open fifth course.

The second course also has two strings which likewise sound a single note in unison as above, tuned a third above the said third course, so that when it is stopped at the third fret it will make an octave with the thicker string of the fourth course and a unison with its cantino.

The cantino, the single first course, is tuned a fourth above said second course, so that when it is stopped at the third fret, it will make an octave with the open third course.[21]

In the works of several composers—like Francesco Corbetta (ex. 6.3), Antonio Carbonchi, Carlo Calvi, and Giulio Banfi—we find tuning charts and checks similar to those of Pesori and Foscarini, but without verbal reference to unisons or octaves. It is likely, however, that they should be interpreted in

Example 6.3. Francesco Corbetta (1639), tuning chart.

Example 6.4. Ferdinando Valdambrini (1646), tuning chart.

the same way. Probably, the charts are a stepwise representation of the act of tuning: first you compare every course in unison to the next and then check the tuning with octaves. This is the procedure that Montesardo, Sanseverino, Millioni and many others followed in their verbal explanations of the tuning, though Millioni and most later sources do not mention the high octaves on the lower courses.

If a composer such as Corbetta used this same tuning chart and check for a re-entrant tuning (which some modern authors have supposed), there would be an octave, not a unison, between the note on the fifth fret of the fourth course and the open third course, as shown in example 6.3. In the *accordatura* chart as well as in the *prova*, octaves and unisons would be mixed up, and consequently there would be no critical difference between the two. This does not seem a practical way to instruct novices. Should we then suppose that the tuning charts are only there to give the intervals between the strings, independent of the actual octave they are in? Most modern authors seem to accept this inference, in particular for works with tuning charts but no verbal instruction about unisons or octaves, some even taking this as a sign of indifference on the part of the composer as to what tuning was to be used and how their music should sound. Following this reasoning, the usual tuning charts (like the one in ex. 6.4) may be considered ambiguous. It is argued that they could have been used for any possible stringing. There are clear instances, however, where there is no such ambiguity, and the charts and checks mean what they say: Foscarini (ca. 1630) and Pesori (1648) have tuning checks that explicitly specify octaves, and thus bourdons on the fourth and fifth courses. Ferdinando Valdambrini's *Libro primo* (1646) is the only Italian tuning chart that clearly indicates re-entrant tuning (ex. 6.4).

Tyler warns the reader not to take tuning charts at face value; he notes the example of a "normal" tuning chart from an anonymous (early alfabeto) manuscript (F-Pn Rés.Vmc. Ms 59), whose confused verbal tuning instructions are assumed to imply that a re-entrant tuning is intended, supposedly proving that tuning charts were not always understood as a direct rendering of the tuning.[22] Sources with conclusive evidence to support his argument (with contradictory information of this kind) are very hard to find. Tyler gives a summary of sources of specific information about the tuning and stringing,[23] ending with the cautionary note that "all other sources are ambiguous concerning tuning and stringing," but in fact Tyler's choice of sources is subjective and incomplete, omitting for instance the octave check from Stefano Pesori (ex. 6.2) and Giulio Banfi's text, both of which imply a tuning with bourdons.[24]

As appears from the examples cited above, re-entrant tuning and the tuning with bourdons seem to have coexisted for several decades in Italy; during the period when the last great highlights of the Italian repertoire appeared in print, in Bartolotti's *Secondo libro* in about 1655 and Granata's *Soavi concenti* in 1659, the bourdon tuning probably was the one most in use. Granata included compositions for the *chitarra atiorbata*, a guitar with seven extra bass strings. This instrument probably had bourdons on the fourth and fifth courses. In any event, this did not keep him from writing campanela passages for it (ex. 6.5). We will discuss campanela scales below.

With regard to the earlier works of Granata, there is no reason to suppose he used re-entrant tuning. In his book of 1646 he copied the tuning chart and the instructions from Foscarini's *Cinque libri* almost verbatim, and therefore we must assume he was very familiar with the works of this composer, written for Italian tuning.[25] There is nothing in Granata's preface that points to any other tuning:[26]

First tune the fifth string, neither too high nor too low, so that the others also can be tuned corresponding to the size of the guitar. If we play the [note of] the fifth fret of this fifth string, it sounds the same as the open fourth course. Similarly, the tone produced on the fourth fret on the third string is the same as the open second. And similarly the one of [again] the fifth fret on the second string is the same as the open first.[27]

The tuning charts for the scordatura pieces in Giovanni Bottazari's *Sonate nuove* (1663) are probably the last directions from the entire battuto-pizzicato repertoire from Italy.[28] Only in the many collections in alfabeto, mostly reprints of earlier editions, can instructions still be found after this time.[29] Tuning instructions were probably considered redundant by then.

The next source of information is the (Italian) preface to Corbetta's *La guitarre royalle*, published in Paris eight years after Bottazari's collection. No guitar music of importance is known to have survived from the intervening years, and it is unlikely that any radical changes in idiom and playing technique had taken place in the meantime. It was the time of the exodus of Italian musicians to France. Only two composers who published music in the mixed style before

Example 6.5. Giovanni Battista Granata (1659), p. 98, Preludio, mm. 24–25. In the second half of measure 25, there is a descending cascading scalar passage, from a' to b.

1660—Bartolotti and Pellegrini—have given *no* information about tuning,. The tuning implications of Bartolotti's *lettere tagliate* have been discussed above, in chapter 5.

Campanela Scales

In The *Guitar and Its Music*, Tyler reviews the subject of octave stringing in some detail.[30] Joan Carles Amat, Girolamo Montesardo, Benedetto Sanseverino, Lucas Ruiz de Ribayaz, Pierre Trichet, Nicolao Doizi de Velasco, Gaspar Sanz, and Francisco Guerau all describe octave stringing on the fourth and fifth courses. Of special interest is the document from the workshop of Antonio Stradivari, briefly mentioned earlier, with a description of string gauges (on a drawing of the neck of a theorboed guitar) indicating high octaves on the "bass side" of the course.[31] This feature, which is also clearly visible in figure 6.2b, was advantageous for the performance of campanelas. Tyler comments: "When playing single line melodic passages (such as cascading scales) on a guitar with a bourdon on the fourth course, for example, many apparent anomalies in the melody line can be resolved (or avoided) if the guitarist decides to pluck only the upper octave string of the course and not the lower."[32] This last idea has found an enthusiastic response in our time, though Tyler obviously is well aware of the lack of extensive historic evidence for this "split course" technique, and presents it as no more than a possible solution.[33] Even so, the French tuning has been widely adopted as the best available compromise.[34] With that tuning, however, there is still a bourdon present on the fourth course in cascading scalar passages, a no less disturbing fact, to some listeners, than the one on the fifth.

Another solution, widely overlooked, depends on the skill of the player in varying how to touch the course, which can sound like a real bass if the bourdon is plucked firmly, or can be made part of the melody, if the high octave string is emphasized. It is not strictly necessary to avoid touching the low octave string, though that is possible. An important factor is the material the strings are made of. In our time, too often metal-wound basses are used, with a very dominant sustained sound (Castillion in 1730, and Rousseau in 1757 noted the deficiencies of overwound strings), disturbing the fragile balance of the campanelas. Plain gut strings, on the other hand, will not overwhelm their high octave pairs, if we touch the bourdons lightly. We do not know whether completely leaving bourdons out was ever the desired mode of execution for campanela runs; nonetheless the practical possibility of playing campanelas effectively even with bourdons means that it is doubtful whether the presence of campanela sections (or the use of the fourth and fifth courses in treble melodies in general) can provide decisive information about stringing. At the very least, it is not at all self-evident that the performance of these effects requires that there are no bourdons.[35]

The significance of campanelas in the evolution of guitar tuning has perhaps been overestimated. They appear, probably for the first time, in Kapsberger's third book of music for the chitarrone (1626). The re-entrant tuning of the first two courses of the chitarrone enables one to play cascading scales.[36] In Bartolotti's first book (1640) there are a modest number of short campanela figures, mainly in first position.

In example 6.6 we see an elementary campanela figure, and in example 6.7, one of the rare longer scale patterns from this same book, including notes in higher positions.[37] This became a characteristic of campanelas of a later period, in Bartolotti's *Secondo libro* (ca. 1655) and in Spain with Gaspar Sanz and Santiago de Murcia. The higher positions are also used in a few cascading scales that we find in Corbetta's book of 1643. Usually, these are scale patterns in D major,[38] which can also be found in his 1648 print, and in Granata's books of circa 1650, 1659, and 1674. Obviously it was part of the palette of standard formulas that the guitarist had at his disposal. It is significant that there are few of these cascading scale passages in Corbetta's collection of 1648, in fact even fewer than in the 1643 book. Perhaps he found the effect somewhat hackneyed.

With Granata there is a similar development. In his first book, *Capricci armonici sopra la chitarriglia spagnuola* (1646), there are some incidental campanela runs. In his next publication, *Nuove suonate di chitarriglia spagnuola* (ca. 1650), there are not many more; by contrast, there are many instances of fast scales in *strascini* (a left-hand slurring technique).[39] Campanela scales are absent from his book of 1651 and relatively scarce in his *Soavi concenti* (1659). In the Italian repertoire, then, the gimmickry of the campanelas was used only to a limited degree, appearing more frequently in just a few works from Bartolotti's *Secondo libro* and in Granata's book of 1674.

The way in which Bartolotti, Corbetta, and Granata take advantage of the peculiarities of guitar tuning may deceive us; while occasionally treble notes are captured on the fourth and fifth courses as part of the melody, these courses are routinely employed to provide the bass in the many (plucked) two- and three-part cadential figures.[40]

Example 6.6. Angelo Michele Bartolotti (1640), p. 66, Sarabande, mm. 23–24, short campanela run.

Example 6.7. Angelo Michele Bartolotti (1640), p. 51, Allemande, m. 13, cascading scale.

Example 6.8. Ferdinando Valdambrini (1646), p. 31, Toccata.

Valdambrini's books (Rome, 1646 and 1647) are particularly interesting, because they are without doubt intended for a guitar in re-entrant tuning, without bourdons on the fourth and fifth courses. They can provide material for an examination of his style of composition in relation to the tuning. Apart from an abundant use of campanela textures, the composer takes great liberties with the disposition of the melodies over different octaves. In example 6.8 we can see that Valdambrini repeatedly wrote leaps of a seventh from the third to the fourth course (from m. 1 to m. 2) and back. It seems not to have bothered him that the note g of the third course is a major seventh lower than the f♯′ of the fourth course. The blatant inconsistency in voice leading distinguishes his work from that of most of his contemporaries. Yet, his passacaglias are full of inventive idiosyncratic effects and, like Granata and Bartolotti, he wrote long campanela trills (ex. 6.9).[41]

The High G

Several composers, including Gaspar Sanz, use the third course in treble melodies in such a way that one could suppose that this course, too, had a high octave string—a minor third higher than the first course. In a tuning with a high g′ on the third course, some apparent anomalies in the melody line can be resolved; however, in the many sources that deal with the tuning there seems to be no truly reliable information about this, just a few ambiguous and uncertain manuscript references; therefore it should not be assumed that such an arrangement was in general use.[42] In the extensive observations by Gaspar Sanz, we find no word about it. It is unlikely that Sanz himself would have used an octave-strung third course, since in his discussion of the disadvantages of octave stringing on the fourth and fifth courses (for performing ornaments and campanelas), he makes no reference to octave stringing on the third course.

In example 6.10, from the *Jacaras* by Gaspar Sanz, we can see that in measure 23, the note g on the open third course occurs in a lower octave than the rest of the melody. With a high g′ string added to the third course, this note would fit perfectly in the melodic line. In measure 25, however, there still is a leap of a seventh that cannot be eliminated, since the second note, an a on the fifth course, and the last note e′ are in different octaves, in any tuning.[43] Besides, this g on the open third course is probably to be played with the finger, not with the thumb, so that even with the bourdon on the treble side, normally helpful in campanelas, the low string is touched first and thus its sound will drown out the high octave string. Clearly, Sanz, for one, took considerable liberties in spreading a melody over different octaves, so we have to exercise

Example 6.9. Valdambrini's trills. In the first measure we see a cross-string trill. In the second measure is the usual trill, made with the left hand.

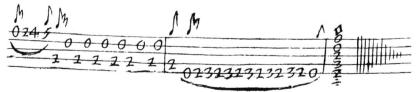

Example 6.10. Gaspar Sanz (1674), tomo 1, p. 7, "Jacaras," mm. 23–26.

great caution with the supposed indirect evidence from melodic lines for a high octave string on the third course.

Also in Corbetta's works from his years in France and England there are melodies with notes on the third course that are apparently displaced (ex. 6.11). We should not jump to conclusions about ideal melody lines too easily; the repertoire for the five-course guitar is full of melodic leaps from one octave to the other. It is the unavoidable result of the limited scope of the instrument.

There are a few manuscript sources that could give rise to speculation about the existence of a tuning with a high g′ on the third course. The formulation of the instructions in these sources is unclear, preventing unequivocal conclusions. On top of that, it concerns collections of very simple music, only in alfabeto. While in the music of certain composers we are confronted with uncommon melodic leaps of a seventh or a ninth, and while unambiguous information on the stringing is often lacking, modern performers have started to experiment with a tuning with a high g′.

There are physical limits to the breaking pitch of a string of given length. A high g′ string made of gut is even closer to that point than the first course at e′, and can only be used on an instrument with a relatively small scale (most surviving baroque guitars have a rather long string length of over 650 mm.), or on a guitar, tuned to a lower pitch. Moreover, an added octave g′ on the third course would sound almost continuously above the melody, especially in strummed chords where the high octave cannot be avoided. In music in mixed battuto-pizzicato style, this would obscure voice leading considerably.

Example 6.11. Francesco Corbetta (1671), p. 28, Allemande, m. 16.

A tuning with only one bourdon (the French tuning) in combination with a high octave on the third course would not be an obvious choice for Italian or Spanish music. We might sooner think of (hypothetical) tunings like aa, d'd', g'g, bb, e' or aA, d'd, g'g, bb, e'.[44]

The "Modern Way of Composing"

In 1674, three years after the publication of Corbetta's *La guitarre royalle* in Paris, Gaspar Sanz gave the following report—speaking of the situation in Rome, but in general musical terms:

> In stringing there is variety, because in Rome some masters string the gui-
> tar with thin strings only, without any bourdon on either the fourth or fifth
> course. In Spain the opposite is the case, since some use two bourdons on
> the fourth and another two on the fifth and at least, as is usual, one on each
> course. These two methods of stringing are good, but for different effects.
> For those who wish to use the guitar to play noisy music, or to accompany the
> bass of a *tono* [a vocal work] or *sonada*, the guitar is better strung with bour-
> dons than without, but if anyone wishes to play with skill and sweetness and
> to use campanelas, which is now the modern way of composing, bourdons
> do not sound as well—as only thin strings do—on both the fourths and the
> fifths, of which method I have had much experience. This is the reason—
> when making trills, slurs and other ornaments with the left hand, the bour-
> don interferes with them because it is a thick string and the other is thin, and
> therefore the hand cannot stop them evenly and hold down the thick string
> as easily as two thin strings.[45]

Although Sanz gives different reasons for using re-entrant tuning rather than bourdons (the difficulties in performing ornaments and the disadvantage for campanelas), his comments also show that stringing with two bourdons was usual in Spain, which is confirmed by the instructions in the next two books that were published there, Lucas Ruiz de Ribayaz's *Luz y norte musical* (1677) and Francisco Guerau's *Poema harmonico* (1694). Perhaps Sanz's concerns about bourdon stringing were not shared by the majority of composers in Italy, where in fact campanela scales seem first to have been used; and we can find many ornaments on the fourth and fifth courses in the works of Foscarini, Corbetta, Granata, and Bartolotti. Possibly his preference for re-entrant string-ing was sparked mainly by his enthusiasm for campanelas, which Sanz consid-ers one of the main characteristics of a "modern" style. On the other hand, the connection he sees between the role of the instrument in basso continuo and the tuning with bourdons probably reflects the common practice of his time.[46]

It would be interesting to know whom Sanz considered as practicing the "modern way of composing." Sanz studied in Rome with Lelio Colista, whom he admired greatly. Very few works for guitar by Colista are still extant.[47] Sanz mentioned other Italian composers, including Foscarini, Granata, Pellegrini, Corbetta (whom he calls "el mejor de todos"), and "Caspergier," confirming that the celebrated lutenist Kapsberger (who had died more than twenty years earlier) played the guitar as well.[48] Bartolotti is not mentioned, and perhaps Sanz was not familiar with his works. What he says about the "new style" obviously does not refer to the fully developed battuto-pizzicato repertoire. It is not known if Sanz ever performed battuto-pizzicato music himself, and it is impossible to tell if he would have used the Italian tuning for it if he had.

His remark that "you may choose whichever of the two [stringing methods] pleases you, according to the purpose for which you are playing," is unlikely to mean that a guitarist would use bourdons to play the music of Foscarini and replace those with high strings for the music of Valdambrini or Colista. Some guitar teachers (*algunos maestros*) in Rome had renounced the use of bourdons; others presumably used another tuning in Rome itself and elsewhere. Since there is no reference at all to French tuning in Sanz's preface, the latter tuning must have been the conventional Italian one, with two bourdons.

Musical analysis as secondary evidence for stringing methods can become a new source of disagreement. Thus, Monica Hall observes: "The development of an elaborate treble-dominated style after 1640 led to a preference for re-entrant stringing." She sees this development reflected to a greater or lesser extent in the works of Pellegrini (1650), Bartolotti (1655), Bottazzari (1663), Coriandoli (1670), Asioli (1674/76), Roncalli (1692), and the seven books of Granata.[49] Her conclusions and emphasis contrast with Gary Boye's views on the dual use of the fourth and fifth courses in most of the Italian repertoire, described above. His remarks on the maestros of Rome notwithstanding, one wonders whether Sanz had a thorough understanding of the style of his Italian predecessors; for while he claims to have studied with Lelio Colista, he mainly wrote rather uncomplicated music himself, compared to the works in the mature battuto-pizzicato style (probably not well-known in Spain) by Corbetta, Bartolotti, and Granata.

Monica Hall supposes that perhaps as early as the 1650s, Corbetta used a bourdon on the fourth course, added to a re-entrant stringing:

> In some ways it is the optimum arrangement, giving a range of two octaves on the fingerboard while retaining the characteristics of a re-entrant tuning . . . the re-entrant tuning is adequate for at least the two earliest collections and is just as likely to be the one intended. As he went on to write more complex music the need to extend the compass downward became paramount— hence the need for a low octave string on the fourth course.[50]

This contrasts with Gill's hypothesis about the bourdons of the Italian tuning being left off one by one. I would take issue with both views. There is good evidence for the general use of the Italian tuning in the (now rarely played)

Italian early-seventeenth-century repertoire, and Corbetta's first book—which has not a single example of campanela—fits perfectly into that tradition. It has a tuning chart and check which, as noted before, if taken at face value suggest bourdons on the bottom two courses. It is hard to see how the music from Corbetta's books of 1643 and 1648 particularly benefits from any other tuning. Any information that would conclusively link the music of Corbetta (or other major composers such as Foscarini, Bartolotti, and Granata) to re-entrant tuning is absent. The counterpoint in the lute-like pieces from Corbetta's book of 1639 would, occasionally, be oddly inverted if played on a guitar without bourdons.[51] Consequently, this issue remains equivocal: although the idea that French tuning was a modification of the re-entrant tuning (and not of the Italian tuning) is convincing, there is little reason to assume that such a transition took place in mid-century Italy.

James Tyler's article on the five-course guitar in *Grove Music Online* tends to gloss over an important body of evidence; matters are presented as if the re-entrant tuning was the one most in common use throughout the first half of the seventeenth century (referring to information on tuning given by Mersenne, Briceño, Valdambrini, Carré, and Sanz, the last of whom are rather late in any case, and only Valdambrini is from Italy), neglecting all the Italian sources from the period in question that have instructions for bourdon tuning. Tyler simply states that "the most common modification to the re-entrant type tuning was a/a-d'/d-g/g-b/b-e' which, judging by the musical requirements of their tablatures, was used by the leading composers of guitar solos of the time."[52]

Thus, we can perceive the contours of a comprehensive theory of the rise and fall of the French tuning. One of its premises is that the Italian tuning (the tuning with two bourdons) rapidly decreased after c. 1640, and that it again gained ground in the second quarter of the eighteenth century. It seems that the paradigm of the unique position of French tuning in the history of the baroque guitar does not allow for the Italian tuning continuing to play a role in Italy and France.

Francesco Corbetta and the French Tuning

Today it is taken for granted that for his two *Guitarre royalle* collections, Francesco Corbetta had the French tuning in mind. The main grounds for this is what he says in the (French) preface to the 1671 collection: "I advise you to add an octave d to the fourth course, because the two unisons do not make harmony."[53] This advice must have been directed at players who strung their guitars in re-entrant tuning. Without doubt there was a population of guitarists in France who strung their guitars in this way; and we know from Sanz and Valdambrini that in Italy and Spain, some people also used this tuning.[54]

Does this mean that we should read it as advice to remove a bourdon from a guitar in Italian tuning? Clearly, Corbetta was not addressing himself directly to players using Italian tuning, and the second part of the sentence ("the unisons do not make harmony") does not apply to their stringing: a guitar in Italian tuning makes even more "harmony" than a guitar in French tuning. That he considered French tuning to be better (for his music) than re-entrant tuning does not automatically mean that he considered French tuning more appropriate than Italian tuning.[55]

But in that case, why does Corbetta not advise us to add an octave to the fifth course, too, if that was how he strung the guitar himself? This may have been a matter of the audience he was addressing. As in Spain and Italy, there must have been some variety in stringing in France. No printed solo repertoire in mixed style is known from before 1663, so we must suppose that mainly simple music (song accompaniment and dances) was transmitted aurally. From the 1640s onward, Italian virtuosi (Foscarini, Bartolotti, and Corbetta) visited Paris, and they may have performed in elevated circles. They would presumably have performed an advanced battuto-pizzicato repertoire, on guitars in Italian tuning. This repertoire would have been out of reach for most French *dilettanti*.

Foscarini and Bartolotti were famous as theorbo players; it may not have been possible to make a living as a guitarist in the French capital in the period 1640–70. Apart from some occasional stage performances in ballet or opera, there may not have been much work playing the guitar. Corbetta left for London at the start of the Restoration in 1660, traveling in the train of Charles II. In France until then, Italian guitar music does not seem to have fallen on fertile soil, and very little has survived (notated in French tablature) in manuscripts from the middle part of the seventeenth century. It is telling that a repertoire of comparable excellence by French guitarist-composers seems not to exist.[56] The books by the major Italian composers are all in Italian tablature, which probably was an obstacle for those who were used to French notation.[57] Hence, for example, Huygens's complaint about having to transcribe this "silly tablature, which puts everything upside down."[58] Even today lutenists transcribe Italian tablature to French, for convenience, and also in manuscripts from the last decades of the seventeenth century we can find transcriptions of that kind of works by Granata and Corbetta.

In 1663 the first book of guitar music in French tablature appeared, by François Martin, with rather simple solo music in a local variant of the battuto-pizzicato style. In 1671 two books were published in Paris: *La guitarre royalle* by Corbetta, dedicated to Charles II, and Antoine Carré's *Livre de guitarre*. Corbetta's privilege to publish *La guitarre royalle* was dated September 21, 1670, but it was not printed until October 1671; Antoine Carré obtained the privilege for his *Livre de guitarre* a few months later, on February 12, 1671. A reference is found to legal proceedings involving Corbetta, the printer Bonneüil, and

Carré, dated December 20, 1670.[59] There may have been a quarrel between the two composers, perhaps over plagiarism. The title page of Carré's book says: "Livre de guitarre contenant plusieurs pièces composées et mise au jour par le Sieur de la Grange," suggesting that all compositions in this collection are his. Yet on page 23 we find a sarabande from Corbetta's *Varii scherzi di sonate* (1648). But how could Corbetta know that his music was borrowed if he had not seen the actual contents of Carré's *Livre de guitarre*? In that book Carré has given the advice "fault mettre a la guitare une octave en quattriesme," and Corbetta in turn may have copied this. In the preface to *La guitarre royalle* he writes that he had a part of the music engraved in London and he had brought the plates with him to Paris, and he may have added the preface last at some moment before October 1671. Probably Carré's book had appeared in print long before that date.[60]

Was the French tuning invented by one of these two composers? It is equally likely that adding a bourdon to the re-entrant tuning was an innovation gaining ground in circles of which Carré formed part. It is not known if Corbetta was much in contact with French guitarists during his stay in England after 1660, but he must have realized that they were potential customers for his new collection.

La guitarre royalle begins with a preface in Italian, clearly written by Corbetta himself. In it he makes personal allegations (about plagiarism) against colleagues such as Giovanni Battista Granata. In the more moderate French version that follows, which was probably edited afterward, some of the more virulent statements were omitted. In the Italian version, for example, he remarks: "Many guitar teachers, especially here in Paris, do not even deserve the second place after me, as they themselves confessed."[61] This probably applies as much to their compositions (including Carré's) as to their performance, and he boasts that in his new book there are "the most beautiful and innovative pieces that have appeared to date."[62] Most French guitarists may not have been prepared to play compositions of this kind, hence in part perhaps Corbetta's complaint: "There are always envious people who say that my style is too difficult, because some of my pieces approach that of the lute."[63] Some people may have connected the Italian tuning with the complexity of lute style, which must have seemed unapproachable for most amateurs.

In the Italian preface Corbetta explains that the two strings in unison (in the re-entrant tuning) do not make the harmony *that his sonatas require*.[64] Probably he found that the re-entrant tuning was not at all suitable for his music, and he may have thought that, under the circumstances, adding a bourdon to the fourth course, to conform to the then-emerging French tuning, was the most viable option for players who were used to the re-entrant tuning. Moreover, he considered himself far superior to them, and he may not have been overly concerned with how others strung their instruments, whether with one or two bourdons. The French tuning, with the additional bass of the bourdon at the fourth course, suits the very particular battuto-pizzicato style of Corbetta's solo works far better than re-entrant tuning, even if a fifth-course bourdon will occasionally be missed.

Corbetta's words from the preface to *La guitarre royalle* have given rise to the supposition that he himself changed the stringing of his instrument at some moment, either by adding a bourdon on the fourth course to the re-entrant tuning, or by removing one from the fifth course, from the Italian tuning. To understand his preferences in 1671, it would be helpful to know how he strung his guitar at the start of his long career. As argued above, he probably used the Italian tuning for his first book, and not the re-entrant or French tunings. Should we assume that he subsequently removed one or two bourdons? The style of the music from his books from 1643, 1648, and 1671 does not clearly support this idea; and for the examples of basso continuo included in these books, removing one or two bourdons would have been at the least very unhelpful. So questions about why and when he could have changed to French tuning are still awaiting satisfactory answers.

Likewise, it can be asked if those who were using Italian tuning simply removed their fifth-course bourdon after having purchased *La guitarre royalle*. It seems that players are always reluctant to reduce the tonal range of their instrument. Everyone knows that Sanz advocated the use of re-entrant stringing for his music; nevertheless, most recordings and countless video clips of Sanz's music on YouTube seem to make use of French tuning—which is about the least likely option, historically speaking. Whatever Corbetta's motive was to formulate his widely discussed advice on tuning, it is still possible that he himself always kept to Italian tuning, even if today his advice is accepted as justifying the claim that he strung his guitar in the French way.

The fact that more than ten years later, Robert de Visée played on a guitar with just one bourdon can be seen as evidence for the acceptance of Carré's and Corbetta's advice. In Viseé's first book there is a tuning chart for an *accord nouveau*, clearly indicating re-entrant tuning (with the word "unissons" on the tuning chart).[65] It may be assumed that, conceptually speaking, for the Frenchman Visée, the guitar was in re-entrant tuning with a low d added, as appears from the preface to his 1682 book, while most Italians would have seen such a guitar as being in conventional tuning with high octaves replacing bourdon strings.

The Tuning at the End of the Seventeenth Century

At the end of her monograph on baroque guitar stringing, Monica Hall tentatively summarizes: "This [the French tuning with one bourdon] became the preferred method of stringing in France, England and the Low Countries and possibly also in Italy and Spain during the last quarter of the seventeenth and first quarter of the eighteenth centuries."[66] This view is widely held today.

However, much evidence would be needed to validate such a thesis firmly, which covers virtually the whole of the musical world of Europe over such a long period. From most countries there are no more than a few sources with unambiguous information; and from those it soon becomes apparent that musical practices varied. In France, England, and the Netherlands there certainly were players who preferred the French tuning, but at the same time other musicians in those countries probably adhered to the re-entrant tuning or to the tuning with two bourdons. It is beyond doubt that Antoine Carré, Robert de Visée, and Nicolas Derosier, at some point, preferred to use the French tuning. Nevertheless, we should not generalize from such a small sample, which cannot serve to prove that François Martin, Rémy Médard, Henry Grenerin, Henry François Gallot, François Lecocq, Jacques Alexandre Saint-Luc, Jean-Baptiste de Castillion, and François Campion, who were all somehow related to a "French school,"[67] strung their instruments in the same way; indeed there is evidence to the contrary.

The tuning with two bourdons was probably accepted for basso continuo everywhere; it is likely that Matteis, Grenerin, Sanz, de Murcia, and Campion (and presumably also Corbetta) used it for accompaniment. Were there reasons for them to use a different tuning for solo music, as was advocated by Gaspar Sanz? Re-entrant tuning evidently persisted into the eighteenth century. In 1730 de Castillion paraphrases Visée's advice on tuning in his own words: "One must put an octave on the fourth course, it is absolutely necessary," but says that he himself also uses a bourdon on the fifth course.[68] Perhaps Corbetta had taken a similarly ambiguous position, half a century before. There is little reason to suppose that guitarists from other countries, like Spain (Sanz, Ribayaz, Marin, and Guerau) and Italy (Asioli, Granata, and Roncalli), preferred French tuning. In the wealth of sources we have from Italy, there is no single unambiguous reference to it, and some of the more prominent composers (Foscarini, Corbetta, and Granata) can be associated with bourdon tuning in some manner, taking into account the instructions from their books. From Spain there is only one very late indication of French tuning, in the writings of Pablo Nassarre.[69]

While in France there seem to have been a variety of tunings, in Spain there probably was more uniformity. Ribayaz describes the use of bourdons, and Guerau at least implies it. In the works of Santiago de Murcia there is no information about the tuning, but since he has included extensive instructions for basso continuo in his *Resumen de acompañar la parte con la guitarra* (1714), he must have been very familiar with the use of bourdons. In his later manuscripts we find music by Visée, Corbetta, and Campion (but nothing by Sanz or Guerau), and therefore it has been supposed that de Murcia had a preference for French tuning. But he also included many arrangements of popular or folk music, which might be characterized as the *musica ruidosa* for which Sanz advocated bourdons. That method of stringing was probably always dominant in Spain.

Chapter Seven

Pandora's Lyre

Odd Chords

One of the most striking idiosyncrasies of alfabeto lies in the C-minor chord, represented by the letter L. Example 7.1 shows Montesardo's alfabeto chart of 1606. It gives us a normal minor chord, as transcribed in example 7.2 (a). This is difficult for the left hand, however, and the vast majority of the charts soon saw the appearance of another shape: a minor chord with a ninth (b). Only a few composers chose to prescribe the shapes shown in (c) and (d). These are technically more demanding—example 7.2 (d) asks for a barre—and harder to play in a sequence with other chords, such as G minor and D major (alfabeto O and C). Thus, for ease of execution, an unexpected dissonance entered a genre that otherwise makes use of major and minor harmonies exclusively, without even basic dissonances such as 4–3 or 7–6 suspensions, or so it would appear from the standard alfabeto tables. Yet, some guitarists may not have played what the plain alfabeto indicates.

By the time Foscarini, Corbetta, and Bartolotti published the first mixed tablature collections, advanced dissonances did occur in instrumental music, and indeed some of this generation of guitar players were also able performers on the lute, or theorbo, familiar with the advanced harmony of the day. Clearly, even before the publication of Foscarini's book around 1630, there were guitarists familiar with plucked string music and tablature. An interesting suggestion that the musically literate were playing something more complex than simple alfabeto from an early date comes in the form of a manuscript (ca. 1614) from the hand of Petrus Jacobus Pedruil, showing that this otherwise unknown guitarist was skilled in tablature notation.[1] In this manuscript, consisting mostly of music in alfabeto, there are a few pages in tablature with cadential elaborations full of suspensions and resolutions. In the first example of these harmonic explorations (ex. 7.3), besides the "deviant" chords in tablature, there are alfabeto letters O, L, and C (G minor, C minor, and D major) written above their respective tablature chords.[2] We see the C-minor chord (chord L) at the beginning of the fourth measure. A feature of this chord is that the third and fourth fingers of the left hand are placed at the third fret on

Example 7.1. Alfabeto chart from Montesardo, 1606.

Example 7.2. Shapes of the L chord.

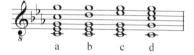

Example 7.3. Petrus Jacobus Pedruil, I-Bc Ms. V. 280, fol. 28v, Passacaglia. In this example, besides the deviant chords in tablature, the alfabeto letters O, L, and C (G minor, C minor, and D major) are also included, notated over their respective tablature chords.

the second and first course (making the notes d′ and g′). This facilitates the connection with the preceding G-minor chord, in measure 3 (chord O).

The use of an ostinato effect on the top strings, prompted by a technical simplification, has implications for the harmony. At the beginning of the first measure, the third and fourth fingers are placed on the first two courses, while the first two fingers complete the harmony and bass line. One wonders if Pedruil was guided by theoretical considerations, like the rules of counterpoint, or found his way through the abundance of possibilities just by ear, as many a blues or flamenco player searches for melody notes to his chords. For them it is often the little finger that has to execute this task; in this case, it is the index and the middle finger which are free to move. Striking variations on chord L can be found again later, in the works of Bartolotti (1640), Corbetta (1643), Médard (1676), and Visée (1686), who exploit the same effect with subtlety (see ex. 7.4).

In a second example from Pedruil's manuscript (ex. 7.5), there are harmonies of increasing tension, on the bass note A. The third chord is a harsh dissonance ($\hat{6} + \hat{7} + \hat{11} + \hat{12}$). Note once again the use of alfabeto: the letter I (A major) over the first and fourth chords. A similar harmony can be found in the *Toccata prima* for lute, from the *Libro primo d'intavolatura di lauto* (Rome, 1611) by Girolamo Kapsberger in the first six-voice chord of example 7.6.[3]

Example 7.4. Francesco Corbetta (1643), p. 16, Passacaglia in O (G minor), mm. 1–3.

Example 7.5. A dissonant chord sequence from Pedruil's Ms, fol. 30v.

Example 7.6. Girolamo Kapsberger (1611), p. 12, Toccata 1, mm. 13–14.

Examples 7.5 and 7.6 share the fingering of the chord, marked here with an X,[4] including the interval of a second, produced by a fingered course next to an open one. In battuto performance it is hard to leave out a string, and it probably was the preferred way to include as many strings as possible when strumming; on the lute, however, it is a matter of deliberate choice to write for more than the usual three- or four-voice texture, and chords of more than four voices have to be at least slightly arpeggiated.

What can we conclude from all this? Kapsberger and Pedruil were in Rome at about the same time. Both made use of the capacity of their respective instruments to produce rich and varied harmonies. For the guitarist, five courses played battuto was a starting point, while the lutenist usually plucked fewer strings. A guitarist playing an instrument connected with popular culture and playing by ear might perhaps have been more inclined to experiment freely with possible left-hand fingerings and resultant harmonies than a lutenist standing in a tradition of polyphonic solo repertoire and used to realizing an accompaniment from a bass line according to the rules of counterpoint. The resulting harmonic innovations may have helped to inspire a composer like Kapsberger, himself a guitarist as well as a lutenist.

Foscarini's Rules of Performance

In the preface to *Il primo, secondo, e terzo libro della chitarra spagnola* (ca. 1630), Foscarini gives nine performance rules. The first rule is an explanation of the alfabeto. The second rule stresses the necessity of striking all the courses distinctly and clearly, with full strokes ("battute piene"), so that all strings will have "their true effect."[5] In our times this rule is sometimes interpreted as a direction to include all courses when strumming, especially in alfabeto chords, but it could as well be an observation about strumming in general. In Foscarini's battuto-pizzicato music there are very many chords with fewer than five voices, which he must have intended to have a full sound. In the sixth rule he stresses that it is necessary to be very careful to play only the strings indicated, implying that nothing is left to chance:

> Sixth, one will observe the corrente named "Nuova Inventione" on p. 68 in which, as in other similar pieces, one must play only those numbers that are notated, without adding to or subtracting from them. Otherwise, instead of delighting, one confounds whoever plays and listens to them. And this one must observe in the *sinfonie, passacagli Spagnoli passegiati* and *ciaccone*, in which one must take the utmost care and diligence, being those proper to this instrument [the guitar]. For in these [pieces], I confess to have used more than ordinary diligence to render them especially charming and rich in new and varied inventions.[6]

However, as we will see below, there are situations in his music in which the strict application of this rule is not so obvious, particularly with regard to open courses. We can assume that on many occasions, open courses would have been strummed even though they are not indicated in the tablature. Today it is often supposed that in alfabeto chords all courses should always be strummed, including those not indicated with an 0 in the chart—some composers' charts do not use a zero at all to show an open string. With respect to the notation of open courses there were different conventions; in the alfabeto chart of Montesardo (see ex. 7.1) they are indicated, while in charts in many other books the lines without a left hand fingering remain blank.

In the books of Foscarini (ca. 1630) and Corbetta (1639) there are separate charts for *alfabeto dissonante* or *alfabeto falso*. In example 7.7 it can be seen that Foscarini only indicates the courses stopped with the left hand. Which open strings should be played here, and when? On some occasions the inclusion of all the open strings will produce an extreme dissonance. A number of the chords from this chart are related to those of regular alfabeto; the tones that are different from the standard chords are usually suspensions that must resolve to a consonance (such as 4–3 or 7–6 progression).[7] In Foscarini's solo works we frequently encounter the 4–3 sequence C$^+$–C, or I$^+$–I. With the

Example 7.7. *Alfabeto dissonante*, Foscarini.

Example 7.8. Giovanni Paolo Foscarini (ca. 1630), p. 68, "Corrente nuova inventione," mm. 1–5.

C⁺ chord, the fifth course can still be played (even though this sometimes gives an unwanted $^6_4$ chord); with the F⁺ chord the fifth course should probably be omitted in strumming.[8] Some of the other chords, such as E⁺, leave one in doubt.[9] The A⁺ chord, for instance, could have been included in the chart for better voice leading of the treble melody. In that case, the sixth of the chord, the open e′ string, should not be played.

There are other situations in Foscarini's tablature where the degree of consonance and the possibility of resolving suspensions seems to be decisive for the admittance of open courses. Knowledge of the particular musical idiom of the composer is needed to make decisions on what should be sounded. In this respect it reminds one of the practice of basso continuo, in which one always has to consider the broader musical context and aspects of style and tradition. A comparison with harmonic formulae from other compositions by Foscarini or the works of his contemporaries would be a fruitful exercise.

The solo works from Foscarini's third book contain many three-voice sections that are to be played battuto, such as the beginning of the "Corrente nova inventione" (ex. 7.8). We are not meant to strum across all five courses here; and to confuse matters, there are chords with nonadjacent strings, which obviously cannot be strummed as written. Foscarini refers to this piece in his sixth rule, which tells us not to touch more (or fewer) courses than are indicated. In this example we can find some striking details. Under strict application of the rule, the last chord of measure 3 would have to be played without the third and the first courses. Proper voice leading however, would justify including the note e′. It is obvious that the g of the third course is to be played as well, although not indicated, because it cannot be avoided if we strum. At the beginning of the fourth measure, there is another chord to which the same g of the third course—not indicated in the tablature—should be added, resulting in a more dissonant harmony. One might like to suppose that Foscarini made

Example 7.9. Giovanni Paolo Foscarini (ca. 1630), p. 21, *Passacaglia*, mm. 1–4.

Example 7.10. L chord and the first chord from example 7.9. The high octaves of the fourth and fifth courses are indicated as quarter notes.

a rule of leaving out zeros from open courses which are *between* courses stopped with the left hand, but as seen in the alfabeto dissonante, there are no unambiguous rules for the inclusion of open courses.[10] In any case, there is a continuing uncertainty about those courses that are *outside* the pattern of the left-hand fingering. In example 7.9 the shortcomings of Foscarini's notation in this respect become apparent.

For reasons of proper voice leading, the bass note d in the second chord should be played, although it is not written; it can be played on the open fourth course, but would not be covered by any (presumed) rule that, when playing battuto, we are to "fill in the gap" by strumming any single vacant string between the two stopped ones. When one considers such ambiguities, one may ask why guitarists kept to the simplified notation for battuto chords, once they started to write more elaborate guitar music? This probably was the result of a practice grounded in a popular tradition. From the moment that Foscarini decided to use mixed tablature, he could have chosen to go further and write out battuto chords completely in tablature, eliminating every uncertainty. But instead he decided to use a simplified notation, often omitting the zeros for open strings. This is the more remarkable because in plucked passages, even within the same compositions, the open strings are indicated conscientiously, as if he found it sufficient to notate battuto in a shorthand form of tablature, assuming players would know how to perform the chords.

A very specific quality of the guitar is revealed in this excerpt. In the first measure of the example there is a C-minor chord, to which the d on the fourth course is added in strumming, in an awkward position (ex. 7.10). This is almost identical in sound to chord L in example 7.2b, with an idiomatic effect that only works on the baroque guitar. The ear can be deceived by the high octaves

Example 7.11. Giovanni Paolo Foscarini (ca. 1630), p. 32, Passacaglia, mm. 1–5.

of the fifth and fourth courses (sounding c′ and d′ here) of the bourdon tuning (aA, d′d, gg, bb, e′) that was presumably used by Foscarini.[11]

Foscarini published his *Il primo, secondo, e terzo libro* in Rome, where Kapsberger also lived for many years. In a passacaglia from this book we find the same dissonant chord ($\hat{6}$ + $\hat{7}$ + $\hat{11}$+ $\hat{12}$, marked with an X) already noted in works by Pedruil and Kapsberger (see ex. 7.11, at the beginning of the third measure).[12] Foscarini probably intends us to play all the open courses in this chord.[13] As argued before, strict application of Foscarini's sixth rule does not always seem desirable, and we face the question which criteria should be followed here with regard to the open strings. We cannot be certain whether Foscarini included the open first course in all the chords, but voice leading would be considerably poorer without an e′ here.[14] The section becomes more dissonant by the addition of this tone, but from other examples of Foscarini's style (see the last two measures of ex. 7.12) it can be observed that he did not eschew such daring harmonic writing. The effect of varying dissonances against open strings appears to be a characteristic of early-seventeenth-century guitar style, particularly in those genres which probably came from Spain, such as the passacaglia, ciaccona, and sarabanda—dances with a battuto "character," used by guitarists as a playground for harmonic experimentation. Traces reminiscent of this practice can arguably be found later, in chaconnes and passacailles in the French lute repertoire of the Gaultiers and the keyboard music of Louis Couperin.

Foscarini's broad-mindedness in matters of dissonance can be seen in a few works that he wrote for guitar in *accordatura differente* (B, d, g, b, d′).[15] Guitarists like Foscarini, Corbetta, and Granata experimented with the possibilities offered by alternative tunings, probably inspired by the French lute school. From around 1620 lutenists had begun to make widespread use of *accords nouveaux*, in one of which the first six courses were often tuned in a D-minor chord

Example 7.12. Giovanni Paolo Foscarini (ca. 1630), p. 101, Sarabanda, mm. 20–24.

(A, d, f, a, d′, f′), instead of the "Renaissance" tuning in fourths, with a third in the middle (G, c, f, a, d′, g′). Among Foscarini's compositions for this new tuning there are a few pieces entirely in battuto style. As a result, many dissonant harmonies appear that could easily have been avoided in plucked, lute-style music. Sometimes suspended notes and their resolutions appear simultaneously as a consequence of the "added" open courses, as in the last measure of example 7.12 (audio ex. 13).[16]

We may conclude that the harmonic language of the guitarist was rooted in the peculiarities of the instrument, resulting from the battuto technique and its tuning. Composers showed great inventiveness in writing unexpected, daring harmonies.

Corbetta's Barres

Foscarini's rules may not be relevant to the notation of the music of some other composers, who developed their own forms of notation. The introduction of new systems by Bartolotti (1655) and Corbetta (1671) shows that they did not take the application of Foscarini's rules for granted. Bartolotti presented a system with note-heads placed on the lines of the tablature. Now for the first time we get more precise information about the action of the right hand. The main drawback of this system is, however, that although it makes it clear on which of the lower courses the strum must start, it does not indicate where the strum ends. Francesco Corbetta, again using a different system, puts dots on the lines of tablature in his book of 1671, indicating which courses should not be played. This could have put matters beyond doubt, but unfortunately Corbetta uses this innovative device with such freedom, not to say carelessness, that confusion is merely increased. We will discuss the subject of Corbetta's dots in more detail below. Composers such as Antoine Carré, Nicola Matteis, and Robert de Visée also adopted his system, and used it with similar negligence.

Example 7.13. Francesco Corbetta (1671), p. 69, Sarabande, mm. 21–23, with two possible transcriptions.

There is a dot on the first line, on the chord on the second beat of the first measure of example 7.13, indicating that the first course should not be played. One wonders if this applies to the next strum as well, and the two transcriptions give alternative readings of the tablature. It seems unlikely that the note d on the open fourth course in the last chord of the first measure is part of the harmony. It is a harsh dissonance, unprepared and unresolved. If the fourth course is to be excluded, the fifth should surely be omitted as well. Like Foscarini, Corbetta would have intended as many open strings to be strummed as "belong to the harmony," but since he did not always specify them, he probably sometimes left his contemporaries in confusion.[17] The note e' of the first measure, last chord, fits into the harmony, but obscures the voice leading c♯'–d'–e'. Therefore it is perhaps better to omit this e' as well.

An almost identical situation, in another key, can be found in a sarabande by Corbetta (ex. 7.14a). The last chord of the first measure is again very dissonant, as in example 7.13, only here Corbetta has written out the whole chord in tablature. In the version of this same sarabande published by Antoine Carré in his *Livre de pièces de guitarre* (ca. 1675), this chord is simplified in the same manner as in the thinner of two transcriptions in example 7.13.[18] Carré has left out a number of tablature letters from Corbetta's original. The simplified harmony can still be played battuto, so that justice can be done to Corbetta's original strum notation. In *La guitarre royalle* there are many chords notated like the one on the last quaver of the first measure of example 7.14a, chords that are always very dissonant. We will return to this below.

The difference with Foscarini is the lack of resolution. Two technical conditions always crop up: the index of the left hand forms a barre and the chord is played battuto. Perhaps Corbetta has used the letters of the tablature—normally supposed to represent exactly which strings should sound—in an improper way to serve as a fingering for the left hand. If that were true, the

Example 7.14a. Francesco Corbetta (1671), p. 65, Sarabande, mm. 8–9.

Example 7.14b. Corbetta's Sarabande, in Carré (ca. 1675), p. 17, mm. 8–9.

Example 7.14c. Transcription of the same Corbetta Sarabande.

tablature letters would only indicate the best fingerings, and not which courses should be played.[19] In that respect it could be seen as a manifestation of an attitude toward the notation of strummed textures similar to what underlies Foscarini's practice of omitting zeros: on paper the battuto chords are treated as something primarily for the left hand. Neither Foscarini nor Corbetta provided more information for the right hand than an ambiguous sign for a strummed chord.

Those familiar with strummed chord accompaniment (and modern songs) will probably understand the rationale behind these shorthand notations. In battuto, the actual number of courses touched by the right hand (and also the intensity of the impact of the stroke on each individual string) can vary widely, depending on the context. Upstrokes, for example, have a tendency to include fewer strings than downstrokes, and a thumb stroke usually puts more emphasis on the lower strings than a stroke with the fingers, whereas an upstroke with the index finger accents the treble strings.

Example 7.15 shows that Corbetta's method of notation can lead to a tablature with harmonies which on paper look extremely dissonant. It is hard to imagine, though, that Corbetta intended to write so many discordant chords in

Example 7.15. Francesco Corbetta (1674), pp. 49–50, Passacaille, mm. 16–17.
Transcriptions in bourdon tuning (upper stave) and in French tuning.

Example 7.16. Francesco Corbetta (1671), p. 56, Passacaille, mm. 1–4.
Transcriptions in bourdon tuning (upper stave) and in French tuning.

a context of otherwise harmonious music. In this case there may be no better
solution than to leave out most of the notes that are on the fourth and fifth
courses. All in all, it seems impossible to draw a hard line. Dissonance was very
much part of the guitar idiom of the time, and chords with "open" barres are
ambiguous in this respect. It is often unclear how many (and which) courses
should be considered to be part of the harmony, as there are many situations
that cannot be satisfactorily explained by any rule.

If the passacaille from example 7.16 is played on a guitar in French tuning,
the bass line will consist of the notes on the fourth course. Starting in measure

2, the fourth and fifth courses produce (parallel) fifths, which give the impression of being the root and the fifth of a different chord, sounding simultaneously with the harmony of the three top courses. To be able to understand such complex harmonic situations by ear, it should at least be clear which of the notes is the root of the chord.[20] When played on a guitar in bourdon tuning, the chords from examples 7.15 and 7.16 contain an accumulation of fourths, which is even more disturbing. Example 7.16 can be heard in audio example 27, played on a guitar strung with bourdons. In audio example 28 we can hear the same fragment, but this time played without the notes on the fifth and fourth courses. It is taken from the "Sarabande et sa Passacaille" from the *Suite in G minor* (audio ex. 29).[21]

Chitarra Flamenca?

It is often assumed that the acciaccature in Domenico Scarlatti's keyboard sonatas were inspired by the guitar music he heard in Spain. Usually *acciaccatura* (a "crushed" stroke) is defined as a simultaneous *appoggiatura*, an accessory note, a semitone below its main note, and there also exists a nonharmonic "passing acciaccatura." The tone clusters in the second measure of example 7.15, however, cannot possibly be explained in this way, and a connection between Scarlatti's stunningly effective dissonances and these strange chords seems very unlikely. Undoubtedly, there are Iberian elements in Scarlatti's music, such as popular dance rhythms, repeated ("strummed") block chords, and characteristic harmonic progressions, often including "Phrygian" cadences; in our time the influence of unwritten popular music on Scarlatti is often assumed. For example, in *The Oxford History of Western Music* we can read:

> [This] passage . . . where the acciaccaturas are maintained throughout like a sort of pedal (or more to the point—like a constantly strummed open string), discloses the reason for Scarlatti's seeming obsession with them. By combining the acciaccaturas with "Phrygian" neighbor notes . . . , Scarlatti unmistakably conjures up the sound of "Flamenco" guitars, the Andalusian gypsy style that has become pervasive in Spanish popular music, and that must have already been a conspicious part of the sonic landscape in Scarlatti's day.[22]

There is one cadential figure in particular that has fueled speculation about "flamenco" acciaccature in seventeenth-century guitar music (see ex. 7.17).[23] The B-major harmony leading to E minor (V–i) is sometimes transcribed from tablature with the open first and fifth courses included. Consequently, the nonchord tone (or inverted pedal point) e′ of the open first course forms a semitone with the d♯, and together with the high octave string of the fourth course it produces the tone cluster d′♯–e′–f′♯. Together with the a of the fifth course. it creates the illusion of the overlapping of harmonies.[24] It may remind

Example 7.17. Francesco Corbetta (1671), p. 15, Sarabande, mm. 19–20. The upper stave shows a transcription with the first and fifth courses missing. On the second stave is a transcription that includes the open first and fifth courses, making use of French tuning.

us of the effect of ♭II–I (C major–B major) of an "Andalusian" cadence, in the (unusual) key of B Phrygian,[25] in which the effect of the open e against the d♯ is explored (even if, in fact, Corbetta's cadence is just a straightforward V–i⁶–V–i in E minor). In Scarlatti's music the overlapping of harmonies and (inverted) pedal points often creates clusters like these. It is not at all certain that Corbetta intended to include the open courses in a cadence like this, because the resulting dissonance is rather extreme—no matter how interesting this "flamenco" harmony from Italy may seem to us—and probably alien to the style of his music.

We should carefully distinguish between different harmonic constructions, in the works of different composers, from different times and places. In Spanish guitar tablatures of the seventeenth- and eighteenth century, for example, of composers such as Gaspar Sanz, Francisco Guerau, or Santiago de Murcia, dissonances of this kind are strikingly absent. Moreover, it is doubtful whether the guitar was ever used in that way before the rise of *toque flamenco*, which took place in the nineteenth (or even twentieth) century. Italian sources may be different in this respect. Perhaps the accessory notes in Foscarini's music (as in exx. 7.9, 7.11, and 7.12), are closer to Scarlatti's acciaccature. Here there are no "Phrygian" neighbouring notes in gypsy style. In Italy there was a tradition of dissonance, from the seconda pratica of Claudio Monteverdi to the keyboard works of Domenico Scarlatti and Francesco Gasparini's thoroughbass tutor *Armonico pratico al cimbalo*, published in 1708. In this book Gasparini (who possibly was Scarlatti's teacher) described the use of acciaccature in accompaniment, and most likely Scarlatti was familiar with his ideas.

Even if some of Scarlatti's sonatas sound truly Spanish, with textural and harmonic effects reminding us of the guitar, there is no firm evidence that his dissonances were also inspired by this instrument. It is even possible that the same unusual harmonies originated from a common source. Scarlatti's frequent vertical "Phrygian" semitones may also be seen as reflecting an Arabic or gypsy style of singing, colored by very characteristic (extra-European) microtonal inflections. Although it is speculative, we might even consider the possibility of an influence in the opposite direction, and that harmonic experiments such as Scarlatti's have created a fertile soil for flamenco harmony from later times. After all, the unusual left-hand patterns for the dissonant chord progressions that we encounter in flamenco today were most likely introduced by famous guitar virtuosos, and not before the twentieth century. We will have to look closer at Corbetta's tablatures, to find other explanations for his odd harmonies.

Corbetta's Dots

In the preface to *La guitarre royalle* (1671) Francesco Corbetta explains that he has inserted dots in the tablature "to avoid dissonances."[26] But is this really what he used the dot for in practice? As we have seen in example 7.13, there are very ambiguous situations in his works in which the composer did not include them, and there are many harmonies, in two to four parts, where adding open strings would lead to problematic dissonances. On the other side, there are the "dotted" chords for which the degree of consonance does not change much if the open fifth course is included (as in ex. 7.18).[27] The question is why dots were added in some cases and not in others.

La guitarre royalle (1671) is Corbetta's first known book of French tablature.[28] It is likely that the absence of alfabeto as a means to indicate standard chords in French tablature spurred him to search for ways to replace the shorthand notation he was used to. In French tablature, chords were written out in full, enabling the composer to redefine the number of courses that he actually wanted to be strummed, which is probably why the five-part chord patterns of alfabeto are now often reduced to four or three. In the chords for example 7.18, the principal reason for the dot does not appear to be to avoid dissonance created by playing added open courses. Nor is it for certain transpositions of the chords in example 7.19. For example, alfabeto G in first position or alfabeto N in second position appear very often as dotless four-part chords, to which the open fifth course can be added with little consequence for the harmony. In these situations, the dot would give ambiguous information, as it can be understood as an indication that the right hand should omit the fifth course, but also that placement of a finger of the left hand (belonging to a former alfabeto chord) is redundant.

The chord patterns with dots in example 7.19 are still recognizable as the former N, G, P, and & from alfabeto. The same chords (the former N, G, P, and

Example 7.18. (a) Francesco Corbetta (1671), p. 36, line 3, m. 4; (b) p. 39, line 4, m. 3; (c) p. 34, line 6, m. 4. The chords in question are N2, &5, and N7.

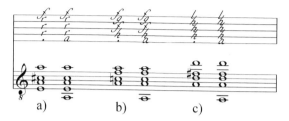

a)   b)   c)

Example 7.19. Reduced alfabeto chords.

N   G   P   &

&, used in similar context) sometimes have dots and sometimes do not, and presumably Corbetta was not completely convinced of the necessity of providing information of this kind. It shows his indecision with respect to the notation of battuto chords in general, which often is far from accurate.

The four-part N of which the fingering of the fifth course is replaced by a dot (as in ex. 7.19) is by far the most current, but P and & (mostly in three parts) and G (in three or four parts) also appear quite often, while their full five-part counterparts are relatively rare. In contrast to this, K and H are often written out completely (ex. 7.20). However, when K5 or H5 (D minor and D major) appear in a reduced form, they almost never have dots. This is understandable, because the open fourth and fifth courses can be added without seriously affecting the harmony.[29]

As distinct from N, G, P, and &, Corbetta only used K and H in very specific situations and transpositions. In *La guitarre royalle* (1671) the three-part reduced K appears exclusively in fifth position. Reduced H seems applicable only in third or fifth position, and in third position it is always replaced by the peculiar shape of the last chord of example 7.20. A possible explanation for the different treatment of K and H could be that, as opposed to N, G, P, and &, these two chords require the fifth course to be fingered with the barre, a *quantité négligeable*, on which Corbetta was not inclined to waste any dots. It has a function comparable to the nut in first position. Within this frame of thought, it would have been unnecessary to indicate with a dot that the first finger is not needed there, just as the open strings in first position chords seldom have dots (see ex. 7.13 and the last chord of ex. 7.20).

Apparently the notation of the "open" barre with tablature letters (as in ex. 7.15) was a way to show that the original chord included more strings (and

Example 7.20. Reduced K and H.

other fingers, apart from the index). If this assumption is valid, then Corbetta would have made use of no less than three different methods to notate the same smaller chords: (1) with dots; (2) without dots (like the three- or four-part patterns from the exx. 7.18, 7.19, and 7.20); and (3) with an "open" barre, written out in tablature. This last idea is the most difficult to grasp (and, perhaps, to accept).

As argued above, in the period of transition from alfabeto to notation in tablature contradictory information was used, indicating that courses should be left out of what would otherwise be a five-part chord. For instance, in Bartolotti's *Secondo libro*, there are many alfabeto chords, originally in five parts, reduced to four by a stroke sign placed on the fourth line of the tablature system (see ex. 5.4). Thus, a discrepancy is created between the instructions for the left hand and those for the right.

Doizi de Velasco's *Nuevo modo de cifra* is probably the most detailed tutor for guitar accompaniment of its time, but in his examples we find contradictory instructions, as well. In Velasco's diagrams (ex. 5.1) there are chords with all strings stopped by the index finger, where he has indicated with an *x* that the fifth course should nevertheless not be touched by the right hand.[30] The *x* is there not only "to avoid the dissonance" of the C on the fifth course, but to tell that no extra finger needs to be placed at the fifth fret. Corbetta's notation is even more elusive, because he avoids putting a dot on a string stopped with a barre. Consequently, he lost his means of showing (like Velasco) that the right hand should not strike this string. In a situation like at the last chord of example 7.20 (compare also exx. 7.21b and c and exx. 7.22b and c), where the F on the fourth course is problematic, perhaps there are no dots because Corbetta was unwilling to combine them with a barre. In example 7.15 we could see the ultimate consequence of this approach, with lost chord shapes, of which only the skeleton of the barre remains.

Barre Notation in Cadences

This last issue is particularly relevant with regard to many standard cadences from *La guitarre royalle*. In his books of 1643 and 1648, Corbetta has placed the letters of alfabeto in the tablature staff (like the H in ex. 7.22a). Here he has combined traditional alfabeto with non-alfabeto chords notated in tablature, such as seventh chords and suspensions. Corbetta's tablatures are packed with stereotypical strummed three- or four-part cadences, as in examples 7.21a and 7.22a; probably voice leading was the reason for using these thinner chordal textures.[31] Gradually he began to write four- and five-part chords instead, which resulted from the inclusion of extra tablature letters for the barre (exx. 7.21b and c and exx. 7.22b and c).

Not all dissonance on open barres is undesirable by definition. Some passing notes are unusual, but can still be understood as suspensions. However, it can be doubted that Corbetta over the years aimed for an extreme increase of dissonance in exactly the same cadences. Is what we see here a progressive development of his harmonic language, or has he made wrong use of tablature, only showing at what point the barre has to be placed, as Richard Pinnell supposes?[32] Pinnell describes an example from a courante, here reproduced in example 7.23a. He observes that it "includes the one frequent nonharmonic tone which I have been unable to justify. . . . The chord is merely V (except for the strident anticipation of I)." The note in question is the F on the fourth

Example 7.21. (a) Francesco Corbetta (1643), p. 14, Passacaglia, mm. 15–16; (b) ibid., p. 14, Passacaglia, mm. 4–5; (c) Francesco Corbetta (1671), p. 41–42, Allemande, mm. 16–17.

Example 7.22. (a) Francesco Corbetta (1643), p. 55, Corrente, mm. 12–14; (b) Francesco Corbetta (1671), p. 23–24, Courante, mm. 26–27; (c) ibid., p. 22–23, Allemande, mm. 25–26. The first two chords of example 7.22b can be understood as modifications of the alfabeto N chord, which would explain the dots on the fifth line.

course (ex. 7.23a, the last chord of measure 26), which would prepare the fundamental of the F-major chord in the next measure. However, the preparation of the bass note does not always occur in this cadence; in example 7.23b the final chord is in $\frac{6}{3}$ position and the nonharmonic F on the fourth course is even more disturbing because the dissonance it creates is never resolved.

In Corbetta's instructions for accompaniment in *La guitarre royalle*, the continuo examples from his 1643 book are transcribed into French tablature (ex. 7.24). In the latter, the fifth course is added. This can be compared to examples 7.21b and 7.21c.

Example 7.23a. Francesco Corbetta (1671), p. 24, Courante, mm. 26–27.

Example 7.23b. Francesco Corbetta (1671), p. 23, Courante, mm. 3–5.

Example 7.24. The same basso continuo example, in Corbetta's books of 1643 and 1671.

It seems unrewarding to try to explain every nonharmonic tone, even if it does not resolve in a comprehensible manner, with reference to the very particular style of the composer. After all, these harmonies can hardly be characterized as "the most delicate and the least awkward," although that is how Corbetta described his style in the preface to his 1674 book.

In the end, the answer to the question whether we should consider these chords as unusual harmonies deliberately included by Corbetta as part of his personal imaginative style or artifacts of a notational practice must be subjective. In all these examples from the works of Foscarini and Corbetta, we can deduce that in the battuto-pizzicato repertoire the information provided by alfabeto or "shorthand tablature" is often incomplete or imprecise, especially in two particular situations. First, open courses that are not indicated may have to be included in a strummed chord, for reasons of harmony or voice leading, judged against the background of the style of a specific composer. Second, in the case of the barre notation of Corbetta and (less frequently) composers like Antonio Carbonchi (1640) and François Martin (1663), simplification of what is notated (as in ex. 7.14b) may be called for. Thus, the inaccurate notational practice of the seventeenth-century guitarist gives rise to persistent uncertainty about how the music should be played.

If we want to perform the music, however, we are bound to choose. Final cadences, for example, which should lead to a chord in root position, often end with the reduced N chord (see exs. 7.18a and c), with the fifth of the chord in the bass ($^6_4$ position). If we avoid playing the fourth course, the chord will be in root position instead and sound more like a true ending (as in Corbetta's "Caprice de Chaconne," audio ex. 20),[33] and Corbetta's music conforms more to the familiar seventeenth-century style of works for lute and harpsichord.

Chapter Eight

The Baroque Guitar Unmasked?

The Guitar and Its Riddles

Writing these chapters, I discovered that unearthing the history of the guitar in the seventeenth century was akin to compiling the biography of a personage who never was a prominent figure in politics, warfare, arts or science, someone who shone only in the ephemeral domain of unwritten, popular culture. In pictures often disguised as a character of the commedia, our subject made music in the company of ordinary people—and of the nobility behaving like them. If it happened to be present, the instrument had to be heard. Gentlemen carried the guitar with them to play where and when they felt like it, following the example of Corbetta. Everyone knew the chitarra spagnuola's role in the sphere of popular song and dance, and as a symbol of an exotic or pastoral world; but at the same time evidence is scarce that would prove conclusively that the music from the guitar books was actually performed in public. Up to the present day, the bulk of this repertoire has remained unknown, even among many who have a replica of a chitarra spagnuola at home. Such neglect seems to be the lot of this unpretentious, seemingly ageless instrument, and wholly in keeping with this, millions of people play the classical ("Spanish") guitar today without much awareness of its history and repertoire.

Of all the hand-plucked instruments, the guitar was perhaps the easiest to manage, and certainly one of the cheapest. Despite its imperfections, it was treated much the same as a lute to play "complete" music on, with a melody and a bass. Educated music lovers like Samuel Pepys and Constantijn Huygens overcame their aversion and learned to play the instrument. In a letter to Utricia Ogle (Lady Swann), Huygens tells that he has composed more than thirty pieces for this "miserable instrument," works that are no longer extant. That fate may have befallen many other compositions, and we can hazard a guess that even printed works were primarily used for personal enjoyment (if they were played at all). Besides, guitarists invented their own little pieces or they assembled sets of variations on the immensely popular ciaccona (to be compared to what is usual in *toque flamenco* today, in genres like *soleares* or *alegrías*), music that was not put on paper. Regrettably, Lully's compositions are also lost, because he did not even care to write them down.

Has the five-course guitar had any impact on musical history? Strummed chordal self-accompaniment, almost a prerequisite for popular music today, was invented in the sixteenth century. Through the ages, light secular songs with guitar accompaniment have flourished in the shadow of the canon of great masterworks. At one point in the seventeenth century, the plain and simple canzonetta, a genre in which the guitar has thrived, was taken as a model for the Italian operatic aria (now accompanied by larger instrumental forces) by composers such as Pietro Francesco Cavalli, Luigi Rossi, and Stefano Landi.

Did the guitar participate in orchestras or continuo groups? Would not the theorbist have brought along his guitar to do some occasional strumming? It is problematic that there is so little evidence to support this idea. The fact that the instrument was used for a specific purpose in one situation does not mean that it was accepted everywhere. It is also a question of chronology. In the middle of the sixteenth century, the four-course guitar had a polyphonic repertoire of a high standard. Fifty years later the guitar (then with five courses) was played exclusively with chord strums. After 1640 alfabeto lost ground again with the rapid decline of the canzonetta repertoire. In guitar books, instructions began to appear for the realization of basso continuo in battuto-pizzicato style. It is unclear how long the tradition of purely strummed accompaniment remained in vogue, since there is no clinching evidence of an all-battuto performance of figured bass (almost a contradiction in itself) from the second half of the seventeenth century. Perhaps it did not even enter people's heads to employ the guitar in that way in ensembles, while strummed accompaniment—and the admission of the guitar in general—most likely had always been confined to certain genres, and to a particular context. What is now considered a possible instrumentation may have been inconceivable then.

Chronology and Geography

Italy

As the wanderings of the guitar through Europe make clear, practices differed from place to place and the playing style and notation did not develop simultaneously everywhere. Italy was a leader in the creation of a song repertoire with alfabeto, which flourished between 1610 and 1640. Besides, a large number of books with solo works in battuto-pizzicato style was published there between 1630 and 1660, while almost all printed matter from other countries appeared after 1670. At the same time the predilection for the chitarra spagnuola in Italy began to fade away.

During its Italian Golden Age, the guitar was played by the nobility, by the clergy, by merchants and members of the professional middle classes, but also by mountebanks and artisans. Taking into account the large number of printed sources from Italy, we must assume that the guitar was one of the most-played instruments of the middle part of the seventeenth century. At that time, very few works for other solo instruments were published in Italy. Initially, the guitar was used for accompanying song and dance, and it played a role in a broad informal musical culture,—Carnival, pastoral, masquerade—colored by images of the commedia dell'arte, spiced with social criticism. This movement was associated with an intuitive, nonintellectual approach to music, in contradistinction to the mannerisms of the late-sixteenth-century madrigal style or the notational precision of melodic embellishments pursued by composers such as Giulio Caccini or Sigismondo d'India.

Italy was the stage for the innovations of the *seconda pratica*, the new vocal monody and opera. Nevertheless many renowned composers also published collections of more modest strophic arias with basso continuo, many of which include alfabeto. Even though there are numerous examples of problematic harmonic clashes in this repertoire, some composers have provided an alfabeto accompaniment which is largely in agreement with both the melody and the bass, and we can suppose that these songs were composed with the guitar in mind (for example, Domenico Obizzi's "Hor que vicin mi sento" or "Rompi, rompi mi core," audio exx. 2 and 4). The broad acceptance of the chordal accompaniment of the guitar probably reflects the changing tastes of the time. One could even hypothesize that the great fashion for the guitar has to some extent shaped the musical preferences of a larger public.

Italian vocal genres of this time stand out through expressive, well-shaped melodies. Although the guitar, due to its limited harmonic resources, could not keep up with the theorbo or harpsichord, the practice of realizing one's own accompaniment to newly composed songs (as opposed to traditional genres such as ciaccona, romanesca, bergamasca, aria de gran duca, etc.) left much room to try out unusual chordal progressions, even more so because there was no general prescriptive theory. As a consequence, a very free treatment of harmony also found a place in solo repertoire from about 1630 onward. For purely instrumental genres such as variations or ostinato works, and stylized dances, the old rules of vocal polyphony were no longer as relevant as they were before. The guitar brought foreign or exotic music into people's homes, in a variety of national styles—licentious ciacconas from Spain (perhaps even stemming from the New World), for example, with a lot of strumming, but also graceful French correntes, predominantly plucked (beginning with Foscarini's transcriptions of French lute music).

Spain

The guitar became a symbol of Spanish music. Although seventeenth-century sources from Spain are relatively scarce, it can be assumed that the instrument was much played. However, the diversity of genres—dances and vocal works—was probably less there than in Italy. Besides, in Spain there were considerably fewer professional theorbists, while Italian theorbo players often had the guitar as their second instrument. The guitar participated in a repertoire of traditional genres (of españoletas, Ruggieros, chaconas, etc.), for the greater part based on stock harmonies. We have to suppose there existed a lively practice of aural transmission, and the lack of notated examples may be one of the main reasons that compositional innovations did not flourish as much.

Until the works of Gaspar Sanz (1674) and Lucas Ruiz de Ribayaz (1677) appeared in print, written in a distinctly traditional folkloric style, the guitar was used primarily for strummed chordal accompaniment. Yet, in contrast to the Italian battuto-pizzicato style, these composers chose to write predominantly in pizzicato (punteado), probably heavily influenced by the typical Spanish tradition of melodic variation (in *diferencias*). Variation works had first appeared in print in the vihuela books of the sixteenth century. This tradition was preserved in the repertoire for keyboard instruments in the early seventeenth century, and it presumably returned to the guitar via that route. The exceptional continuo part in tablature, from the large manuscript collection (ca. 1699) of songs by José Marin (GB-Cfm Ms.Mus.727), is completely without rasgueado chords. This shows that plucked guitar accompaniment had already gained much ground in Spain before 1700.

France, England

In France and England, the fashion for the guitar as a solo instrument only came into full swing after 1660. In these countries the instrument initially seems to have had its devotees primarily in circles around the royal courts in Paris and London. From the 1620s onward, the guitar appeared in ballets at the court of Louis XIII. By mid-century the instrument came to be used in the Comédie Italienne in Paris, in commedia dell'arte performances. Outside Spain and Italy, no great tradition of guitar songs based on vernacular music ever emerged, nor was there an extensive repertoire with accompaniment in battuto style. The French made little use of chord notation like alfabeto or Spanish cifras. Because the instrument had no roots in traditional culture, guitarists largely depended on a repertoire of foreign songs and dances, like villanos, las vacas, sarabanda, and folias, which were probably passed on aurally. After about 1640 a repertoire began to evolve, so simple and accessible that amateurs could take pleasure in playing it. We can find examples in a manuscript from circa 1649, which belonged to Monsieur Dupille, "Commissaire des guerres" (see ex. 2.1), and in François Martin's *Pièces de guitairre* (1663). Unfamiliarity with Italian tablature probably was an impediment to accessing the more advanced repertoire from Italy. In the last quarter of the century, ciacconas in particular must have been immensely popular, since there are interchangeable sets of variations (often in C major, like the ones that first appeared in printed books from Italy) to be found in several manuscripts, notated in French tablature.

The Count of Grammont is known to have remarked on the "whole guitarery" and the universal strumming in Whitehall, where the entire court made attempts to master a certain sarabande by Corbetta. Corbetta's personal success with British royalty, as a teacher of Charles II (and his brother James and sister Henriette Anne), probably contributed greatly to the popularity of the instrument. At the Royal court in Paris, the guitar had an ambassador in the person of Lully, who must have been a fervent player, especially in his younger years. In his stage works he incorporated characters from the commedia dell'arte, and the special liking for Italian song and dance that he shared with Louis XIV probably contributed greatly to this vogue. Perhaps more than in Spain or Italy, the role of the guitar here was to represent an image of otherness, as an instrument of Spanish *chaconistas*, Italian comedians, Egyptians (gypsies), or Moorish slaves.

From the close of the century, there are French manuscript sources in which many works of Corbetta, Granata, and Bartolotti can be found. We may conclude that from the 1670s onward, the solo repertoire was dominated by the Italian legacy, as appears from the many dance suites in the books of Médard, Grenerin, and Carré, strongly influenced by the mixed style of Corbetta's *Guitarre royalle*. At the same time a change of taste took place that is reflected in collections compiled by amateurs; in those manuscripts, simple but elegant allemandes, courantes, menuets, and gavottes (often anonymous) appear in great numbers. These influences together created the conditions for a last flare-up of the battuto-pizzicato style in the works of Robert de Visée and François Campion.

Toward a Coherent Theory of Guitar Tuning

The application of the two different styles of playing, battuto and pizzicato, has probably been decisive for the music's stylistic development and the way it was performed and notated. An analysis of the compositions, both of solo works and accompaniments, is hampered by vexed theoretical problems, where all the arguments are inextricably intertwined. No satisfactory answer to the question how voice leading and chord position were treated can be formulated if we cannot tell how the guitar was tuned, the solution to which riddle can only be helped by reviewing the significance of campanelas for how the instrument was strung and examining the importance attached to the position of the bass in accompaniment. The outline of a comprehensive explanatory model, in which the problems are resolved in relation to each other, can be summarized in the next premises:

1. Tuning charts were generally understood as an instruction to compare the strings in unison. The tuning was normally checked in octaves, as can be seen in the tuning checks in tablature.

Tuning charts and verbal tuning instructions are probably the most concrete indicators we have. Taken literally, they tell us to compare adjacent courses in unison. Usually, the charts do not show if there were high octave strings present on the fourth and fifth courses as well, presumably because such information was considered redundant and made a quick overview of the presentation more difficult. In verbal instructions on tuning, we sometimes find statements about these octaves. In a number of books a tuning checking chart, making use of octaves, is provided as well. If we follow the tuning charts stepwise, they normally result in a tuning with low strings on the fourth and fifth courses. We still have to decide about adding high octave strings, but tunings without those seem to have been rare.

2a. Pizzicato gives a clearer presentation of the position of the chord than does battuto. By making use of pizzicato, chords can be played in any possible inversion.

2b. Basso continuo asks for bourdons.

In different eras, accompaniment was shaped in different ways, particularly with regard to battuto or pizzicato. The way guitarists have applied the principles of counterpoint and voice leading is confusing, and the widespread lack of respect for theoretical rules probably had a background in popular traditions. Yet we should distinguish between different composers, as there were various approaches with regard to voice leading. The early alfabeto practice departed from a permanent use of all courses of the guitar. This made it possible to strum without too much concern about notes that would be foreign to the chord. For Foscarini, who as a lutenist was familiar with basso continuo, the absence of a true bass in alfabeto would have been unsatisfactory. Around 1640 the use of the guitar in accompaniment changed dramatically. Foscarini began to add elements of lute music to his compositions, and his instructions for basso continuo (the first of their kind) show an awareness of the position of the chord. Likewise, a mixed style of accompaniment is to be found in the continuo examples of Corbetta (1643 and 1648) and Granata (1659). Figured chords, like sixth chords and suspensions, are always played pizzicato, and they are mostly followed by a solution in battuto (notated in alfabeto). Thus, the limited vocabulary of conventional alfabeto could be enriched by new harmonies.

It is telling that in Nicola Matteis's *False Consonances of Musick* (1680), perhaps the most important tutor for basso continuo on the guitar, the bass is often not at the bottom when we play battuto. However, if the chords are played pizzicato, it usually is the lowest note. It appears that the choice for battuto was inspired by a long tradition. The principle that the bass should be the lowest note of the (plucked) chord is reflected in the continuo exercises of Grenerin, Matteis, Sanz, and Murcia. The endeavour to conform to current practices was probably strengthened by the potentialities of the bourdon tuning. Moreover, re-entrant or French tuning will never produce a true bass line (the succession of the lowest notes, as given in examples in staff notation).

3.   Campanelas were used on a modest scale only. Therefore it is not likely that they had a decisive influence on the method of stringing, with respect to leaving off bourdons.

The rediscovery of the campanela effect has caused much uncertainty about how the guitar was strung in the seventeenth century. Many have supposed that bourdons would be a handicap for the performance of cascading scale passages. This has led to the assumption that the heyday of the Italian solo repertoire (1630–60) saw a growing tendency to leave off the bourdons of the fifth and fourth courses, prompted by the technical conditions posed by the performance of campanelas. It must be stressed that for a sound judgement, experience is needed with appropriate historical stringing (without metal-wound basses) and an adequate right-hand technique. Although the music from the first books with campanelas (Bartolotti's *Primo libro* of 1640 and *Varii capricci* by Corbetta of 1643) has remained virtually unknown in our time, it seems that hasty conclusions still have been drawn. Furthermore, it is often assumed that the French tuning became the standard in the last quarter of the century in order to facilitate campanela passages. This theory is, however, based on scant evidence. Campanelas were probably seen as an idiomatic gimmick in the first place. Many composers alternated them with *strascini*, longer groups of left hand slurs. Both are ways to perform scalar passages.

4.   The tuning with two bourdons was much in use during the second half of the seventeenth century, both in basso continuo and the solo repertoire.

Different from what is often supposed today, only a very few composers (Carré, Visée, and Derosier) seem to have used French tuning. The geographical spread of this tuning probably was confined to France, Britain, and the Netherlands. In Spain (with composers such as Sanz, Ribayaz, Marin, and Guerau) and Italy (Pesori, Pellegrini, Bartolotti, Asioli, Granata, and Roncalli), there appears to have been no widespread preference for this tuning. Presumably, changing from re-entrant to French tuning became an issue in certain circles, around 1670. Yet we cannot generalize from such a small sample, and there is little reason to assume that François Martin, Rémy Médard, Henry Grenerin, Henry François Gallot, and François Campion—who could be considered to be part of a "French school"—all used the French tuning. It appears from how the basso continuo on the guitar was shaped in the tutors of Grenerin, Sanz, Matteis, and Murcia that bourdons were considered necessary for accompaniment.

Once we recognize that in Italy the guitar was often strung with two bourdons—almost as a reduced version of the lute—our perception of its solo repertoire changes. Around 1640, after the introduction of the mixed style, the bass became increasingly important. Foscarini and Bartolotti started writing polyphonic textures in a repertoire of lute-like dances. Without bourdons the counterpoint would often be oddly inverted, and, as a consequence, the music would be difficult to comprehend.

Notation and Performance

The guitar always maintained the image of accessibility, very different from the scholarly lute, which, with its ever-expanding number of strings, was more and more becoming an instrument of specialists. In the seventeenth century, the lute took its position as an instrument for music of a higher, esoteric order, especially in France; while the guitar, with its simple songs and dances, kept pretending to be everybody's friend. But there is a snake in the grass. To fully appreciate the highly idiomatic nature of this music, a basic insight in the mechanics of guitar playing (and the inner logic of the mixed-style tablature notation) is required.

From the time that battuto chords were notated in tablature, and no longer in alfabeto, the figure 0 indicating an open string was often omitted. This probably was done because it saves labor and costs in writing or engraving. When the composition of the chord and voice leading are obvious, leaving out the 0s (and later, the a's from French tablature) does not cause many problems. In other situations, however, the performer is compelled to make difficult decisions, in particular when the inclusion of open courses not indicated in the tablature would lead to increased dissonance. Sometimes it seems impossible to reach a definitive conclusion about what should or should not sound, even more so if we take the existence of a tradition of harmonic experiment into account, firmly linked to the instrumental idiom of the guitar, and composers who persistently refrained from the strict application of theoretical rules.

Much confusion has been caused by the ways that certain composers indicated barres. Unusual chord shapes can be found in several tablatures, and in Corbetta's works in particular, there are many strummed chords including tablature letters that may not actually represent notes. These letters may be there only to serve as left-hand fingering. This should, of course, be considered an improper use of tablature. In certain genres (in particular in works with a predominant battuto character, such as passacaglia, ciaccona, and sara-banda) there were always unusual harmonies; but normally these dissonances resolve happily, albeit sometimes with much delay. In contrast, Corbetta's odd chords, which even occur in more modern dance genres such as the menuet or gavotte, often remain unresolved. In such cases, a literal performance of the tablature results in inexplicable harmonies and unintelligible chord progres-sions. Supposing that some of the tablature letters were written with the inten-tion not to be sounded, but only touched by the left hand, we would in fact be playing "notes" that should remain unheard.

The modern performer is imbued with the notion that leaving out notes (apart from obvious errors) is not acceptable, because it would be an assault on the integrity of "the work" and the original intentions of the composer, as they have come down to us in written form. Particularly the music of celebrated virtuosos is supposed to be based on great experience with the instrument, and a deep knowledge of what to write and what not to write. Still, a musician may feel compelled to make use of secondary information about notational conven-tions, style, and instrumental technique in order to reach a performance that does justice to contextual implications. In the works of Foscarini and Corbetta it is occasionally necessary to go into the compositional process itself, since their notation is open to interpretation. This applies especially to battuto, because in certain situations there are different possible ways to strum a chord, ranging from a single interval to five-part harmony.

Today it is sometimes supposed that guitarists never played their chord strums the same way twice. In this respect the capriciousness of Corbetta's barre notation can be misleading, since it does not necessarily imply that there was great variation in his performance. In the pizzicato sections from the same compositions there is not the slightest sign of indecision. It seems unlikely that his hesitancy would have been confined to battuto only, and to chords with barres in particular, which leads to the conjecture that not everything he put in tablature is music.

This has wide implications for performance. If we eliminate the extreme dissonances from Corbetta's two *Guitarre royalle* collections, a style emerges that is generally comprehensible, and occasionally very different from what appears in the tablatures at first glance. There is little doubt that Corbetta had a clear idea of the position of the bass, in strummed textures as well as in pizzicato passages. Therefore, we should probably consider his music as normal two- or three-part writing, not essentially different from compositions for lute or harp-sichord (leaving aside the inherent miniature character of most guitar music). Thus, it appears that the five-course guitar had a high-quality repertoire even before the time of Visée.

In summary, we can say that for a satisfactory performance, two crucial issues must be resolved: (1) the question of appropriate stringing; and (2) the inter-pretation of the tablature notation with regard to strummed chords. Another issue is how to integrate the battuto chords in the performance of music in the mixed style. The importance of this last point has not yet been broadly recognized. Inadequate right-hand technique can be one reason that music for the baroque guitar often sounds chaotic, because displaced battuto accents in a pizzicato context can potentially ruin the phrasing. The music will sound incoherent, as if the accented chords—often on unstressed beats—are not part of the same composition. It might well be, however, that a well-balanced and more fluent performance can change our opinion on battuto-pizzicato music in general, making it more accessible to wider audiences. It could make a good starting point for an in-depth exploration of the repertoire.

In the seventeenth century, the guitar was not generally held in very high esteem, and the instrument was often seen as "imperfect"; for the most part, its repertoire consists of small-scale pieces. Nevertheless, some of the leading Italian guitarists, such as Foscarini, Bartolotti, and Corbetta, created more ambitious and original compositions. This book was written as a tribute to their work.

Appendix

Source Texts

The following original texts in Italian, Spanish, and French are referenced in translation in the main text. The translation of "Charles Sorel's Dispute of the Lute and the Guitar" from the French is my own.

Agazzari, Agostino

1607 *Del sonare sopra il basso*

Per tanto dividerno essi stromenti in duoi ordini: cioe in alcuni, come fondamento: et in altri, come ornamento. Come fondamento sono quei, che guidano, e sostengono tutto il corpo delle voci, e stromenti di detto Concerto: quali sono, Organo, Gravicembalo etc. e similmente in occasion di poche e soli voci, Leuto, Tiorba, Arpa etc. Come ornamento sono quelli, che scherzando, e contrapontegiando, rendono più aggradevole, e sonora l'armonia: cioe Leuto, Tiorba, Arpa, Lirone, Cetera, Spinetto, Chitarrina, Violino, Pandora et altri simili.

Medesimamente li stromenti di corde, alcuni contengono in loro perfetta armonia di parti, quale è l'Organo, Gravicembalo, Leuto, Arpadoppia etc: alcuni l'hanno imperfetta, quale è Cetera ordinaria, Lirone, Chitarrina: et altri poco, ò niente, como Viola, Violino, Pandora etc.

Noi per tanto trattaremo primamente di quei del primo ordine, che sono fondamento, et hanno perfetta armonia, e nel secondo luogo diremo di quei, che servono per ornamento.

Amat, Joan Carles

1596 *Guitarra española.* Edition of circa 1761. (The first edition, Barcelona 1596, is no longer extant.)

Al lector.
La colera de España ha sido la causa mas principal (discreto Lector) que aya facado á luz esta obrecilla, porque veo que ninguno es tan flematico como es

menester para enseñar el arte de tañer la guitarra, y assi no se maravillen los que deseavan ser instruydos en esta arte, si al cabo de tres dias sus maestros estavan muy cansados de enseñarles, porque nos tiene tan oprimidos à todos los Españoles este humor colerico, que qualquier cosa que emprendamos, por corta quesea nos parece muy larga. Considerando pues yo la falta que avia en toda esta tierra por no haver algun Autor tratado desto, (alomenos que no sepa) he querido escrivir con este estilo, el modo de templar, y tocar rasgado esta guitarra de cinco, llamada Española, por ser mas recibida en esta tierra que las otras, y el modo de poner en ella qualquier tono, para que sirva de maestro, y tambien paraque los dicipulos delle no estèn sujetos à tanta miseria como es la que nos dà este humor. Lo que quiero suplicar à todos los que se aprovechan de este mi trabajo, que consideren que la buena voluntad ha sido la causa de todo.

Capitulo octavo.
De una tabla con la qual puede qualquier cifrar el tono, y cantar por doze modos.
No será de menos provecho lo que trataré aqui, que lo tratado, aunque aya necessidad de saber lo susodicho, para entender lo que diré: quiero dezir, que para poner, ò ajuntar en la Guitarra qualquier tono, no es de necessidad entender esta Tabla que verán, porque yá pueden sin ella acomodar el tono que quisieren: pero será tan dificultoso, quanto facil, haziendolo con el estilo que verán luego.

Para confirmar esto, quiero contar lo que me acontició con unos Musicos de Guitarra, que pretendian ser en esso de ajuntar, ò poner, la prima de España; los quales estavan saneados (y eran quatro) y sabiendo muy bien que yo tenia cierto estilo, con el qual luego sin dificultad ponia en la Guitarra qualquier tono: una tarde passeandome encontré con ellos; hecho el devido acatamiento, me dixo uno de ellos: Amigo, nosotros tenemos entendido que sabeys una arte maravillosa (y esto lo hazian para hazer burla de mi, como lo afirmaron despues) con la qual presto poneys en la Guitarra qualquier tono; estos mi compañeros, y yo, os suplicamos querays enseñar à los que os deseamos servir el modo que teneys, y el estilo que usays, en esto que tenemos dicho; y si lo hazeys, quedarémos satisfechos, y lotendremos à grande dicha, para que en otras cosas os podamos servir. Yo viendo tantas flores en Ivierno, entendida la maraña, sin darles à conocer que la entendia, les dixe: Señores, el modo que yo tengo en lo propuestro, es de poco momento, y delante de vs. ms. fería como un grano de mostaza puesto à los lados de una grande montaña: vs. ms. estense con sus riquezas, y yo con mis miserias. No satisfechos de mi repuesta, de nuevo me lo dixeron; y yo diziendo, que era cosa muy poca, no es dava muestras de quererlo hazer. Al fin dixeron; Amigo, este estilo que vos teneys, puede ser que para acomodar solas tres vozes fea, qual dizen; pero que pueda servir para mas, tenemos por cierto que es falso, y cosa muy impossible; y tened por averigado, que solo para deziros esto viendo tan buena ocasion, hemos venido aqui. Yo sin mostrar el animo turbado, les dixe: Señores, la verdad es esta, yo tengo el estilo que dezis en una Tabla muy pequeña, que yo fuy el inventor de ella (aunque alguno se ha alçado con ella) y con ella no tres vozes solas, pero quatro, cinco seys, y quantas quisiereys acomodaré en la Guitarra; y para que entendays que es verdad lo que digo, vamos à donde quisiereys para hazer de esto experiencia; y vereys si es verdad lo que digo. Fueron contentos; pensando que seria mejor ocasion para burlarse de mi, y suymonos à un aposento del uno de ellos, que era Estudiante en Artes, y en entrando por él, me dieron unos papeles de Prenestína à cinco vozes; y yo cifrando todo el tono, me dieron una Guitarra, y començeamos à cantar cada uno su voz, juntamente con el instrumento, y vieron ser verdad lo prometido: de fuerte, que admirados de lo hecho, mirandose unos à otros quedaron satisfechos. Desuerte, bolviendo à nuestro proposito, que será cosa muy facil entendida la prometida Tabla, hazer lo que à muchos ha parecido impossible.

Banfi, Giulio

1653   *Il maestro della chitarra*

Prima accorderanno la 5. corda a suo piacere purche non sia trop alta; e poi tasteranno la detta 5. al 5. tasto, & a quella accorderanno le quarte.

Al quinto tasto delle quarte accorderanno le terze. Al quarto tasto delle terze accorderanno le seconde. Al quinto tasto delle seconde acorderanno il cantino.

Avertiendo nell'accordare qualsivoglia corda dovveranno ricercar la voce, cioe l'unisoni per essempio nell'accordar le quarte se la voce sara accordata al quarto tasto della quinta bisognera alzar le dette corde quarte. Se la tutte voce sara al sesto, o piu, o meno anderanno abbassate, e questa regola servira per l'altre.

First tune the fifth course at a convenient pitch but not too high; then press the fifth course at the fifth [fret] and tune the fourth [course] to it. Tune the third [course] at the fifth fret of the fourth [course]. Tune the second [course] at the fourth fret of the third [course]. Tune the cantino [the first course] at the fifth [fret] of the second [course].

I advise you to tune every string by searching for the tone, that is to say the unison [;] for example when you tune the fourth [course,] if the tone is at the fourth fret you have to raise the tone of the fourth course. If the tone is at the sixth [fret], or [slightly] higher, or [slightly] lower you have to lower [the fourth course] and this rule applies to all others.

Bermudo, Juan

1555   *El libro llamado declaracion de instrumentos musicales*

Book 2 chapter 32, fol. 39.

El temple de la guitarra a los viejos no diffiere de esta a los nuevos: sino que la quarta cuerda suelen abaxar un tono. Avia desde la quarta a la tercera a los nuevos un diatessaron: y a los viejos ay un diapente, que es quinta perfecta. Pues queda esta guitarra a los viejos una dezena mayor. Este temple mas es para romances viejos, y Musica golpeada: que para Musica de el tiempo. El que uviere de cifrar para guitarra buena Musica: sea en el temple a los nuevos.

Briceño, Luis

1626 *Metodo mui facilissimo para aprender a tañer la guitarra a lo español*

La Guitarra es vn instrumento el mas favorable para nuestros tiempos que jamas se bio porque si el dia do hoy se busca al ahorro de la bolsa y de la pena. La Guitarra es vn theatro verdadero deste ahorro. demas de esto es acomodada para cantar. tañer. dançar. saltar. y correr. baylar y Zapatear Ruando con ella cantando y representando mil amorosas pasiones con su ayuda. Es salsa para el contento. desterradora de pesares y cuidados Pasatiempo a los tristes. consuelo a los solos. Alegria a los melancolicos. templança a los colericos. Da seso a los locos y enloquece a los sanos. es esclaua del tiempo. no la ofenden ninguna de las incomodidades que el delicado laud tome. no hay humo ni calor. ni frio. ni humedad. Que la incommode es como la rosa siempre viua. si presto se destempla bien presto se torna a templar. si se rompe con dos sueldos se acomoda. de suerte que la Guitarra segun mi opinion y de muchos lleba gran ventaja al laud. porque para hallarle bueno son necesarias muchas cosas. ser bueno. ser bien tañido. buen encordado y bien escuchado con silencio. pero la Guitarra Señora mia, sea bien tañida. o mal tañida. bien encordada o mal encordada. se haçe oyr y escuchar. atirando con la breuedad de su çiença y facilidad. los mas ocupados injenios. y los haçe dexar otros exercicios mas subidos por tenella entre sus manos.

Castillion, Jean Baptiste de

1730 B-Bc Ms.S5615. Recueil des pièces de guitarre composées par Mr. François le Cocq. Receuil des pièces de guitarre de meilleurs maitres du siecle dixseptième

S'il est vrai que la Guitarre soit le Cithara de l'Ecriture sainte, ainsi que Mr. Furetière semble le dire dans son Dictionnaire, on remarque aussitôt son antiquie, et combien cet instrument a de la douceur et des charmer. Ce seroit d'elle que la Genese feroit mention au chapitre quatrieme et que Isaie auroit dit, que sa douceur s'est contituit dulcedo citharae, lorsqu'au Chapitre vintquatrième il represente l'image afreuse de la desolation et de la ruine de

Babylone et de Jerusalem. J'en laisse la recherche aux curieux, en si les scavans ne s'accordent pas sur cette longue antiquité, on en convient que la Guitarre est un instrument de plus harmonieuxz et qu'elle a fait de tout tems les amusemens des Princes dans les heures de leur precieux loisirs. Mais comme dans ce Monde tout est sujet à la vicissitude, il paroit que Louïs XIV, ce grand Roi soit le dernier qui s'y est exercé, et que ce soit presentement le tour de la Guitarre de languir. Le fameux François Corbet l'avoit reveillé dans ce Pais bas, et apres qu'il avoit dedié son livre aux Archiducs Albert et Isabelle, tout ce qui etoit noble à Bruxelles se faisait gloire d'en jouer, et à la fin du siècle dernier, et au commencement du present J'ai encore veu que la Guitarre étoit seule à la mode, et que Madame l'Electrice de Baviere se faisait enseigner par le Sᴿ. François le Cocq, actuellement musicier jubilaire de la Chapelle royale de la Cour. La manière et la tour aisé qu'il donne aux pièces qu'il a composé dans le goût de la musique de ce tems, montée à une si haute perfection font que on le juge le plus habile maître; qui ait paru jusques à present. C'est après l'avoir ouï plusieurs fois toucher la guitarre avec une justesse et une delicatesse suprenante, que j'ai repris ce noble et melodieux instrument que j'avois abandonné depuis plus de vint ans, occupé par mes emplois à des afaires trop serieuses; et que je tache de joüer ces mêmes airs, avec les quels il a eu l'honneur d'amuser plus qu'une fois son Altesse serenissime l'Archiduchesse, sœur de l'Empereur Charles VI nôtre Auguste souverain et Roy, Gouvernante des Païs-bas, dans le cabinet de cette illustre Princesse.

Quelque petit service que je lui ai casuelement rendu, et l'ancienne connoissance l'ont porté de me les gracieusement presenter écris de sa propre main et authentiqués par sa signature, que j'ai copié pour mon usage pareillement de ma propre main dans ce livre que j'avois preparé et reglé aussi moi-même a ce sujet. Je joins dans ce recueil après les airs de Monsᴿ le Cocq quelques pieces d'autres maîtres qui ont excellé au siecle dernier. On trouve dans celles de Monsᴿ Francis Corbet beaucoup de gravité. Monsᴿ Lelio a feint aux sienes une agréable douceur. Michel Perez Zavala espagnol et maitre de mon honoré Pere à Madrid vers l'an 1690 me paroit n'avoir pas mal imité ces deux excellens autheurs. Les pieces de Monsᴿ Gaspar Sanchez aussi espagnol et de Monsᴿ Jean Baptiste Granata Italien ont leur merite: les chaconnes et passacilles de ce dernier passent pour bonnes. Monsᴿ Robert de Visée a été renommé par toute la France par l'honneur qu'il a eu de joüer si souvent devant Louis XIV ce grand Roy et de luy avoir didié son livre de Guitarre en l'an 1682, ouvrage a ce qu'il marque, de plusiers années. Mᴿ Saint-Luc a été ce meme tour de grande reputation, et touchoit la guitarre d'une grande habileté. A fin Mᴿ Nicolas Derosier Ordinaire de la Musique de son Altesse Electorale Palatin, tres entendu dans la musique, a fait une étude toute particuliere de la Guitarre, et s'y est si fort perfectionné qu'il a inventé la Guitarre Angelique, de huit cordes de plus que l'ordinaire [a theorboed guitar].

Il a donné au Public un livre de l'une et de l'autre en l'année 1692. C'est de tous ces autheurs que j'ai copie quelques pieces, et que l'on trouvera apres celles de Monsr Francois le Cocq.

Je donne au commencement de ce livre les Principes de la guitarre où j'explique les signes et les marques que l'on trouve dans sa tablature. Bien de maitres en ont des singulieres je tache de les eclairer, et surtout les harpege-mens de M^r le Cocq, qui donnent à ses pieces un agrement incomparable. J'ÿ explique pareillement tout que ce que l'on doit scavoir de musique pour bien joüer de cet instrument. Et après tout je donne un abregé alphabetique des noms des airs et des termes de musique le plus usités, avec leur explication pleine d'instructions. Fasse le Ciel que ce livre après ma mort tombe entre les mains d'un amateur qui puisse joüer de mes peines. Fait à Gand, pendant le ceurs de l'année 1730.

Foscarini, Giovanni Paolo

Correspondence with Constantijn Huygens.

All the excerpts from Foscarini's letters to Constantijn Huygens are taken from Rasch (2007). All English translations are mine.

Letter of July 26, 1647.
Illustrissimo Signore mio Padron mio Colendissimo,
    Retrovandomi in Francia per esser stato chiamato da questa Maestà, per valersi di me in un'opera musicale, che fu rapresenta l'iverno passato, e di la prese animo di metere insieme un'opera intitulata *L'armonia del mondo*, prendendo ardire di far veder in Francia l'operatione Italiana, capitandomi casualmente un virtuosissimo personagio, nomato il Signor Walter Kriger, abitante costì, il quale m'informò delle rare qualità e virtù di Vostra Signoria Illustrissima, e di la prese animo appo-giarle soto la Sua protetione la sopradeta *Armonia*, como spero che à questa hora l'haverà ricevuta in un fagotino, consignata al detto Signore Walter; mi fu ancora deto che, oltre l'altre sue qualitadi, sii protetor w posessor della musica; dove ciò considerando, prendo baldanza di mandarLi qualche compositioni, qui incluse, fate da me. Le quale, se consterò che siino gradite da Vostra Signoria Illustrissima, non mancherò di continuar le mie fatiche, abenche deboli, per poterGliene pre-sentar altre, conforme il Suo gusto. Fra tanto La suplico di gradire questa poca dimostratione per l'infinita reverenza che Li porto, e conosendomi abile di poter esser ascritto nel numero de servidori del Serenissimo Principe Suo signore, me Gli esebisco per qualche tempo, e ciò sarebbe bona occasione per levarmi di queste parti, mentre però fusse proteto e favorito da Vostra Signoria Ilustrissima. E non mi estendendo più in oltre, humilissimamente Li baccio le mani, e Li fo riverenza. Di Parigi, li 26 Luglio 1647.

Di Vostra Signoria Ilustrissima
Devotissimo et obbedientissimo servidore
Gio. Paolo Foscarini.

Letter of January 1, 1649.

Illustrissimo Signore mio Padron mio Colendissimo,

Ricevo la gentilissima di Vostre Signoria Illustrissima, nella quella vedo che Lei si compiace di honorarmi in lodare le mie debole compositioni, del che Le rendo infinite gratie. Vedo ancora, che Lei desidera di havere delle compositioni à due e à tre, dove che Le invio presentamente un dialogo, che spero che haverà la medesima lode che hà havuto in questa corte. Le dò poi nova, che ho fatto epilogo di tutte le mie compositioni, e no ho scelto 50, à tre, à quattro, à cinque ed à otto, con la sua partitura, acciochè Vostra Signoria Illustrissima possa considerare il più eccellente studio della musica. Le ho fatto scrivere in buona forma, ben corrette, che non Gli daranno niuna sorte di fastido nel cantarle, e questo sarà per mia memoria appresso di Vostra Signoria Illustrissima ricevendo questo picciol dono per segno della moi devoto osservanza, chiedendo Gli licenza, dovendo partire alli 20 di questo alla volta d'Italia per servire et accompagnare la Maestà della Regina Sposa di Spagna.

E subito che sarò in Italia, non mancarò d'inviare al Signor Tarsin la musica degli cinque liuti di Bologna di Laus Maler, i quali son sicuro che delli più pari e degli più conservati non ve ne saranno simili altrove. Resta solo che Vostra Signoria Illustrissima li potrà fare accomodare all'uso moderno per esser con il manico piccolo all'antica. Le inviarò con le sue casse, perché son tanto belle che mi pare peccato il lasciarle indietro, essendo infodrate di veluto chemesino, con le chiavi e serrature dorate. Cosi La supplico ancora di attender à far comprita del liuto della vera taglia per il che so che in Fiorenza ve ne è un para, che sono eccelentissimi e ben conservati, e gli ricuperarò dal proprio gentillhuomo, che gli tiene, con assai meno prezzo di quello che Li potrei havere in Parigi.

In tanto accetti il moi buon animo, resti servita della mia poca inhabilità, assicurandoLa che al moi salvo arrivo à Madrid non mancarò di fare il moi dovere condarGliene parte, e tutte quelle musiche, che si faranno in così gran sposalitio, le invariò a Vostra Signoria Illustrissima, alla quale facio riverenza, e Le bacio le mani, augurandoLe li buon capo d'anno con altretando di felicità appresso. Di Parigi, il primo di Genaro 1649.

Di Vostra Illustrissima
Devotissimo servidore
Gio. Paolo Foscarini.

Letter of March 29, 1649.
Illustrissimo Signore et Padrone moi colendissimo,

Il primo giorno di Gennaro ressposi alla gentilissima Sua delli x di Desembre et asieme Le inviai un dialogo à 3, che spero che non deve esser stato dispiasuto à Vostra Signoria Illustrissima. Dopoi andai conforme il Suo ordine dal Signore Tarssino, il qualle è stato la causa che io mi son consumato al tutto qui in Parigi con queste rivolitioni, che son statto nesesittato vender tutto quello che io havo per vivere, essendome manchato le provesione della corte e tutte le mie speranze, che, se il Signor Tarssino me havesse datto subito quella cortesia che Vostra Signoria Illustrissima si compiaque per Sua innata benignità, me ne sarei andato à Lione, la dove me posso prevalere al moi bisogno nesesario. Si che ricevi Linidi passato 25 scuti daldetto Signor Tarsino, al qualle ne ho fatto ricupata. Et mi è restratto da consegnarLi un libro di arieta à una, doi et à 3, che sono in tutte 50, ne le qualli ne feste mentione nella mia, che, per non havere il danaro per pagare la copiatura, non le ho potutto inviare à Vostra Signoria Illustrissima.

Mi arosescho à poner in carta la mia miseria, che mi trovo, che, se io potessi havere credito appresso di Vostra Signoria Illustrissima, La suplicarei di un segnalatissimo favore, di agiuntarmi in questa mia nesesotà di qualche danaro, atio io mi potesse condure sino à Lione con la mia famiglia, che in contracanbio di questo favore prometo à Vostrea Signoria Illustrissima in parola di gentilhuomo honoratto, que sonno, de Le inviare la musicha delli miei leuti di Bologna, subito harivatto in Itaglia. Et se Vostra Signoria Illustrissima havesse qualche amico à chi le potessi consegnare, non mancherò al moi harivo farlo, et Le prometo in parola di honore de inviarLi doi leuti della vera forma di Anz Frai, che sono belissimi et di una belissima vernice. Suplico Vostra Signoria Illustrissima per amor di Dio à conpatirme della gran presentione che io piglio con esso Lei, assichurandoLa che mepassa l'anima, che, oltre haver consumato quel pocho che si ritrovavemi, ancora siamo statti con pericolo della vita, si che lasciarò iudicare à Vostra Signoria Illustrissima il resto. La suplico donque à non mi arbandonare in questa mia nesesità, che oltre alla riconpensa ne restarò con perpetua obligatione.

Consegnai al Signor Tarsino alchuni concerti, con il partimento, di studio grande in materia di compositione, i qualli fano mirabel effetto, sonati sopra le viole, che in Roma nelle academie sonno statti stimati. Il libro di ariete à una, doi et à 3, le ho detto il tutto, vi è ancora una cosa curiosa di una pazza amorosa, la qualle Li piacerà. Pensavo ponerla alla stampa et inviarGela stanpata. Le barichate di Parigi à guastato il tutto. Riceverà il bon hanimo con la scritura à mano, se conpiacerà di giustarla in quel modo, con assichurandoLe che la mia divota osservanza non mancherà mai, et pruchurerò con quanto potrà le deboli forsi mie continuarla.

Li dimando perdone del tropo ardire che ho usatto, confidatto nella carità generosa di Vostra Signoria Illustrissima, alla qualle viverò in perpetuo obligatto. Mi schuserà se io non ho scrito di prop[r]ia mano, per esser con una defluctione da un brazzo dalla gran malinconia che mi son preso di vedermi fori di casa per 3 anni, et non havere mai pottuto fare aquisto di sugetto da potersi prevalere di un bever di aqua. Laciarò considerare il resto à Vostra Signoria Illustrissima. In tanto starò atendendo con ardente core la gratiosissima Sua rissposta, et per fine Li fascio riverenza et Le batio le mani. Parigi, li 29 Marzo 1649.

Di Vostra Signoria Ilustrissima
Devotissimo et obbedientissimo servidore
Gio. Paolo Foscarini.

Giustiniani, Vincenzo

1628 *Discorso*

Perché avendo lasciato lo stile passato, che era assai rozzo, et anche li soverchi passaggi con li quali si ornava, attendono ora per lo più ad uno stile recitativo ornato di grazia et ornamenti appropriati al concetto, con qualche passaggio di tanto in tanto tirato con giudizio e spiccato, e con appropriate e variate consonanze, dando segno del fine di ciasun periodo, nelche li compositori d'oggi dì con le soverchie et frequentate cadenze sogliono arrecar noia; e sopra tutto confar bene intendere le parole, applicando ad ogni sillaba una nota or piano, or forte, or adagio, or presto, mostrando nel viso e nei gesti segno del concetto che si canta, ma con moderazione e non soverchi. E si canta a una o al più 3 voci concertate con istrumenti proprii di Tiorba o Chitarra o Cimbalo o con Organo, secondo le congiunture; e di più in questo stile si è introdotto a cantare o alla spagnola o all'italiana, a quella simile ma con maggior artificio e ornamento, tanto in Roma, come in Napoli e Genova, con invenzioni nuovedell'arie e de gli ornamenti; nel che premono i compositori, come in Roma il Tedesco della Tiorba nominato Gio. Geronimo.

Granata, Giovanni Battista

1680 *Nuovi soavi concenti di varie sonate*

[f. 3r] Cortese Lettore. Essendo si sparsa voce per il Mondo, che le mie Compositioni sopra la Chittara Spagnola son difficili da suonare, e che non sono da Principianti, mà solo da Maestri, stimolato io da questo, sono sforzato à rispondere con la presente lettera, che non hò mai havuto in pensiero di comporre cosi facili, e triviali, mà ben sì di andare tirando di grado in grado all'ultima perfettione di sonare bene tale istrumento per quello però, che hà potuto arrivare il mio debole talento, mà non per questo sono tanto difficili, che non solo le possino suonare li Virtuosi di tale istrumento, mà ancora moltissimi Signori miei Scolari, che in varie parti del Mondo si ritrovano, quali essendo stati in varij tempi à Bologna à studiare, hebbi io fortuna di servirli per Maestro, mà che dico? non solo questi, mà ogni sorte di persone, purche habbino qualche poco d'intelligenza dell'intavolatura, e modo di suonare tale istromento conosservare però quello, che sono per insegnarti. Primieramente, che non bisogna spaventarsi per vedere, che nelle mie compositioni li tempi delle note di sopra caminano di Crome, Semicrome, e Biscrome, perche questo è fatto per aggiustare il tempo, e la battuta, e non per questo si devono suonare con prestezza grande come devono pensare questi tali, mà bensì deve pigliare un tempo adagio proportionato, con osservare il tempo delle note, e della battuta, e con suonarle più volte così verrai ad intendere l'aria della fuga, ò cantilena della suonata. Secondariamente osservarai il modo, che si devono fare li strasci, dritti, e roversci avvertendo, che non sempre si devono far caminar veloci, mà conforme il tempo delle note di sopra, e così ancora nel fare li passaggi, e campanelle. Terzo osservar ai il modo di fare li trilli segnati con un T. e nel fare il trillo per b. molle, e per b. quadro, quando si deve fare per b. molle trillerai la corda vuota cioè il zero à primo tasto, e quando sarà b. quadro à due tasti, seguitando poi primo, secondo, e terzo, & altri numeri si deve fare il trillo avanti à ciascheduno numero dove sarà segnato trillare dolcemente la detta corda, ò più appresso, ò più lontano dal numero con destinguere l'armonia del suono del b. molle, e del b. quadro, e con trillar la corda più ò meno conforme il tempo della nota, che vi sarà sopra. Trovarai ancora numeri segnati con li diesis, per farli devi spiccare affatto la mano dalla Chittarra ponendo le dita più commode al numero, che mostrerà, e squassando, e premendo la mano si procurar à di fare quanto sia possibile sostentare à poco à poco la voce di detta corda, il che servirà per regola generale dovunque si troverà. Quarto dovrai osservare le qui inserte suonate di farle spiccare armoniose, cioè suonarle piano, forte, come ne gli andamenti cromatici, che vanno à poco à poco risolvendo, come nelle suonate patetiche, e malenconiche, e poi arrivando nelli passaggi, e campanelle farle più allegre, e granirle di quando in quando con qualche trilletto dolce, e con suonarle affettuose, così verrai ad imitare con l'armonia la voce humana, che canta. Quinto dovrai osservare il modo d'Arpeggiare li passaggi, che nelle suonate troverai di farli uniti con toccare li soprani con li bassi uno doppo l'altro senza intervallo di tempo sempre in fino al fine. Trovarai ancora, che per mancanza de numeri grandi mi sono servito nelli dieci del X. dell'undici, dodici, tredici, e quatordici, de numeri piccioli, come vedi qui segnati. 11. 12. 13. 14. Devi ancora condonare à gli errori della stampa, poiche dove è quantità di numeri, note, trilli, slissi, lettere, botte, & altre cose sempre vengono stampati de gli errori, però li vedrai con la penna emendati, e per farti conoscere il mio desiderio, che hò di servirti, vorrei potermi trovare in qualunque luogo, dove anderanno i miei libri per poterti con la voce ammaestrare e con le mani insegnare le presenti Compositioni. Stimo in questa mia opera di haver sodisfatto al genio di molti, perche à chi piace il patetico, à chi l'allegro, à chi le sinfonie, à chi le fughe, & altre sonate di più sorti in tutti i generi, crederei, ch'in quest'opera trovasse ciò che desidera. Troverai ancora molte suonate concertate à due Violini, e Basso, & ancora si possono suonare à Chittara sola, & in questo devi osservare l'istesse regole. Finalmente non ti maravigliare se non in tutte le Chittare si possano suonare queste mie Compositioni, perche essendomi io affatigato per ridurre alla maggiore perfettione ch'hò possuto l'harmonia di questo istromento, hò fatto fare le mie Chitare col manicio d'undici tasti, e trè altri tasti d'Ebano in collati sul fondo della Chittara; Adopra anco tù, o studioso Lettore un simile istromento, ch'io t'assicuro, che conoscerai l'affetto, con cui hò inteso giovarti in quest'Opera, e Vivi Felice.

Huygens, Constantijn

Excerpt from a letter to De Nielle of May 1, 1670.

J'ay aperceu d'abord que ces pièces pour la tiorbe sentoyent le stile du Sieur Angelo Michel, et suis marri d'avoir negligé de luy en demander durant le temps que j'ay eu le bien de le converser chez la Signora Anna. Il est vray que pour lors j'avois moins d'inclination pour cest instrument, si non pour l'accompagnement de la voix: du depuis la fantaisie m'en a si bien pris, j'en ay produit plus de soixante pièces par toute la varieté et l'estendu des tons. En voyci quelques eschantillons que j'expose humblement à vostre censure.

Excerpt from a letter to Sébastien Chièze, May 30, 1673.

Je suis fort ayse de veoir ces airs Espagnols en notes de musique, y trouvant le véritable génie de la nation, fort Africaine, à mon avis, et qui jamais ne se despouillera bien de *Punicum et Lybicum* d'outre mer. Pour la tablature de la guitarre, il m'en coustera encor une fois (*y no mas*) la peine de traduire ceste sotte manière de *sotto sopra* en bonnes lettres d'alphabet, en esperance d'y rencontrer quelque-chose qu'il vaille la peine d'avoir épluché. Vous diriez que c'est de la tablature pour les antipodes. Ces messieurs m'obligeront fort de s'expliquer à la mode de deça des Pyrenées, ce qui leur seroit plus ayse qu'à moy. *Miraremos* si le jeu vaudra bien la chandelle.

Kapsberger, Girolamo

1619   *Libro secondo di villanelle*

Libro secondo di villanelle a 1.2. & 3. voci. Con l'alfabeto per la chitarra spagnola. Del Sig. Gio. Kapsberger nobile alemanno. Raccolte dat Sig. Ascanio Ferrari. Roma, Robletti, 1619.
Al molto Ill. Sig. Mio Osser. Il Sig. Gio Girolamo Kapsberger.

Natural' proprietà delle Gratie è l'andar' ignude, ne perciò avviene ch'elle dalla nudità, non havendo corpo, ricevan vergogna. A modeste verginelle non possono le parti loro ancor' più belle, senza biasimo grande far palesi, ne senza rossore. Lacere in mille guise e squarciate i panni andavano queste Villanelle, che parto di V.S. usciron' già delle sue mani sì nobilmente adorne. Io per atto di pietà non meno che d'Amore l'ho unite ensieme, e ricopertele per quanto io ho potuto, delle loro primiere spoglie, ho risoluto per mezzo della Stampa d'inviarle a V.S. sicuro che se forse non havrò fatto cosa interamente grate a lei, havrò sodisfatto almeno al commun' desiderio di chi ama l'altrui valore, al qual deve alle, per non si mostrare troppo severa, conformar' la sua volontà.

Montesardo, Girolamo

1606   *Nuova inventione d'intavolatura*

[fol. 5v]
Avertendo ancora che chi vorrà farlo più soave bisognarà sonare su la rosa, alcuna volta vicino il manico, & anco per addolcire alcuna volta sù l'istesso manico.

[fol. 5r]
Del modo di sonare con la mano dritta. Chi vorrà haver una bella e leggiadra mano su la Chitarra, è necessario prima, e principalmente tener la mano relassa dall'attaccatura di essa, quanto sia possibile, tanto che diventi leggiera; che cosi farà molto leggiadra al sonare, e poi batter le corde dolcemente con tre, ò quattro dite in modo di arpeggiare, e non tutte insieme che cosi farebbono un gran fracasso, & oltre che il suono sarebbe crudo, darebbe gran noia all'udito.

Sanseverino, Benedetto

1622   *Il primo libro d'intavolatura*

p.vii.
Modo d'accordare le Chitarra alla spagnuola.
   La chitarra vuol'havere cinque ordine accompagnati à due corde per ordine eccetto il cantino.
   Il quinto ordine detto il Basso haverà un cantino di sopra accompagnato con una corda più grossa, che venghino à far ottava tutte due insieme, tirandole à voce corista, come si usa nelli altri strumenti, overo à voce proportionata secondo la grandezza della chitarra.

Il quarto ordine parimente vuol havere un cantino accompagnato con il suo basso, che facciano ottava tutte due insieme come di sopra, l'incordarete con il quinto ordine, tirandole quattro voci più alte del quinto ordine, che mettendo il deto sopra il secondo tasto farà quinta con il basso, overo toccando il quinto tasto del quinto ordine faranno unison tutti duoi li ordini.

Il terzo ordine faranno due corde accompagnate insieme d'una sola voce al unisono, tirandole quartri voce più alte del quarto ordine, che mettendo il deto sopra il secondo tasta, farà ottava con il quinto ordine voto.

Il secondo ordine, faranno due corde parimente d'una sola voce al unisono come sopra, tirandole tre voci più alte del sodetto terzo ordine, che mettendo il deto sopra il terza tasto farò ottava con la corda grossa del quarto ordine, e unisono con suo cantino.

Il cantino primo ordine solo, l'accordarete quattro voci più alte del sodetto secondo ordine, che mettendo il deto sopra il terzo tasto faccia ottava con il terzo ordine voto.

Sanz, Gaspar

1674   Instruccion de música

[fol.8] primer tratado p.1:

En el encordar ay variedad, porque en Roma aquellos Maestros solo encuerdan la guitarra con cuerdas delgadas, sin poner ningun bordon, ni en quarta, ni en quinta. En España es al contrario, pues algunas usan de dos bordones en la quarta y otros dos en la quinta, y a los menos, como ordinario, uno en cada orden. Estos dos modos de encordar son buenos, pero para diversos efectos, porque el que quiere tañer guitarra para hazer musica ruidosa, ò acompañarse el baxo con alguno tono, ò sonada, es mejor con bordones la guitarra, que sin ellos; pero si alguno queira puntear con primor, y dulçura, y usar de las campanelas, que es el modo moderno con aora se compone, no salen bien los bordones, sino solo cuerdas delgadas, assi en las quartas, como en las quintas, como tengo grande experiencia; y es la razon, porque para hazer los trinos y estrasinos y demas galanterias de mano izquierda, si ay bordon impide, por ser la una cuerda gruessa, y la otra delgada, y no poder la mano pissar con igualidad, y sujetar tambien una cuerda recia, como dos delgadas; y a mas desto, que con bordones, si hazes la letra, o punto E, que es Delasolre, en la musica sale la quinta vacante en quarta baxo, y confunde el principal baxo, y le dà algo de imperfeccion, conforme el contrapunto enseña; y assi puedes escoger el modo que te gustare de los dos, segun para el fin que tañeres.

Sorel, Charles

1644 *Nouveau recueil des pièces les plus agréables de ce temps, ensuite des jeux de l'inconnu et de la Maison des jeux*, 170–83. Paris. [See for original text http://gallica.bnf.fr/ark:/12148/bpt6k715706.image. r=luth.f155.pagin]

THE DISPUTE OF THE LUTE AND THE GUITAR

Preface of the Musician.
Although I am not an expert in music, I know enough to entertain myself and any other person who, out of affection for me, will like anything I do. I have always cared more than others to make good my shortcomings, and now I have found out that I have instruments that can speak, as if they were enchanted by a Fairy or the Gods had gifted them with that ability. So, one day I amused myself dreaming in my room when I heard my lute murmuring something, and it seemed that he was talking in prose instead of in verse, as was usual. This made me think that he had something important to tell me. At the other side, my guitar was not mute, and we together had a discourse that I will report word by word.

THE LUTE
My Master, I see that you have the kind of worries which I am able to banish, if you would just take my advice. All the books you consult are not enough to relieve your sorrow. This direction leads to melancholy.

THE GUITAR
My dear Master, do not listen to this deceiver. You know well that the Lute has that certain something that leaves you in the state you are in, but if he would do anything to change your passion, he would rather enhance it. He is not like me, who can ease the problems of men, being always happy and pleasant.

THE LUTE
You are always impudent, my sister. You do not respect me, as the eldest in the house. Why do you hide the truth? Is it not clear that when our Master was passionate in love with Sylvie, Amaranthe, and Dorimene, I was his only diversion? Did he not reveal all his thoughts to me? And did he not spend whole nights making me produce his complaints, and did I not grieve with him?

THE GUITAR
You condemn yourself; while it is certainly true that you grieve with him who complains, instead of comforting him and giving him help, to the extent that you increase his torture, I myself have never been so unhelpful.

THE LUTE

It has occurred that my Master has taken you with him when he was already in a good humor, because if he had been sad, he would have soon rejected you. But I foresee that soon you will not be any more in favor, since he is threatened again by misery, and he can only take me as a remedy. That is why I beg him to listen to me.

THE MUSICIAN

Tell me frankly what you have to say to me, because it is of great importance to me.

THE LUTE

I believe that at first you did not dislike me, and that despite the persuasions of my malicious sister you did not believe that I was the cause of all the troubles you had to endure. However, if you did not enjoy that which you have desired, it must be easy to bear that loss and it would be best to find out what you have now in mind. Well, if I am not capable of bringing you relief on my own. you should know that if you would be willing to give me a companion I can give you complete satisfaction.

THE MUSICIAN

If you want, I can adapt my voice to the sound of your strings.

THE LUTE

Your benevolence is very kind, but I think this is not what is needed. Something from outside you is required, so that I can have company. To say it more clearly, I should marry an instrument of my own sort. I know that my well-being and yours depends on it.

THE GUITAR

Lutes normally harmonize with other lutes. This one wishes to be married to another of his own kind. Please do avoid that scandal, my Master; I knew well that he had that wicked desire, because he is from a country where many are suspect of male love. If anyone of your family should marry, I beg you that it may be me. You know that I am of the age to be taken care of. I as a female do ask for a man. Please give me in marriage to a cittern or a violin.

THE LUTE

It is generally known that the Guitar is an imperfect instrument that cannot come to an agreement with the others, and it is more involved in cohabiting than in marriage. Let us leave her with her voluptuousness. While she is used to serving buffoons, she is not entitled to spread gossip about me and speak badly of me. But I will demonstrate that I have nothing but honest intentions.

Though recently I have indeed developed affection for someone, the young Espinette of my neighbours that I have heard singing yesterday, so beautifully that I am overjoyed. Ha, my Master, please permit this engagement. You will have the pleasure to see me married to the Queen of all musical instruments, I do not know if you know her. She deserves more honor than the Lyre of Orpheus, or that of Apollo.

THE GUITAR

Do you still listen to that troublemaker? You know, my Master, that if I marry the Cittern, of which you have already heard, you will be perfectly satisfied. He is rich and very much favored by the Muses, and will give you joy as a member of your household.

THE MUSICIAN

I have already dreamt of what you say, my Guitar. And you my Lute, I appreciate that you have had the courage to direct your affection at such a virtuous object, but you will have to realize that you are not in a state to be married. You are as badly dressed as possible, most of your strings are broken and the rest are out of tune. Your table is warped and your sides are split. It will take much time to repair you and bring you back to a proper tuning. To present you to your mistress in your present state will make you lose her completely. She will have more respect for a dishonorable violin than for you. If you will not be judged worthy of being her servant, you will be thrown into the fire.

THE LUTE

This affair truly is worth putting myself in good order, which I am not now, and you should help me with that, please. I confess that some in Paris are more beautiful and more harmonious, but it is important that I belong to you and that you take the trouble to talk to the parents of my Espinette, and if you present me to her with your hand, I have no doubt that I will obtain the object of my desire.

THE MUSICIAN

I will do what I can, but apart from that we should remember to put you well in order. It will take time to ensure that you leave behind the bad habits that you acquired until now. I have brought you in contact with unruly men, who made you say obscene words and who dragged you into serenades for persons who do not deserve them. You will have to be purified after so many profane occupations. I have heard that the young Espinette who you wish to serve is of a good family, which demands that one lives next to her in honor and respect. I know that she is still Virginal, and that she has not been touched other than by the graceful fingers of a Nymph who occasionally appears to her. You cannot charm her if you do not observe the rules of modesty. And then, what would your beautiful mistress think of me? Would she not detest me because I have instructed you so badly?

THE LUTE

I admit that one can never prepare enough for such an investigation. My beautiful Espinette will refuse to sing with me if I am out of tune, and I do not know any other airs than the ones I have learned recently. Instead of the drinking songs, there should be only love songs. O, perfect and divine Espinette, I am prepared for it, from now on I will have no more strings that are not in tune to serve you. Even if I am not with you, I will love you as if you were here. What a joy it will be to marry you one day. Together we will produce a marvellous harmony. The sweet chords born from us two will be the children of our marriage. My master will be charmed, and possibly even your beautiful Nymph will be satisfied by it.

THE GUITAR

Now you see that the Lute already ensures his happiness, while I will remain here, just like now. My looks will fade, and no one will want me anymore.

THE MUSICIAN

I do not refuse to take care of you, but I also have the responsibility to put you in good shape. You will have to forget those frivolous songs, which you have learnt during Carnival and sung at our farces. A person of your sex should be honorable in her words and deeds. He whom you wish to marry wants a virtuous wife, who is not at all coquettish.

THE GUITAR

I am prepared to arrange myself in modesty, and I will do my utmost for that, but I fear that it will be useless, because I have heard that it is ordered that you may give away only one of us two. If the Lute marries his mistress, I will be no more than the servant of this beautiful Espinette.

THE MUSICIAN

I should tell you both, frankly, nothing like that has yet been ordered. I will see what is the best thing to do.

THE GUITAR

O, my Master, I will complain no more: I will obey everything that you decide; you have power over us like the Gods have over mankind. Whatever will be, I will always love my Cittern.

THE LUTE

And I will love my Espinette.

Trichet, Pierre

circa 1640   *Traité des Instruments*

La guiterre ou guiterne est un instrument de musique grandement usité parmi les français et italiens, mais encore davantage parmi les espagnols, qui les premiers l'ont mise en vogue, et qui s'en scavent plus follastrement servir qu'aucune autre nation, ayant une adresse particulière à chanter et sonner leurs sarabandes, gaillardes, espagnolettes, passemezzes, passecailles, pavanes, alemandes et romanesques avec mille gestes et mouvements du corps autant crotesques et ridicules que leur jeu est bigearre et confus. L'on trouve néanmoins en France des courtisans et des dames qui se rendant singes des espagnols taschent de les imiter, monstrant bien qu'ils s'aggréent plus aux choses estrangères qu'à celles qui leur sont naturelles et domestiques. En quoi ils resemblent à ceux la qui, pouvant faire bonne chere en leur propre maison, aiment mieux aller manger chés autrui du lard, des ognions et du pain bis. Car qui ne scait que le luth est propre et familier aux français et qu'il est le plus agréable de tous instruments musicau? Toutesfois quelques-uns de nostre nation le quittent tout à faict pour prendre et apprendre le jeu de la guiterre. N'est-ce pas à cause qu'il est plus aisé de s'y perfectionner qu'au jeu du luth, qui requiert un long et assidu estude avant d'y pouvoir acquérir quelque addresse et disposition recommandable? Ou bien est-ce à cause que la guiterre a je ne scai quoi d'efféminé qui leur plaist et leur flatte le cœur et les rend enclins aux voluptés?

Notes

Introduction

1. Tyler and Sparks, *The Guitar and Its Music*, 49.
2. In alfabeto the most common harmonies appear in just one fixed position, in convenient finger patterns. Therefore, alfabeto harmony is completely uniform, with very little concern for voice leading. In example 1.2a the rhythm of the strumming and the direction of the strums (up or down strokes) are indicated on a time line. At downstrokes the hand moves in the direction of the floor, and at upstrokes to the ceiling. The example begins with two downstrokes.
3. See the transcription of a gigue by Angelo Michele Bartolotti (ex. 4.11).
4. Books by Francesco Corbetta (1671 and 1674), Antoine Carré (1671 and c. 1675), Rémy Médard (1676), Henry Grenerin (1680) and Robert de Visée (1682 and 1686).
5. Hudson, *Folia, Saraband, Passacaglia, and Chaconne*. I will treat passacaglia as a dance, although it probably originated from the *ripresa* or *ritornello*, an instrumental interlude between the stanzas in a few (mostly four) chords. It was used in dance songs and is therefore most likely to have been used for dancing, as well.
6. Treadwell, "The 'Chitarra Spagnola.'"
7. Strizich, "L'accompagnamento di basso continuo."
8. Dean, "The Five-Course Guitar."
9. Gavito, "The Alfabeto Song in Print."
10. Murphy, "The Tuning of the Five-Course Guitar."
11. See Katritzky, *The Art of Commedia*, 429, 450, and 471.
12. Musée du Louvre, Paris. There exist other early Italian guitar paintings, by artists such as Rutilio Manetti and Domenico Fetti.
13. The Wallace Collection, Hertford House, London.
14. NL-DHgm MS 133. K6.
15. On the cittern in the Netherlands, see Grijp, "The Cittern of Sweelinck and Vermeer."
16. By artists like Rutilio Manetti (1571–1639) and Valentin de Boulogne (1591–1632), who lived in Italy, and somewhat later, Mathieu Le Nain (1607–77), in France.
17. See Fischlin, "The Performance Context of the English Lute Song 1596–1622."

Chapter One

1. As described in Juan Bermudo, *El libro llamado declaración de instrumentos musicales*.
2. Ibid., fol. 39v (For Bermudo's original text, see appendix, Bermudo).
3. Ibid., fol. 97r.

4. Thomas Christensen had noted that "Spanish theory predating these guitar tutors [Amat, Doizi de Velasco, Sanz] was by no means uniformly conservative. The Spanish mathematician Ramos de Pareja, for example, was the first Western theorist to recommend a just tuning for all imperfect consonances (thirds and sixths) that was to prove essential to the development of triadic composition. . . . To all this theory should be added consideration of the remarkable genre of homophonic *villancico* songs cultivated in Spain during the fifteenth and early sixteenth centuries; these songs display strikingly tonal characteristics. . . . [The] examples do suggest that *rasgueado* [*sic*] guitar music in seventeenth-century Spain flowered in well-tilled soil." Thomas Christensen, "The Spanish Baroque Guitar," 39n31.

5. "Todo lo que ahora se usa de cantar y tañer es a lo rasgado, y ninguna cosa se canta ni tañe de sentido" (fol. 47–47v). Translation in Corona-Alcalde, "The Players and Performance Practice."

6. Amat, *Guitarra española* (Barcelona, 1596). This first edition is no longer extant. See appendix, "Amat, Joan Carles," for the original.

7. See the preface to the edition of 1626.

8. *Grove Music Online*, s.v. "Amat, Joan Carles," by Craig Russell and Monica Hall, accessed September 15, 2007, http://oxfordmusiconline.com.

9. Amat, *Guitarra española*, capitulo octavo. For original text, see appendix, Amat, "Capitulo octavo."

10. See Sayce, "Development of Italianate Continuo Lutes," 50–58. Bass strings were added to the lute, allowing a bass line and chords to be played in a lower register than the voice of the singer and increasing the volume of the instrument. Because of the greater string length, it was necessary to change to a re-entrant tuning of the first two courses; otherwise, the tension of these strings would become too high. This tuning is the principal feature of the chitarrone. In fact, the name *tiorba* (Fr. *theorbe*) is a pet name for a specific type of instrument with this tuning that has a very long neck and a "shepherd's-crook" pegbox for the diapasons.

11. To compare with what was usual on the lute, see Mason, "*Per cantare e sonare.*"

12. See Ayala Ruiz, "Vicente Espinel." Ayala Ruiz lists a considerable number of primary sources in which the addition of the fifth course to the guitar was attributed to Espinel. In his younger years, the poet fought as a soldier in Italy, and after that he lived for some time in Sevilla. Later he returned into the fold of the Church, and at his death held the office of chaplain at the Chapel of Obispo in Madrid.

13. Lope de Vega, *La Dorotea* (Madrid, 1632), 121: 'Perdóneselo Dios a Vicente Espinel que nos truxo esta nouedad y las cinco cuerdas de la guitarra, con que ya se van olvidando los instrumentos nobles, como las danças antiguas, con estas acciones gesticulares y mouimientos lasciuos de las chaconas, en tanta ofensa de la virtud de la castidad y el decoroso silencio de las damas.'

14. "Quién duda que pudiese del infierno / suspender los tormentos y la ira / al dulce son de la famosa lira" Ayala Ruiz, "Vicente Espinel," 14.

15. "Este instrumento ha sido hasta nuestros tiempos muy estimado, y ha avido exelentissimos músicos; pero después que se inventaron las guitarras, son muy pocos los que se dan al estudio de la vigüela. Ha sido una gran pérdida, porque en ella se ponía todo género de música puntada, y aora la guitarra no es más que un cencerro, tan fácil de tañer, especialmente en lo rasgado, que no ay moço de cavallos que no sea música de guitarra.' Sebastián de Covarrubias, *Tesoro del lengua Castellana o Española* (Madrid, 1611), f. 209v. http://fondosdigitales.us.es/fondos/libros/765/16/tesoro-de-la-lengua-castellana-o-espanola.

16. See Yakely, "New Sources of Spanish Music for the Five-Course Guitar." It is evident from this article's bibliography that there are very few sources dating back to the first half of the seventeenth century. The existing sources, mostly from after 1650, are almost without exception in chord notation (cifras or alfabeto), and not in tablature.

17. An exception is the *Libro secundo de tonos y villancicos*, published by the Spanish composer Juan Aranies in 1624 in Rome. In this collection there are works for one to four voices, with alfabeto. The music is mainly in a typically Spanish style, but with Italian influence. This is apparent from the addition of a basso continuo, which was unusual in Spain at that time. See Stein, "Accompaniment and Continuo in Spanish Baroque Music."

18. Stein, "Spain," 349: "While the seventeenth century was a Golden Age for Spanish culture, music held a subsidiary, even a subservient place, next to theater and the visual arts, in terms of private and ecclesiastical patronage, public financial support, commercial appeal, and influence in contemporary society. One obvious symptom of its lesser status is that Spanish music from this period survives largely in manuscript copies."

19. Louise Stein, "The Origins and Character of *Recitado*," *Journal of Seventeenth-Century Music* 9, no. 1 (2003): par. 3.3, http://sscm-jscm.press.uiuc.edu/v9/no1/stein.html.

20. Stein, "Accompaniment and Continuo in Spanish Baroque Music," 359: "Guitars, harps, lutes and theorbos are consistently mentioned as accompaniment instruments in the descriptions of the 1605 festivities [the court entertainments celebrating the birth of Philip IV, that took place in Valladolid] and other court spectacles throughout the early seventeenth century."

21. Possibly the best known theoretical polemic is the Artusi–Monteverdi debate. See Carter, "Artusi, Monteverdi, and the Poetics of Modern Music." The theoretician Artusi took a position as a defender of the established rules of polyphony, while at the other side, Giulio Cesare Monteverdi (the brother of the celebrated composer) advanced arguments to prove that the innovations were based on both *ragione* and *senso*. Artusi asked for mathematical evidence for the correct use of dissonance and the irregular application of modality. Monteverdi did not give a straight answer. Carter comments: "One can see why. That Monteverdi's dissonances are explicable in terms of contemporary improvisation and ornamentation practices, that they are fleeting enough not to offend the ear, that such dissonances are somehow metaphorical substitutes for consonances, that these pieces have to be judged as performed by good singers and not from score, were all arguments roundly (and rightly, given his frame of reference) dismissed by Artusi. . . . Needless to say, Artusi neglected to point out that in Part III of Zarlino's *Institutioni harmoniche* (Venice 1558), the author had also argued that some dissonances could pass almost unnoticed by the ear."

22. "Il secondo modo di cantare all'unisono s'introdusse per mio avviso dopo l'uso delle consonanze; et questo è quando un solo canti allo strumento, del quale siano percosse molte corde tra le quali sia ancora la parte di quello che canta nel tempo medesmo, sposte si che faccino tra di loro diverse consonanze." Vincenzo Galilei, *Dubbi intorno a quanto io ho detto dell'uso del'enharmonico, con la solutione di essi*. Translation from Carter, "An Air New and Grateful to the Ear," 134.

23. See Wistreich, *Warrior, Courtier, Singer*, chapter 5 "Per basso solo." Wistreich demonstrates that in Italy in the second half of the sixteenth century, many multipart

songs were arranged for a bass singer and lute. This is probably also the type of repertoire Galilei referred to. Galilei's own arrangements are essentially polyphonic. It is not known if he was familiar with the practice of chord strumming on the guitar, which was only beginning to emerge at that time.

24. The troupe of Zan Ganassa (Alberto Naselli) resided in Madrid in the early 1580s. In the contract in question, it reads that these actors were to "Servir de tañer con nuestras guitarras y cantar las tonadas á nuestro uso castellano." Cited from Katritzky, *The Art of Commedia*, 39.

25. Hill, *Roman Monody*.

26. Montesardo, *Nuova inventione d'intavolatura*. For a detailed description of the role of the guitar in the rise of monody, see Tyler and Sparks, *The Guitar*, 37–45.

27. Hill, *Roman Monody*, 1:110. For Giustiniani's original text, see appendix.

28. See Stein, "The Origins and Character of *Recitado*," par. 5.1: "Because I find most *romances* to be more song-like than recitational, it surprises me to read that Giustiniani included singing *alla spagnola* and *all' italiana* in the same sentence. But perhaps the importance of the Spanish *romance* to his discussion of early recitative had to do not only with the declamatory character of the *romance* but with Spanish performance practice. *Romances* could be performed as solo songs with strummed chordal accompaniment or by groups of two or three singers, just as described by Giustiniani in his sentence: 'And one voice, or at most, three voices sing to the accompaniment of one's own instrument: a theorbo, guitar, harpsichord, or organ, according to the circumstances.' ... The pervasive Spanish tradition of accompanied solo song ... provides a clear antecedent for Spanish continuo practice. Musical, iconographical, and literary sources attest to the unbroken continuity of this tradition, in which *romances* new and old were performed to the accompaniment of a polyphonic instrument, preferably the strummed guitar or the harp."

29. De Goede, "*Del Suonare Sopra il Basso*," 87. De Goede gives an example from the *Breve regola* (Siena, 1607) by Francesco Bianciardi that includes a number of parallel fifths.

30. See Christensen, "The Spanish Baroque Guitar," 11: "The 'theory' of *rasgueado* guitar music in the seventeenth century was surprisingly progressive in light of later developments in tonal theory. We find explicit recognition of chordal identity and root, extravagant invocation of octave/inversional equivalence, and finally a reduction of modes to two transposable major and minor species."

31. Ibid., 29: "As elementary and unpretentious as these scale triads appear, their theoretical implications are profound: they reflect the beginnings of a subtle, but ultimately decisive, shift in music theory away from a melodic conception of mode based upon the ordering and articulation of particular intervals and toward a tonal conception of key based upon the context and function of its indigenous harmonies. As we follow the evolution over the course of the seventeenth century of these scale triads as prescribed in guitar tutors, we are in essence observing the emergence of a scale-degree-based conceptualization of tonality—a kind of primitive *Stufentheory* [*sic*], if you will. And while many of the same formulations may be found in coterminous theorbo and keyboard tutors, it is in the literature for guitar that we find their most explicit and unencumbered depiction."

32. Gavito, *The Alfabeto Song in Print*, vii. Compare also Silke Leopold, "Remigio Romano's Collection of Lyrics for Music," 57: "It is remarkable that, after the theoretical controversies from Florence, there is no longer any surviving written theoretical discussion of solo song, although in this very century such an extraordinary

amount was changing in the nature of musical composition. Theory says nothing about the canzonets—they were sung, and not discussed."

33. Giustiniani, *Discorso sopra la musica*, translation by Carol MacClintock in *Musica disciplina* 15, 223.

34. Other printed collections of lyrics with alfabeto include those of Pietro Millioni (1627), and Giacinta Fedele (1628). Francesco Gabrielli, known as Scapino, included the text and alfabeto of the "Aria di Scapino" in his *Infermità, testamento e morte di Francesco Gabrielli* (1638).

35. Gavito, *The* Alfabeto *Song in Print*. Gavito recognizes a core repertoire of poetic texts, repeatedly used in songs by different composers. Many of these texts were of Neapolitan provenance, which establishes a firm link between alfabeto song and the south—Sicily and the Kingdom of Naples.

36. Leopold, "Remigio Romano's Collection of Lyrics for Music," 55.

37. Praetorius, *Syntagma Musicum*, 1:17.

38. See Miller, "New Information on the Chronology of Venetian Monody," 22–23. Some of Berti's songs appeared in Romano's booklets even *before* the composer published them in one of his two collections.

39. Kapsberger, *Libro secondo de villanelle a 1.2. & 3. voci. Con l'alfabeto per la chitarra spagnola* (Rome, 1619). Translation in Leopold, "Remigio Romano's Collection of Lyrics for Music," 52. For the original text, see appendix.

40. Gavito, *The* Alfabeto *Song in Print*, 173: "For the purveyors and composers of *alfabeto* songs, adherence to Caccinian models and other musical systems that emphasized compositional control through elaborate musical notation seems not to have been a prime motivation. In fact, the aesthetic premise that characterizes much of the repertory is an outward avoidance (if not rejection) of the florid style of melodic notation that dominates the publications of Caccini. This is effectively illustrated in the *Musiche* books of Sigismondo d'India, where the composer discriminates between *madrigali* and *arie* of the Caccini mold and the unmistakable character of the *alfabeto* song. Naturally this has led scholars to interpret the repertory (or, rather, the practice of *alfabeto* inscription) under the guises of 'unwritten' and 'oral' traditions. While the elusive nature of *alfabeto* notation strongly resonates with such practices, notation and dissemination through the printed medium are still some of the hallmarks of *alfabeto* song tradition."

41. A few exceptions to this are the arias from guitar books like Benedetto Sanseverino's *Il primo libro d'intavolatura*, in which notation for chord strums is also included (see ex. I.2a).

42. An exception (but from a very late date) is the remarkable *Sinfonia* 2^{la} *pizigata* on p. 128 of Foscarini's fifth book (ca. 1640). This is an exemplary realization of a figured bass, in which we recognize Foscarini's experience with the lute. It is questionable, however, whether such an example relates to the actual practice of guitar accompaniment of that time. There appears to be an unbridgeable gap between the alfabeto from the song collections (mostly from the decades before) and the strict lute style of this example, which is far more demanding even than the continuo instructions in the same book.

43. However, it should be noted that to improvise "in style" one has to be familiar with the implications of counterpoint and mode.

44. The same applies for Doizi de Velasco's *Nuevo Modo* and the accompaniment instructions of Corbetta's books from 1643 and 1648.

45. Translation from Strunk, *Source Readings in Music History*, 3:68.

46. In his treatise, he only touches briefly at the *chitarrina*, as we will see in chapter 3.
47. Sanseverino, *Intavolatura facile . . . opera terza*, fol. 3r: "Finalmente mi pare, che la Chitarra alla Spagnuola, si debba suonare con le botte piene, e non altrimente, perche suonandola con diminutioni, legature ò dissonanze, sarebbe piústosto suonare di liuto, che di Chitarra alla Spagnuola & diminuendo tal'instromento non solo se li viene à levare il proprio, natural, & antico stile, mà anco se li toglie affrato l'armonia." Translation from Boye, "Giovanni Battista Granata," 44.
48. Normally the guitar was played *on* the stage as a consequence of its emblematic role (and to compensate for its low volume).
49. Yet there are also a few examples of women accompanying themselves on the chitarrone. See Sayce, *The Development of Italianate Continuo Lutes.*
50. For a more detailed description of this important event, and the role of the guitar, see Treadwell, "The 'Chitarra Spagnola,'" 15–20. According to Treadwell, this is the earliest mention of the guitar in Northern Italy. We can suppose that Vittoria Archilei had learned to play the guitar in Rome. See also Ayala Ruiz, "Vicente Espinel." Espinel was in Milan, in 1581–84, in the service of the Duke of Medina Sidonia. It doesn't seem far-fetched to think that his singing to the guitar made an impression there, too.
51. See Treadwell, "The 'Chitarra Spagnola,'" 25, n67. According to Treadwell, in one of the surviving scores of the *Rappresentatione* there was alfabeto, written in by hand.
52. Carter, "Resemblance and Representation," 129. According to Tim Carter, numerous passages in Monteverdi's late madrigals and operas make it clear that the triple-time aria was the musical language of love, a connotation that certainly applies to pastoral intermezzi with shepherds, nymphs, and allegorical figures singing and dancing on the stage.
53. Gavito, *The* Alfabeto *Song in Print*, 31–63.
54. Several guitar books bear a dedication to Mattias de' Medici, like Carbonchi's collection of 1640 and Granata's book of 1646.
55. Many alfabeto songs are *canzonette*. As a literary genre, the *canzonetta* is noted for its metric and strophic formalism and pastoral subject matter. See Gavito, *The* Alfabeto *Song in Print*, 31, and Tomlinson, *Monteverdi and the End of the Renaissance*, 153, 210–14.
56. Giulio Cesare Monteverdi, *Dichiaratione* (1607). Translation in Strunk, *Source Readings in Music History* 3:48.
57. The cast list of this performance is included in Tim Carter, "A Florentine Wedding," 89–107. In this inventory the names of the singers are linked to specific instruments.
58. "Scena boschereccia con maschere e al centro musico con chitarra." See Treadwell, *The Guitarra Spagnola*, 37: "An engraving of Act II, Scene V of the opera depicts a scene with angel musicians seated in clouds playing a variety of instruments, including the guitar."
59. In Monteverdi's *L'Orfeo* (1607), for which the instrumentation is known, the guitar is not mentioned, either.
60. In Hammond, "Orpheus in a New Key," 103–25 there is a document from the Biblioteca Apostolica Vaticana (Ms. Barb. Lat. 4059) with a remark about the *sinfonia* which opens the opera: "Avanti all'aprir' della Scena fù fatta una sinfonia con 20. Viole, 4. Cimbali, 4. Tiorbe e 4. Violini; 2. Liuti, e 2. Chitarre, che sonavano tutti." In act 2 scene 9, the dryads dance "una sarabanda bellissima," of which an

eyewitness (Ménestrier) remarked that it was performed with castanets. Castanets were often used in combination with the guitar.

61. See Stein, *Songs of Mortals*, 149 n62.
62. Bacci, "Lettere inedite di Baccio del Bianco," 68–77. Letter of Baccio del Bianco to Ferdinand II or Mattias de' Medici, of July 19, 1653. Translation from Louise Stein, *Songs of Mortals*, 149. Stein comments: "Baccio del Bianco was startled and irritated when four guitar players disturbed the ambience that he carefully had created for the spectacular prologue to Calderón's mythological play *Fortunas de Andrómeda y Perseo*."
63. Translation from Stein, *Songs of Mortals*, 275. According to Stein, "The phrase 'il cuatro di violino' is difficult; that a group of four violins played, as in the Spanish 'el cuatro de violines,' or that one of four violins played. It is also possible, but less likely, that he referred to the *violino piccolo*, a small violin tuned higher than the ordinary treble violin." It is not known what piece they performed.
64. See Rebours, "Lully guitariste," 14–16.
65. In Antonio Carbonchi, *Lo dodici chitarre spostate*, there is music for no less than twelve guitars of various sizes, all tuned to a different pitch.
66. Briçeño, *Metodo mui facilissimo*, preface. Translation from Corona Alcalde, *The Players and Performance Practice*, 302. See appendix for the original Spanish text.
67. Jensen, *The Development*, 27.
68. Ibid., 28.
69. "per compiacer . . . all'allegra, e nobile gioventù."
70. Parisi, "Acquiring Musicians and Instruments," 123.

Chapter Two

1. One of these aristocratic families were the Pepoli. Francesco Corbetta's first book, published in 1639, was dedicated to Conte Odoardo Pepoli.
2. For a description of the cultural climate of that time in Bologna, see Schnoebelen, "Bologna 1580–1700." See also Oleskiewicz, "The Rise of Italian Chamber Music."
3. Pasqual and Regazzi, *Le radici del successo*, 68.
4. Granata, *Nuovi soavi concenti di varie sonate* (1680): "Ancora moltissimi Signori miei Scolari, che in varie parti del Mondo si ritrovano, quali essendo stati in varij tempi à Bologna à studiare, hebbi io fortuna di servirli per Maestro."
5. The two books by Agostino Trombetti, printed by Nicolò Tebaldini, were also from Bologna. In the *Libro secondo d'intavolatura sopra la chitarra spagnuola* (1639), there is one early piece in mixed style, in tablature.
6. Giovanni Paolo Foscarini, *Il primo, seco[n]do, e terzo libro della chitarra spagnola*. Although it is not known how many copies were printed, a relatively large number of Foscarini's books have been preserved. His works were printed in Macerata, Rome, Venice, and other cities. Foscarini probably kept the plates in his possession, so that he could add different front pages with dedications to various patrons, depending on the circumstances. Many individual pieces within the book bear the names of dedicatees, other than the ones from the front page(s). The dedicatees would have been familiar with his work. From his correspondence with Constantijn Huygens, it is clear that he often took the initiative to have his music printed.
7. See example 5.6.

8. Tyler and Sparks, *The Guitar*, 69.

9. Specifically the stroke signs, placed *in* the tablature, in the *Secondo libro* (1655), are easier for an engraver to add. It has been suggested that Bartolotti engraved the tablatures himself. See Chauvel, preface to the facsimile edition of *Libro primo et secondo di chitarra spagnola*.

10. Granata, *Nuovi soavi concenti* (1680): "Ogni sorte di persone, purche habbino qualche poco d'intelligenza dell'intavolatura, e modo di suonare tale istromento conosservare però quello, che sono per insegnarti . . . e per farti conoscere il mio desiderio, che hò di servirti, vorrei potermi trovare in qualunque luogo, dove anderanno i miei libri per poterti con la voce ammaestrare e con le mani insegnare le presenti Compositioni."

11. The registers of the court document Corbetta's annual salary of 160 thaler. See Sievers, *Die Musik in Hanover*, 46 and 134.

12. See Boye, "Giovanni Battista Granata," 102–4. In fact, Granata seems to have held the post of a *sopranumerato*, a substitute player.

13. Translation from Boye, "Giovanni Battista Granata," 108.

14. Granata, *Nuovi soavi concenti* (1680), preface. For Granata's original text, see appendix.

15. In Richards, *The Commedia dell'Arte*, there is a long fragment from the diary of Giuseppe Pavoni from 1589, with a colorful description of the quarrel of the star actresses and a report of the comical action on the stage.

16. Michael Praetorius, *Syntagma Musicum* vol. 2, 53: "Und brauchens in Italia die Ziarlatini und Salt'in banco (das sind beyn uns fast wie die Comoedianten unnd Possenreisser) nur zum schrumpen; darein sie Villanellen und andere närrische Lumpenlieder singen."

17. See Ciancarelli, "Modalités de réadaption," 143–46. Stefano della Bella's well-known etching of Carlo Cantù, standing before the Pont Neuf, was probably made in Paris around 1645, during della Bella's stay in the French capital from 1639 to 1650.

18. Carlo Cantù, *Cicalamento*, 43.

19. In Giovanni Ambrosio Colonna's *Intavolatura di Chitarra alla Spagnola* (1620), there are two vocal compositions: "Aria alla Piemontesa" and "Cantata dal Virtuoso Signor Francesco Gabrielli detto Scapino." Of Gabrielli there are two works left, *Villanelle di Scapino* (1624) and a posthumously published work, *Infermità, testamento, e morte di Francesco Gabrielli detto Scapino* (1638), which includes the famous "Aria di Scapino" with alfabeto.

20. The name *Scappino* is related to the Italian verb *scappare*, "to flee." Scapino was a stock character of the commedia dell'arte, a comic servant noted for his cowardice, taking flight at the first sign of a conflict. *Encyclopædia Britannica Online*, s.v. "Scapino," accessed December 17, 2008, http://www.britannica.com/EBchecked/topic/526629/Scapin.

21. "Fermeve sù, ò subianti / Acquieteve, ò ignoranti / Ande à subiar à Lio / Stamegne maledette / Bulli da tre gazette / Treve in rio—Sei tali, che ne sprezia / I no sà che a Venezia / Scapin se tien à mente / Chi è bravo, e chi e poltroon / Chi è ricco, e chi è guidon / E chi è insolente / O quanti tien subià—Che da tena i non hà / E se i tir a` l sò conto / I hà' l mantel d' Istà / E'l zipon ripezzà / Con el cul'onto—Chi è nassù nobilmente / No può esser' insolente / Ma che ze vagabondo / De manco no puol far / De no se far nasar / Da tutto el Mondo—Però concludo, e digo / Che i varda che nemigo / Scapin no so dichiara / Perche'l canterà el nome / El vestir, e'l cognomen / In la Chitara." Translation in Dean, *The Five-Course Guitar*, 193–94.

22. Trichet, *Traité des instruments* (F-Psg Ms.1070, n.p., c. 1640). For the original text in French, see appendix. Translation by Grunfeld, *The Art and Times of the Guitar*, 106.

23. Sorel, *Nouveau recueil*, 170–83. For the full text, see http://gallica.bnf.fr/ark:/12148/bpt6k715706.image.r=luth.f155.pagin. An English translation is included in the appendix.

24. "Lulli commença par cet instrument; & la guitare plus à la mode qu'aucun autre en Italie, & celui dont on y joue le mieux, fut celui qu'il connut d'abord. Il conserva le reste de sa vie de l'inclination à en jouer. . . . Au contraire, lorsqu'il voyoit une Guitare chez lui ou ailleurs, Il s'amusoit volontiers à battre ce chaudron-là, duquel il faisoit plus que les autres n'en font. Il faisoit dessus cent Menuets et cent Courantes qu'il ne recueilloit pas, comme vous le jugez bien: autant de perdu." Le Cerf de La Viéville de Fresneuse, *Comparaison de la musique italienne et de la musique française*, 183–88.

25. They appeared in a *Récit grotesque*. See Rebours, "The Baroque Guitar in France," 198: "The situation was similar in the theatre: the guitar appeared in 'charivaris,' in comical and grotesque situations, associated with Spaniards or Italian characters like Harlequin, Brighella, Pantalone, the Ziarlatini and Salt'in banco. And that was not all: the guitar players sometimes came down amongst the public, moved, sang, and danced. The instrument was, in fact, perfectly adapted to these situations: light, not too big, transportable, generally flat-backed and so more stable and easier to handle than the viola da gamba or theorbo."

26. From a letter by Sir Richard Bulstrode to Lady Harvey April 1673. In Richards, *The Commedia dell'Arte*, 277.

27. John Evelyn, *The Diary of John Evelyn*, 387.

28. See Fontijn, *Desperate Measures*, 62. Fontijn suggests that Fiorelli and Corbetta had met in 1651 at the court of Carlo II Gonzaga in Mantua. Clearly they moved in the same circles. According to Anne Macneil, *Music and Women of the Commedia dell'Arte*, the Mantuan court was a place of refuge for the commedia dell'arte.

29. GB-Ob. Ms. Mus. Sch. C94, "Pieces de guitarre de differend autheurs receuillis par Henry François Gallot."

30. Médard, *Pièces de guitarre*, preface: "Je pretens avoir entierement suivi la maniere du fameux Francisque Corbet . . . avec cette difference que j'ay trouvé pour mes pièces une facilité quil ne se'st pas donné la peine de chercher."

31. Corbetta called this book his *Libro quarto*. Because only two earlier books are known (from 1639 and 1643), a third book must be considered lost.

32. See Pinnell, "Role of Francesco Corbetta," 161. Johann Friedrich traveled through Italy and had converted to Roman Catholicism in 1651.

33. Jacques Bonnet (1644–1723), *Histoires de la musique* (Paris, 1715), 331, Bayerische Staatsbibliothek Digital. http://reader.digitale-sammlungen.de/de/fs1/object/display/bsb10598304_00353.html. Also see Tyler and Sparks, *The Guitar*, 107. According to Tyler, this could have been Foscarini, who was in Paris around that time. But there were more Italian guitar players around, notably in the circles of the commedia dell'arte and opera (Carlo Cantù for example). It is even possible that Corbetta was his teacher for a time. In 1649 Foscarini wrote to Constantijn Huygens that he had been from home for three years. In his correspondence, there is no mention of such an honorable position. See his letter of March 29 of that year, below.

34. Benjamin de Laborde, *Essai sur la musique ancienne et moderne III.* (Paris, 1780), 503, http://gallica.bnf.fr/ark:/12148/bpt6k503809q/f509.image. Laborde most likely

based his information on the obituary for Corbetta from *Le Mercure Galant*, from April 1681.

35. See Tyler and Sparks, *The Guitar*, 108.

36. This suffering ended with the successful surgery of the King's anal fistula on November 18 of that year.

37. "Le soir S M se promena longtemps à pied dans ses jardins; il se recouche toujours sur les huit heures et soupe à dix dans son lit; il fait d'ordinaire venir Vizé pour jouer de la guitare sur les neuf heures. Monseigneur, Madame La Dauphine et toute la maison royale sont auprès de lui jusqu' à son souper.' *Journal du Marquis de Dangeau*, 1:332: May 11, 1686. http://gallica.bnf.fr/ark:/12148/bpt6k116691/ f444.image. This text has caused some modern writers to accept, perhaps too readily, that Visée provided bedtime music to the monarch, and even on a regular basis.

38. Pinnell, "Role of Francesco Corbetta," 191.

39. August 5, 1667. Samuel Pepys, *The Diary of Samuel Pepys*, 7:52.

40. Ibid., 5:138, November 17, 1665.

41. Pinnell, "Role of Francesco Corbetta," 256.

42. Ibid., 254. The title *Easy Lessons on the Guittar for Young Practitioners; Single and Some of Two Parts. By Signor Francisco* appeared in *The Term Catalogues* for November 26, 1677. The title suggests that there were guitar duets in this book, as was the case in his 1674 collection. See *The Term Catalogues*, http://babel.hathitrust.org/cgi/pt?id= mdp.39015033678411;view=1up;seq=345.

43. Ibid., 181–86.

44. Anthony Hamilton, *Memoirs of Count Grammont* (n.d.; Project Gutenberg, 2009), chap. 8, http://www.gutenberg.org/files/5416/5416-h/5416-h. htm#link2HCH0006.

45. For a description of the position of musicians in France, see Anthony, *French Baroque Music*.

46. On page 251 of Adam Ebert's *Auli Apronii* we read about an unsuccessful trip from England to Turin, in about 1678: "The world-famous guitarist Corbetto [*sic*], who taught all the Potentates of Europe, who came here from England, had the misfortune to break a fingernail, and with elderly people they grow slowly; it was impossible for him to play at the festivities, however much he may have wanted to." Adam Ebert, *Auli Apronii*, http://vd18.de/de-slub-vd18/content/pageview/39885297.

47. In the preface to *Li cinque libri*, Foscarini tells that he had been in the service of Archduke Albert of Austria (1559–1621) in Flanders. This must have been in his young years—before 1621, when Albert died. Presumably Foscarini held a post as theorbist or lutenist in Brussels.

48. Foscarini received payments for services to Huygens, to whom he sent several of his own compositions. Foscarini repeatedly promised Huygens to send five sixteenth-century Italian lutes of superior quality, by Laux Maler. This is characteristic of mid-seventeenth-century French tastes. Old Italian lutes were much sought after, and retrofitted with a longer neck, according to newer taste. See Sayce, "The Development of Italianate Continuo Lutes."

49. Rasch, *Driehonderd brieven*. For a transcript of the original letter see appendix.

50. From this letter it is not clear if he played the theorbo or one of the two guitars that were present in the première of *L'Orfeo*.

51. It is often assumed that this was an Italian translation of Kepler's *Harmonices mundi*. In fact it is another treatise on music theory (probably written by Foscarini himself), with many references to astrology and Greek mythology. On pp. 10–11, the

different plucked instruments (lute, theorbo, and cittern) are summed up, but there is no mention of the guitar.

52. In an e-mail discussion on Foscarini's book, Monica Hall reported that a copy was sold at Sotheby's in 1992. Its title page reads "Li sei libri della chitarra spagnola," i.e., "The six books . . . ," although it includes only the five that we know about. It is dedicated to Hipolito Bracciolini, Baron of Monte Oliveto in Pistoia and dated from Rome, November 25, 1644. Monica Hall to vihuela mailing list, May 30, 2009, http://www.mail-archive.com/vihuela@cs.dartmouth.edu/msg03013.html.

53. Rasch, *Driehonderd brieven*, 925. Letter by Foscarini to Huygens, January 1, 1649. For a transcript of Foscarini's original letter, see appendix.

54. It is not known what Foscarini had to do in return. His allowance from the court perhaps was for taking part in performances as a theorbist, but he could even have been the Italian guitar master of the dauphin.

55. Rasch, *Driehonderd brieven*, 937. See appendix for original text of the letter.

56. Ibid., 941. The booklet is described as "un libretto di conpositioni sopra la tiorba al modo di Francia."

57. "Point de guerre, point de guerre / Nous en sommes saouls. / Paris et Saint Germain / Ont fait assez les fous. / Un bon beuveur, La, la, la / Vaut bien un bon frondeur— On y berne, on y berne / Le gouvernement. / Aussi le Mazarin / Comme le parlement / Un bon beuveur &c.—Estudie, estudie, / Prince de Conti / Te voila en repos / Tu n'as plus de souci / Et tu pourras, La, la, la / Lire Macchiavelli." F-Pg MS 2344, pp. 26–27. I wish to thank François-Pierre Goy and Gérard Rebours for their help with the transcript of this Mazarinade. Originally there were five couplets.

58. The instructions in the manuscript give an unequivocal representation of re-entrant tuning in staff notation. According to his tuning instructions, Dupille's guitar was tuned a fourth higher than the usual chitarra spagnuola. The transcription is transposed a fourth down in example 2.1, for reasons of easier understanding. It is not known if tuning at this higher pitch was much in use in France, or if there was a relation with re-entrant stringing.

59. Bartolotti, *Table pour apprendre*. Bartolotti's only known solo pieces for theorbo are in one of the "Goëss-Vogl" manuscripts and in "Vienna 17706."

60. Rasch, *Driehonderd brieven*, 1099. Huygens did send two of his compositions to De Nielle, to whom he addressed this letter. For the original text of this letter, see appendix: "Huygens, Excerpt from a letter to De Nielle of May 1, 1670."

61. Huygens's original letter is in the Koninklijke Bibliotheek at The Hague. In the 1916 Worp edition of Huygens's letters, the name of the guitarist was transcribed mistakenly as "Signorita Corbetta." http://resources.huygens.knaw.nl/retroboeken/huygens/#page=364&accessor=toc&source=28.

62. Rasch, *Driehonderd brieven*, 1125. Letter to Lady Swann (Utricia Ogle), March 10, 1673.

63. Ibid., 1121. "Je suis, par hazard, devenu guitarriste, et ay produit de mon chef une trentaine de pièces sur ce miserable instrument, que je ne possède encor que par emprunt." March 7, 1673.

64. Ibid., 1121. Letter to Sébastien Chièze, May 2, 1673.

65. Ibid., 1143. For the complete text of the letter, see appendix: "Huygens, Letter to Chièze, May 30, 1673."

66. Ibid., 1153. "Mes plus aigres invectives se portent contre la guitarre de vos esconcheurs d'harmonie, car pour los tonos à chanter, il s'y en trouve d'assez raissonnables, *pro captu gentis*." Letter to Chièze, June 27, 1673.

67. Ibid., 1139. Letter by Chièze, May 24, 1673. Chièze mentioned "los Maestros de la Capilla [José] Marino, Osorio, Juan Sanchez y el Maestro Galan."

68. Ibid., 1132. Huygens to Chièze in Madrid, May 2, 1673. "Ce qu'on vous a fouré dans la main sont *niñerias*, et des plus pauvres. Gautier m'a conté qu'ayant joué deux heures durant sur son excelentissime luth au Cabinet du Roy à Madrid, *los Grandes d'España*—grandes *aselli*—dirent: *Gran lastima es que no tañe la guitarra*, qui le tenta de leur donner de son luth par les oreilles, et cecy me faict croire qu'encor y doibt il avoir quenque scavant qui sçait faire dire à cest instrument quelque chose de bon."

69. Ibid., 1160. Letter by Chièze, July 19, 1673. "Los tonos, Señor, son muy Griegos, pero en la garganta de los músicos de aca, y en sus enredados parosismos, no les falta gracia, mayormente siendo ayudados de harpas, vihuelas y xirimias, a qui vienen unos muy celebrados. De la cifra de guitarra no hablaré mas palabra, y procuraré hallar algun discreto virtuoso, a quien se pueda enseñar la música que Vuestra Señoría fue serbida remitirme de su composición." It is certainly remarkable that Chièze mentioned vihuelas in 1673. He probably knew the difference between the guitar and the vihuela very well, but it could be that he nevertheless used the term *vihuela* to indicate a guitar, or even a viol.

70. Ibid., 1164. Letter to Chièze August 11, 1673. "*Los tonos humano-bestiados* me sont venus, et *ad nauseam sufficit* d'avoir veu, à quoy est decheu le beau génie Espagnol, qui a autrefois inspiré les grandes ames des Seneques, des Lucains et du reste de ces demi-dieux que je vous ay nommez par le passé. Je ne comprens pas cependant que veult dire cest *humano* en musique; est-ce que les bestes chantent le reste?"

71. Ibid., 1173. Letter to Chièze, October 3, 1673. "Vostre derniere du 13ᵉ Septembre m'a porté le dernier de vos *tonos*, et je suis fort content que ce soit le dernier, jugeant de plus en plus, à quel point de bestialité ces mi-Africains sont parvenus. Qui a jamais ouy nommer un *villancico*—que je pourroy nommer une gigue ou vaudeville—*al santissimo Sacramento*? Et puis, au lieu d'un motet ou pièce d'église des plus graves, aller faire rouler cela sur un fa, la la la. Quel diable a tourné l'esprit de ces nepveux de Séneque, de Lucain et de tant d'autres lumières de l'antiquité?"

72. Ibid., 1217. Chièze to Huygens, August 12, 1677. "Voicy des erres de la guitarre que je vous ay promise, Monsieur, et des pièces de la main du même homme qui s'est chargé du soin de vous en faire une, qu'il dit devoir estre de vostre goust, car il y a icy, à ce qu'il dit, un des plus célèbres ouvriers de l'urope. La guitarre est achevée, mais il désire de la garder pendant l'hyver pour, au cas que le bois vint à se tourmenter, y porter le remède *yassentar la obra*. Pour toute récompense on demande vostre censure, Monsieur, sur les pièces incluses, un peu de communication des vostres et de celles que vous pourrez avoir de France, *con advertencia* que la tablature cy-jointe est à l'Italienne."

73. As can be gleaned from the catalogue of the auction of Huygens's estate in 1688 (pp. 61–62), now in the Museum Meermanno in The Hague (MMW 112 D 012), Huygens was in possession of a large number of tablatures for the lute, as well as other important instrumental and vocal works from France and Italy.

74. B-Lc Ms. 245; B-Bc Ms. S5615 and B-Bc Ms. II5551.

75. B-Bc Ms. S5615, Gent, c. 1730, preface. See appendix: Castillion, "Recueil des pièces de guitarre."

76. Ibid. The dedication in Corbetta's book of 1648 is to Archduke Leopold Wilhelm, and not to Albert, who died in 1621.

77. Ibid. "Fasse le Ciel que ce livre après ma mort tombe entre les mains d'un amateur qui puisse joüer de mes peines."

Chapter Three

1. Fortune, *Italian Secular Song*, 136–37: "The Spanish guitar was becoming more and more popular in Italy, and this led to a new practice favored by music publishers, especially by the commercially minded Vincenti: the practice of providing every song with letters for the guitar, even when, as in more serious songs, they were wildly inappropriate (in the same way do the publishers of popular sheet-music of today pepper their pages with tablature for the ukelele)."

2. Tyler and Sparks, *The Guitar*, 80. Also see Christensen, "The Spanish Baroque Guitar," 1–42. Christensen supposes that very often a second continuo instrument, for example the viola da gamba, would have reinforced the bass. See also Hall, *Baroque Guitar Stringing*, 19: "The bass line would often have been doubled by another instrument."

3. On the use of bass-line instruments, Borgir, *The Performance of the Basso Continuo*, 37: "When occurring in a dramatic work the monody was accompanied by at least two instruments, while a similar piece performed in a drawing room required only a chordal instrument. Since the musical style is the same, the difference in performance is very likely a result of acoustical considerations." The guitar's place was primarily in the drawing room, in an informal context. The guitar was mainly used for self-accompaniment, for which the support of a second instrument is not a matter of course. Borgir is much opposed to routinely including bass-line instruments in Baroque music.

4. Leopold, "Remigio Romano's Collections," 52.

5. From the title page of Martino Pesenti's *Arie a voce sola* (Venice, 1633), one of the many examples from the aria repertoire. Vincenti almost always includes the reference to the guitar, but printers from Rome also frequently mention the guitar as a possible instrument for accompaniment.

6. Compare Dean, *The Five-Course Guitar*, 253–54. Dean has found many examples of this typical "Phrygian guitar cadence," with a ♭VI replacing a iv⁶, resulting in a parallel ♭VI–V progression instead of iv⁶–V. On page 240 Dean remarks, "My use of Roman Numerals, then, is necessarily anachronistic. But there is an element of truth in this anachronism, in that cadences were becoming more indicative of larger-scale tonal function as the century progressed, with guitaristic dissonances being part of that trend." See chapter 7 for a discussion of dissonance and alfabeto.

7. "Avvertino, che se non troveranno in qualche loce di quest'opera l'Alfabetto concorde il Basso, l'animo dell'Autore è d'accompagnar la voce più che sii possibile, non curandosi in questo d'obligarsi à quello, essendo la Chitariglia priva di molte bone consonanze." Marini (1622), preface.

8. Milanuzzi, *Terzo scherzo*, 38, translated in Leopold, "Remigio Romano's Collections," 53. "Avverdovi che per esser vario l'affetto che rende il Chitarrone ò Spinetta, da quello della Chitarra alla Spagnola nel sonar queste Ariette, in molti luogi hò variata la notte nella ditta Chitarra da quella, che è assignata nel Basso fondamentale, poste per gl'altri stromenti, il tutto fatto per dar gli maggior vaghezza."

9. See Carter, "Caccini's *Amarilli*." A very early multipart version of "Amarilli" has been found in the so-called Bologna manuscript (I-Bu Ms 177/IV), a partbook that, according to Tyler (*The Guitar*, 39), was written around 1590. In the *Cancionero de Bezón* (ca. 1599) there is a version in alfabeto-text format, with very simple alfabeto harmonies. See Zuluaga, "Spanish Song."

10. We will see examples of that in the chapter about solo repertoire (chapter 4).

11. Strizich, "L'accompagnamento," 8–27.

12. Castaldi, *Primo mazzetto di fiori*, 18; translated in Gavito, *The Alfabeto Song*, 148. "Il quale digratia non si torca, perche l'Autore, come benissimo sà fare, non habbia messo l'A.B.C. della Chitarra Spagnolissima sopra ciascheduna di quest' Arie che si faria pur anch'egli lasciato portare a seconda dal uso moderno, s'ei non si fosse accorto che poco serve simil Pedanteria a chi non sà se non scartazzare, per mille spropositi che ne le cadenze occorrono mediante il geroglifico sudetto, e colui che sà non ha bisogno che se gl'insegni."

13. See O'Donnell, "Le rôle de l'alfabeto," 124. O'Donnell has found this song with similar alfabeto harmonies in two early alfabeto/text manuscripts, F-Pn Rés.Vmf. Ms. 50 and F-Pn Rés.Vmc Ms. 59. In Biagio Marini's *Arie, madrigali et corrente* of 1620, there is a song that has the same text, but a completely different melody. In Kapsberger's *Libro secondo di villanelle* (1619), the song "Aurilla mia" has almost the same melody but a completely different bass line.

14. Millioni, *Primo scielta di villanelle* (1627).

15. We find a similarly independent treatment of the basso continuo and the alfabeto, applied with some success, in works of Giovanni Pietro Berti (1627) and Carlo Milanuzzi (1622). The very simple bass lines from Andrea Falconieri's *Arie* (1616) and the charming ariette from Domenico Obizzi's 1627 collection, completely in accordance with the alfabeto harmonies, give the impression that perhaps here the guitar accompaniment even came first.

16. Treadwell, "The 'Chitarra Spagnola,'" 50. Treadwell gives examples from works by Landi (1620), Veneri (1621), Marini (1635), Francesca Caccini (1618), and others.

17. Ibid., 49–50. Rontani's collections from 1620, 1623, and 1625 state on the title page: "con l'alfabeto per la Chitarra in quelle più a proposito per tale stromento."

18. Ibid., 76–78.

19. See Baron, "Secular Spanish Song," 20–42.

20. The anonymous manuscript I-Rvat MS Chigi cod. L.VI.200 with Spanish texts and alfabeto from circa 1599 belonged to the "Duchessa di Traetta." In the Biblioteca Riccardiana in Florence, there are several manuscripts with Spanish and Italian song texts and alfabeto, in the hand of Francesco Palumbi. See Tyler and Sparks, *The Guitar*, 78–80.

21. Baron, "Secular Spanish Song," 24–25.

22. Perhaps the first collection of alfabeto songs from Venice, which includes tablature for the theorbo as well, is *Le stravaganza d'amore* (1616) by theorbist-guitarist Flamminio Corradi. Benedetto Sanseverino's *El segundo libro de los ayres, villançicos, y cancioncillas a la Española, y Italiana* was published in the same year in Milan. In two other early Venetian collections listed in Dean ("The Five-Course Guitar," 56) there is no alfabeto, even though the guitar is mentioned as an option for the accompaniment.

23. As Gary Boye has argued convincingly in "The Case of the Purloined Letter Tablature," Foriano Pico's tutor (from Naples) was not published in 1608, as was often supposed, but probably in 1698.

24. Manuscript sources with alfabeto from around 1600 appear all to have a southern origin.

25. This is also the case in Benedetto Sanseverino's *El segundo libro de los ayres, villançicos, y cancioncillas a la Española, y Italiana* (1616).

26. Dean, "The Five-Course Guitar," 89.

27. Ibid., 138–39.

28. Ibid., 205.

29. Ibid., 127. "This influence operates not only at the editorial level, in the choice of alfabeto symbols, but also at the compositional level, in that these songs tend to be composed in a style that is amenable to strummed guitar accompaniment. It follows, therefore, that the adoption and adaptation of alfabeto symbols in Italian canzonettas reflects an ongoing, mutual influence between an orally transmitted performance practice and the composition and performance of strophic chamber song with continuo notation."

30. In his dissertation, Alexander Dean gives good examples of this practice.

31. Millioni's version (ex. 3.4) ends with a typical guitaristic "minor passacaglia" cadenza O-L-C-O (G minor, C minor with an added ninth, D major, G minor). See also example 3.5b.

32. Strohm, "Unwritten and Written Music," 229.

33. For example, in I-Bc MSV 280 (see ex. 7.3) and I-Fn MS Fondo Landau Finaly Mus. 175 (see ex. 4.2b). Also see example 4.4, a spagnoletta for three guitars by Foscarini.

34. Variations on the ciaccona and the passacaglia in battuto-pizzicato style can be found in a great number of sources after 1630; the first printed ostinato variations in mixed battuto-pizzicato style from Italy appear in Foscarini's *Libro terzo*, which was published in that year.

35. Dean, "The Five-Course Guitar," 239–58.

36. Cadences like this, resulting in a minor harmony (V–i), are another characteristic feature of alfabeto repertoire.

37. See example 7.3, measures 3–5. In chapter 7, we will discuss the use of the L chord in more detail.

38. Griffiths, "Strategies," 69–70: "No trained polyphonist would have written a passage of deliberate parallel fifths . . . such as the one that concludes the refrain of this song. The most probable explanation is that it is a progression transposed directly from the fingerboard of the guitar into a polyphonic context. This progression falls under the fingers with the greatest of ease, moving along the upper three strings using common chord positions, and is highly effective guitar writing." As Alexander Dean shows, this method stands in marked contrast to the way in which polyphonic Neapolitan villanelle were provided with (non-practical) alfabeto.

39. Even if Millioni had created the alternative alfabeto accompaniment to "Tirinto mio" and other songs himself, we have no way of telling whether he had identified the alternative chord progression in measures 4–5 of example 3.4 as a passacaglia pattern, or if it was merely used as one of the most common cadential formulas of the time.

40. See Leopold, "Remigio Romano's Collections," 56. Leopold has discussed concordances of songs from the collections of Giovanni Pietro Berti and Remigio Romano. If, for example, we compare Romano's alfabeto for "Chi con lima pungente" (1618) with the version from Berti's *Cantade et arie* (1627), it appears that Romano (or whoever else was responsible for it) has made his own alfabeto settings to Berti's bass line, making use of the *scala di musica per B quadro*. Apparently, this song was available to Romano long before it appeared in the printed collection of the composer, and Berti may have added his own, different alfabeto chords at a later stage, when preparing the publication of his 1627 collection.

41. See Miller, "New Information," 27–28.

42. "Gabriello Chiabrera (1552–1638) was an influential Italian poet and librettist. The short, varied verses and novel, often symmetrical internal schemes of his

canzonettas and *scherzi* (the latter a term he introduced) were natural aids to musical organization and attracted many song-writers in the early 17th century, such as Caccini, Peri, Monteverdi (the majority of the *Scherzi musicali* of 1607 are to Chiabrera's texts), Francesco Rasi, Stefano Landi and others." *Grove Music Online*, s.v. 'Chiabrera, Gabriello,' by Barbara R. Hanning, accessed April 4, 2010, http://www.oxfordmusiconline.com.

43. See Murata, "Guitar *Passacaglie* and Vocal *Arie*," 81–116. Also see Dean, "The Five-Course Guitar," 141.

44. Russell, "Radical Innovations," 153.

45. See Montesardo, *Nuova inventione d'intavolatura* (Florence: Marescotti, 1606), fol. 5v: "Avertendo ancora che chi vorrà farlo più soave bisognarà sonare su la rosa, alcuna volta vicino il manico, & anco per addolcire alcuna volta sù l'istesso manico. . . . Chi vorrà haver una bella e leggiadra mano su la Chitarra, è necessario prima, e principalmente tener la mano relassa dall'attaccatura di essa, quanto sia possibile, tanto che diventi leggiera; che cosi farà molto leggiadra al sonare, e poi batter le corde dolcemente con tre, ò quattro dite in modo di arpeggiare, e non tutte insieme che cosi farebbono un gran fracasso, & oltre che il suono sarebbe crudo, darebbe gran noia all'udito."

46. See example 4.7.

47. In a few collections with arias, there are also purely instrumental battuto dances, as in Carlo Milanuzzi's *Secondo scherzo delle ariose vaghezze*. See also the accompaniment by Sanseverino in example I.2.

48. In the stock harmonic progressions of ostinato variations, the bass (the lowest notes) is a result of the successive chords. In the entry on the chaconne in the *The New Grove Dictionary of Music and Musicians* (1980), Richard Hudson observes: "The *chacona* originated as a dance-song apparently in Latin America and became popular in Spain early in the seventeenth century. At the same time it was imported, together with the five-course guitar, into Italy, where certain harmonic progressions that had developed as accompaniment to the dance were transformed into bass melodies that were used throughout Europe during the Baroque period in a technique of variation similar to that of the *passacaglia*."

49. Compare example 5.14, showing how Foscarini realized accompaniment in sixteenth notes.

50. In Spain, continuo groups with guitars were probably normally used for theatrical performances, to accompany vocal genres and dance. There is little evidence, however, showing a link between ensembles including guitars and the sonata repertoire with solo instruments from the later seventeenth century.

51. The extant song accompaniments in chord notation, mostly cifras, are almost without exception from the second half of the seventeenth century or later. The accompaniments of the songs of José Marin, an unique example of a realized basso continuo for guitar from Spain, date probably from the last decades of the century.

52. Biagio Marini, opus 22 (1655).

53. Selfridge-Field, "Instrumentation and Genre," 63. It is very well possible that the alfabeto was included with a certain player in mind, from the circles around the then nineteen-year-old Ferdinando Maria (1636–79), elector of Bavaria, to whom this work is dedicated.

54. Even in Marini's opus 22, there are many alfabeto chords that are troublingly in conflict with the prevailing harmonies, particularly when more uncommon chords are concerned, such as E-flat major or C minor, as at the ending of the "Corrente

quarta" or in the entire *Sinfonia sesto tuono*. Major and minor harmonies are frequently mixed up. Occasionally it seems as if the alfabeto chords belong to only one of the instrumental parts, which could perhaps be performed as a solo with guitar accompaniment.

55. The two guitar parts in tablature from the *Pièces de concer* [*sic*] from Antoine Carré's *Livre de pieces de guitarre* (ca. 1675) are both indicated as "dessus,"—solo parts to be performed with a bass instrument.

56. Corbetta, *La guitarre royalle* (1671), 8: "I'y ay mis l'exemple dans les chansons à trois parties avec la basse continue, et dessous, la mesme basse en tablature, c'est pour accompagner."

57. For this type of accompaniment a guitar strung with two bourdons is needed, as will be argued in chapter 5.

58. See example 5.12.

59. In his preface, Grenerin describes the instrumentation of the Simphonies, with two *dessus de violon* and a *basse de viole*. Grenerin probably used a guitar with two bourdon strings for basso continuo.

60. The subject of how the guitar was used in basso continuo will be discussed in more detail in chapter 5.

61. There are plucked chords even in Matteis's most archaic *Examples* (see ex. 5.16).

62. Campion, *Traité d'accompagnement* (1716), 19. Also see chapter 5. There is one important manuscript from Spain with more than fifty songs (*tonos humanos*) by José Marin (GB-Cfm Ms. Mus. 727), with a fully realized guitar continuo, in pizzicato only.

63. For Agazzari's original text, see appendix.

64. "Medesimamente li stromenti di corde, alcuni contengono in loro perfetta armonia di parti, quale è l'Organo, Gravicembalo, Leuto, Arpadoppia etc: alcuni l'hanno imperfetta, quale è Cetera ordinaria, Lirone, Chitarrina: et altri poco, ò niente, como Viola, Violino, Pandora etc."

65. Calvi, *Intavolatura de chitarra e chitarriglia* (1646), 24: "Le seguenti suonate possono servire anche per la chitarriglia, ma sono veramente per la chitarra."

66. See chapter 6. Taken like this, it would show that for Calvi the music in pizzicato from the second part of his book was better suited for a guitar with bourdons.

67. Boye, "Giovanni Battista Granata," 65.

68. An anonymous Neapolitan painting from the seventeenth century shows a guitar with endpins, reproduced in Caliendo, *La chitarra battente*, 125, illus. 27–28.

69. Barbieri, "Cembalaro, organaro, chitarraro," *Recercare* 1 (1989): 170–71. My thanks to Mimmo Peruffo for this information.

70. Millioni, *Corona*, preface: "Chi volesse ancor"imparare à far le lettere per sonar il Chitarrino, overo Chitarra Italiana per via di numeri, e linee, si servi delli medesimi numeri, e linee, lasciando però la quinta corda, & osservi la medesima regola."

Chapter Four

1. There are a modest number of manuscripts with songs (texts only), accompanied by *cifras*, in a format comparable to the alfabeto books by Remigio Romano. Often these were written on single sheets, with music from *entremeses*, songs and dances (*bailes*), that were performed in theater plays. See Yakely, "New Sources."

2. Ayala Ruiz, "Vicente Espinel," 10.
3. Stein, *Songs of Mortals*, 340.
4. This book was recently rediscovered. It could very well be the same as the *Guitarra española y sus diferencias de sones*, mentioned by bibliographer Nicolas Antonio in the earliest known edition of *Biblioteca Hispana*, printed in 1672. *Guitarra española* by "Francesco Corbera" was dedicated to King Philip IV. The actual date of print is uncertain. A number of Spanish manuscripts has been preserved, with *cifras*, the Spanish chord notation, as only a few Spanish manuscripts with alfabeto exist. From this it can be deduced that in Spain the influence of Italian guitar music must have been limited. See Yakely, "New Sources."
5. Certain cities in Italy had strong political ties with the Spanish kingdom. The city of Milan was under Spanish rule until the early eighteenth century. A number of books with alfabeto were printed there. Giulio Banfi's *Il maestro della chitarra* (Milan, 1653), with music in alfabeto and in mixed tablature, came out with Philip IV's imprimatur. Corbetta's second book (1643) was also printed in Milan.
6. Even the fingering of this fragment is identical with the usual guitar ciaccona. This is possible because Piccinini only used the first five courses of his lute, with the exception of the third course, which is tuned differently.
7. *Nuova inventione d'intavolatura, per sonare li balletti, sopra la chitarra Spagniuola, senza numberi, e note; per mezzo della quale da se stesso ogn'uno senza Maestro potrà imparare.*
8. As we will see in chapter 7, such harmonic experiments can be found already in a Roman manuscript from about 1614.
9. "Terzo, Quando à detti Segni ò in giù, ò in sù doppo la lettera, si troverà un Punto simile V.g.B; si darà al suono di detta botta un poco più di tempo delle altre; e quando saranno due V.g.B: altrettanto di più, cioè, alla botta d'un punto solo, si darà il tempo della semiminima, & à quella di due punti, il tempo della minima." Foscarini circa 1630, preface.
10. Thomas Christensen writes: "Comparing the notation, sound, and function of this music to popular music today, it is astonishing to see how little has changed over the last 400 years." Christensen, "The Spanish Baroque Guitar," 8.
11. See the last line of example 4.3. For an overview of ornamental strums, see Boye, "Giovanni Battista Granata," 31–34, or Charles Wolzien, *Early Guitar Anthology II*.
12. See Foscarini, *Cinque libri*, 135.
13. Tuning instructions for guitar ensembles, "Regola per incordare le Chitarre per sonare di concerto," can be found in Giovanni Ambrosio Colonna's *Intavolatura di chitarra alla spagnuola* (1620). In Foscarini's first book there are also works for three guitars, tuned a fifth apart (e.g., e, a, d', f♯', b'; A, d, g, b, e' and D, G, c, e, a), an ensemble that is not described in Foscarini's own introduction.
14. On p. 14, below the pieces in alfabeto, it reads: "Il fine delle Sonate semplice."
15. For a discussion of Foscarini's dissonances, see chapter 7.
16. See example 7.12.
17. Equal fret-placing was advocated by Nicolao Doizi de Velasco in his *Nuovo modo de cifrar* of 1640.
18. Parallelism, as a compositional technique with a free handling of harmonic theory, found a place again in classical guitar music in the twentieth century, with the quotatation of Debussy's *Soirée dans Grenade* in the *Homenaje* by Manuel de Falla. In the works of Heitor Villa-Lobos, particularly in the studies, the shifting of complete chords is a structural principle. After the 1950s, it became a standard way of playing rhythm guitar in rock music, made even more blunt with the introduction of so-called power chords in the last decades of the millennium.

19. "Delle Sonate, dette Pizziccate, non ne parlo più che tanto, havendo poste più per abbellimento dell'opera, che per altro rispetto; poiche sò benissimò esser più proprie del liuto, che della Chitara." Foscarini (ca. 1630), fol. ii.

20. Corbetta, *La guitarre royalle* (1671), 8: "Et parcequ'il y a tousjours des envieux qui pouroient dire que ma maniere de iouer est trop difficile, a cause qu'une partie de mes pieces aproche de la maniere du Luth, je leur pourrois responder avec verité, que je ne scay pas un seul accord sur cet instrument, et je n'ay iamais eu d'autre inclination que pour la Guitare seule."

21. Dinko Fabris, program notes for Paul Beier's CD *Michelagnolo Galilei: Sonate from Il primo libro d'intavolatura di liuto (1620)*, Magnatune, accessed November 25, 2008, http://www.magnatune.com/artists/beier.

22. Foscarini (ca. 1630), preface.

23. In Foscarini's third book, there are transcriptions of two "Corrente francese" by René Mesangeau (the originals are in CZ-Pnm IV.G.18, fol. 69v–70v; Mesangeau, *Oeuvres*, no. 4 and 5). See Goy, "Three versions," 59.

24. James Tyler (*The Guitar*, 66) has localized the concordant source, a *Courante Gauthier* for lute, found in GB-Cfm MS Mus 689, f. 37.

25. Albert was married to Isabella, the Infanta of Spain, daughter of Philip II.

26. *Grove Music Online*, s.v. "style brisé," by David Ledbetter, accessed February 14, 2015, http://www.oxfordmusiconline.com.

27. As in example 5.9.

28. Such chord chains are shown in example 7.8.

29. Foscarini (ca. 1630), preface: "'Le Sonate, come Corrente, Balletti & Gagliarde, che vanno nello stile Francese; si devanno sonare quietamente, solo con darle spirito conveniente, conforme al tempo, che haveranno sopra."

30. See Paolo Paolini's preface to the facsimile edition of Corbetta's *Varii scherzi di sonate* (1648). This incipit probably appears for the first time in guitar music in an allemande from Bartolotti's *Libro primo*, 71.

31. Bartolotti, *Secondo libro*, 64. The prelude concludes with a section notated in long "measures" of unequal length.

32. For the original text, see appendix.

33. A-Ila Ms. Nr. 533. The second part of the manuscript is in Italian tablature, possibly written by another hand. It contains very simple pieces with a more Italian character, like the ciaccona and passacaglia. There is no indication of the tuning. Commissaire Dupille describes the re-entrant tuning he used.

34. For example, in the Suite in A minor, tracks 14–19 of the audio files.

35. Corbetta's songs are published in *La guitarre royalle* (1671), 83–98.

36. It can even be asked if the guitar is at all adequate for the scale of the music of Robert de Visée. With respect to voice leading and the representation of harmony (and even the tessitura), the alternative versions for the theorbo of the dances, known from his guitar books, are somehow more comfortable.

37. In a few works by Santiago de Murcia and François Lecocq of around 1730, the guitar was used in a different way, with more emphasis on *cantabile* lines, as in an Adagio of Lecocq (B-Bc.Ms.S5615, 67). De Murcia also arranged some compositions of Corelli.

38. In the preface to his book of 1682 he remarks: "J'ai tasché de me conformer au goust des habiles gens, en donnant a mes pieces, autant que ma foiblesse me la pû permettre le tour de celles de l'inimitable Monsieur de Lulli."

39. Corbetta, preface to *La guitarre royalle* (1674): "Pour satisfaire l'inclination que j'ay tousjours euë pour la Guitarre, J'ay voulu voir en plusieurs endroits de l'Europe

ceux qui en faisoient profession: Et comme ils me prioient avec instance de donner au public quelques compositions suivant leur maniere. J'en ay fait imprimer
a plusieurs fois pour les contenter. Il y a deux ans que Je fis parestre un Livre qui
contenoit differentes sortes de manieres. Il y a avoit des pieces pour ceux qui jouoi-
ent mediocrement de cet Instrument et pour ceux qui se picquent d'en bien jouer.
Aujourdhuy que l'occasion se presente de donner encore quelques Nouvelles compositions, J'ay voulou me conformer a la maniere qui plaist le mieux a sa Majesté,
veuque parmis les autres elle est la plus chromatique. La plus delicate, et la moins
embarrassante. J'espere que ce grand Monarque qui m'a quelquesfois honoré de
ses Commandemens, ajoustera a ma felicité l'honneur de son approbation et de sa
protection. Pour vous si vous en faites cas par leur propre merite, ou par la cous-
tume des François de marcher tousiours sur les traces de leur grand Roy Je vous en
seray tous iours oblige."

40. Corbetta's earlier books were in Italian tablature. It is likely that some French guitarists made transcriptions in French tablature for their own convenience.

41. Pinnell, "Role of Francesco Corbetta," 226.

42. In certain works, Milhaud wrote harmonies with an accumulation of fourths.
Especially at the lower end of Corbetta's most dissonant chords, we find this accumulation of fourths, corresponding with the tuning of the guitar (the "open" barre
brings forth a transposition of the tuning in fourths); see example 7.15.

43. Tyler and Sparks, *The Guitar*, 124.

44. Pinnell, "Role of Francesco Corbetta," 228. Pinnell supposes that several composers from England were influenced by Corbetta, such as Matthew Locke, Michael
Farinel, and perhaps even Johann Jacob Froberger, who was in London in 1662.
Pinnel does not give supporting information for these assumptions. His judgement
of Corbetta is very positive: "Corbetta is a major figure, if not the innovator to have
permanently stylized the later folia, the slower French sarabande, the passacaglia
and the allemande. The medium of guitar music was unusually forward-looking in
the baroque period, as witnessed by the development of these forms in Corbetta's
output" (295).

45. GB-Ob. Ms. Mus. Sch.C94 (the "Gallot manuscript") and B.Lc 245; also Carré's
book from circa 1675.

46. Pinnell, "Role of Francesco Corbetta," 267.

47. For example, the *Allemande du Roy*, from page 1 of *La guitarre royalle* (1671). In
Gallot's version, the music is changed considerably (mostly simplifications). It gives
the impression that the tablature was not copied from *La guitarre royalle*, but rather
was written from memory. Because of the confusing tuning of the instrument, this
must have been a very difficult task. It remains possible that the tablatures were
copied from an alternative source, possibly even also by Corbetta. Considering the
poor solutions, however, this is not very likely.

48. Pinnell, "Role of Francesco Corbetta," 226–27.

49. It is remarkable that at other places in the Gallot manuscript there are the same
"barre fingering harmonies" that were removed from Corbetta's works. Apparently,
this way of indicating a barre was used more often, even if it was confusing for
performance.

50. About Remy Médard's book, James Tyler remarks (*The Guitar*, 110): "Médard's
book is an interesting collection of preludes, sarabands, minuets, and the like that
require the same degree of technical skill as the music in Corbetta's two books
of French-style music. Unlike Corbetta's, however, Médard's music is distinguished

by its ingratiating melodies, and foreshadows the *galant* style of de Visée and Campion." And (on page 109) about the *Pièces de guitaire* (1663) by François Martin: "Stylistically, the only comparable guitar music is found in Corbetta's second *Guitarre royalle* of 1674, to which Martin's compares most favorably." Richard Pinnell ("The Role," 264) is less enthusiastic about Médard: "The pleasant, simple style is typical of the ordinary guitar music of the period: it makes up for its lack of excitement with charm. It would be good music for instructing beginners, however, for dissonances are few and the rhythms are totally regular." Tyler (*The Guitar*, 109) is also very positive about Antoine Carré's music from his book from about 1675: "A larger collection than his first, it contains solo music of the same high calibre." Notably, the mediocre pirated versions of compositions by Corbetta in this book still compare favorably to Carré's own works.

Chapter Five

1. Tyler speaks of the situation in southern Italy, but doesn't comment on any other region. Tyler, "Role of the Guitar."
2. They appear in the books of Briceño (1626) and Mersenne (1636), both published in Paris.
3. Amat (1596), Montesardo (1606), Sanseverino (1620 and 1622), and Foscarini (1629). As will be argued in chapter 6, the tuning instructions by Abatessa (1627) and Millioni (1627) also imply bourdons.
4. "When the chords are played on a guitar without bourdons, any inversions are virtually inaudible. Even on a Baroque guitar strung *with* bourdons, the effect is still one of nearly inversion-free block harmonies." Tyler and Sparks, *The Guitar*, 40.
5. Hall, *Baroque Guitar Stringing*, 4–5.
6. For the thumb, this would happen with the upstroke.
7. Rousseau comments: "Les bourdons filés ont deux inconvéniens, l'un d'user de couper les touches; l'autre plus grand, est de dominer trop sur les autre cordes, & d'en faire perdre le son final par la durée de leur, principalement dans les batteries. Il est des accords où ils peuvent bien faire, c'est lorsqu'ils produisent le son fondamental; mais comme cela n'arrive pas le plus souvent, il vaut mieux s'en tenir aux bourdons simples, a-moins qu'on ne veuille que pincer." Translation in Hall, *Baroque Guitar Stringing*, 27.
8. "Y a mas destro, que con bordones, si hazes la letra, o punto E, que es Delasolre, en la musica sale la quinta vacante en quarta baxo, y confunde el principal baxo, y le dà algo de imperfeccion, conforme el contrapunto enseña." Sanz, *Instrucción*, fol. 8 (translation by Monica Hall).
9. As shown in example 5.15.
10. "Y quando se quiera tañer con fugas no son tanpocos sus puntos que passen diez y siete, termino bastante a dilatarse en qualquier fuga, y por esta razon me parece mejor el encordarla con bordones en la quarta y quinta cuerda, y no sin ellos, porque asi es mas sonora, y mas semejante a los puntos de las bozes naturales. Que aun que de una, o de otra manera no se libran algunas consonancias de las quartas en las bozes baxas, esto se puedo suplir, quando se tañen de rasgado." Translation from Hall, *Baroque Guitar Stringing*, 6.
11. Also compare Bartolotti's chord notation in example 5.3, below.

12. Boye, "Performing Seventeenth-Century Italian Guitar Music," 189.

13. Hall, *Baroque Guitar Stringing*, 14.

14. Tyler and Sparks, *The Guitar*, 69, concerning campanelas: "Although Bartolotti provides no details of tuning or stringing, this particular technique requires a guitar
that is strung without a bourdon on the fifth course (that is, with both strings tuned
an octave higher than the fifth string of a modern guitar), and probably with none
on the fourth course either."

15. See Mattax, *Accompaniment on Theorbo and Harpsichord*, 19: "Seventeenth-century theorbo players were not overly troubled by mistakes in voice leading or chord inversion resulting from the peculiar tuning of the top strings. Bartolotti, for example,
writes out a progression of seventh chords in which . . . [the] chords are inverted."
Lynda Sayce, however, makes it clear in her dissertation ("The Development of
Italianate Continuo Lutes," 133) that methods for the theorbo from France, like
the *Livre de theorbe* by Henry Grenerin and Bartolotti's *Table pour apprendre facilement
à toucher le theorbe sur la basse continuë*, were in fact most likely written for amateurs
playing theorbed lutes in archlute tuning. On those instruments, the first two
courses were not tuned down an octave, as on the theorbo proper. On those lutes,
all chords will be grammatically correct.

16. There is a very thin, G-major chord with just the highest three courses in Corbetta's
alfabeto falso chart. It consists only of the root, third, and octave (g-b-g'). A position
like this is not possible for G minor, because of the B. We could play the B♭ on the
third course, but that would result in a more difficult P chord in third position.

17. Today this "small F major chord" (alfabeto G tagliate) is frequently used on the
six-string guitar. The difference is that on a modern guitar, a full barre would be
needed to include all strings.

18. Compare Boye, "Giovanni Battista Granata," 79: "This older style demonstrates that
guitarists could be more concerned with chord inversions than has been previously
thought. Inversions frequently found among the alfabeto chords are rarely present
when the chords are written out; indeed, when using pizzicato notes in general
most guitarists of the period were careful with the bass. Strummed chords, on the
other hand, are frequently found in inversion, even at cadence points, and were
apparently thought of as harmonic units without a true bass."

19. This corresponds to the tuning information from Corbetta's book of 1639; see
example 6.3.

20. See example 5.15.

21. Sanz, *Instrucción*, Primer tratado, 1: "For those who wish to use the guitar for noisy
music, or to accompany the bass of a song or a sonata, the guitar is better strung
with bourdons than without them."

22. Many of the works in the first and second section of Sanz's book (*tomo* 1 and 2) consist of thin pizzicato textures, for which re-entrant tuning would work well. In *tomo*
3 there are the Passacalles, of Italian inspiration, with a stronger battuto-pizzicato
character.

23. Sanz, *Instrucción*, Primer tratado, 1.

24. Visée, *Livre de guitarre* (1682), 4: "Et ie prie ceux qui scavrons bien la composition,
et qui ne connoistreront pas la guitarre, de n'estre point scandalizez, s'ils trouvent
que ie m'escarte quelque fois des règles, c'est l'instrument qui le veut, et il faut satisfaire l'oreille preferablement a tout."

25. Strizich, "L'accompagnamento," 26.

26. Like Corbetta, Visée often uses the notes of the high octave of the fourth course in treble melodies (see ex. 5.10).

27. If the French tuning were used, with only a bourdon on the fourth course, this chord would be in $^6_4$ position.

28. The same applies to Grenerin's basso continuo instructions.

29. Strizich, "L'accompagnamento," 18: "Benché i suoi esempi contengano alvuni accordi rasgueadi (batteries), predomina il pizzicato, È anche significativo il fatto che Grenerin sembri evitare di accompagnare le note alte di basso con accordi che contengano suoni piú gravi della nota scritta di basso."

30. In 1647 Ferdinando Valdambrini published his *Libro secondo d'intavolatura di chitarra a cinque ordini*, in Rome. In this book, intended for re-entrant tuning, there is a chart for accompaniment, with chords in every possible inversion. The chart includes many alfabeto chords with barres, providing three to five different positions to choose from (with different alfabeto chords) for every given bass note. The result is that the inversion of the chords is random. It is the inevitable consequence of the limited range of the guitar in this tuning; the only practical way to play continuo on it was probably to completely neglect the bass line and just choose the "correct" harmony, irrespective of inversions. It is probably not for nothing that Sanz, unlike Valdambrini, recommended the use of two bourdons for continuo, despite his preference for re-entrant tuning for solo repertoire.

31. Matteis, *The False Consonances of Musick*, p. a4.

32. By coincidence, only the very first chord of this example seems to be strangely inverted; however, if we emphasize just the high octave (the B♭) of the fifth course, it can be used for the middle voice.

33. Jocelyn Nelson has compared the chord positions in Matteis's tutor with three different tunings. In her article "Matteis and Seventeenth-Century Guitar Accompaniment," Nelson concludes that "there is not much difference in the accuracy of chord position between the tunings: bass note position is not a priority with guitar accompaniment." It should be taken into account, however, that Matteis did distinguish between battuto and pizzicato. The vast majority of the plucked chords would be in proper position in the tuning with two bourdons, but not in French tuning.

34. Campion, *Addition au traité d'accompagnement*, 38: "On ne doit pas se piquer pour l'accompagnement de cet instrument, de monter du ton grave à l'aigu. Il suffit que la verité de la notte y soit; & nous voyons même que, sur le clavecin, òu le ton grave & aigu sont possibles, les accompagnateurs, par plaisir ou par indifférence, prennent un degré pour l'autre. . . . Cette indifférence étant rendue suportable aux oreilles."

35. See on the use of bass-line instruments: Borgir, *The Performance of the Basso Continuo*, 37: "When occurring in a dramatic work the monody was accompanied by at least two instruments, while a similar piece performed in a drawing room required only a chordal instrument. Since the musical style is the same, the difference in performance is very likely a result of acoustical considerations." The guitar was used for informal music making in the first place, at home in the drawing room. The instrument was mainly used for self-accompaniment. Borgir criticizes the routine inclusion of bass-line instruments in baroque music.

36. Italics mine. "Qu'on ne se prévienne point sans raison contre la Guitare. J'avoüerai avec tout le monde qu'elle n'est pas aussi forte d'harmonie que le Clavecin, ny le Théorbe. Cependant je la croy suffisante pour accompagner une voix: au moins

est-ce la justice qu'on luy a rendu, quand on me l'a etendu toucher; pour ce qui est des accords, je ne luy en connois point d'impossibles, elle a par dessus les autres la facilité du transport & du toucher, & par-dessus le Theorbe, les Parties d'accompagnement non renversees, par consequent plus chantantes" (Campion 1716, 19).

37. Kevin Mason, "François Campion's Secret," 83.
38. See chapter 4. The style of Corbetta's accompaniment is very ambiguous. It is midway between a harmonic-rhythmic chordal support in the old alfabeto tradition (characterized by the typical *trillo* and *repicco* strokes); in certain places the bass line is followed more carefully, and then played pizzicato. Still, an approach like this, making use of an abundance of non-alfabeto chord patterns, is far removed from the simple alfabeto chord strumming of the 1620s. Because Corbetta has made allowance for the harmonic implications of the figured bass, the accompaniment can be performed together with other bass-line instruments, without any harmonic conflict.

Chapter Six

1. This is what others had supposed before, as well. See, for example, Eugen Schmitz, "Zur Geschichte der Guitarre," *Monatshefte für Musikgeschichte* XXV (1903), reprinted in *Gitarre und Laute* 5 (1990): 21–25.
2. "In transcribing the tablature, stress was laid above all on preserving the correct musical impression, even occasionally at the expense of an all-too-literal transcription which would have given a false effect. It was necessary, for example, to make allowance for the original octave-tuning of the two lowest pairs of strings." Karl Scheit, from his introduction to the transcription of Visée's *Suite in G Minor*.
3. Murphy, "The Tuning of the Five-Course Guitar," 49–63.
4. Murphy presents the French tuning as aa, dd′ [*sic*], gg, bb, e′. with the high and low strings of the fourth course inverted.
5. See example 6.11.
6. Tonazzi, *Liuto, vihuela, chitarra*, 100. Tonazzi gives a description with an example in staff notation of campanela passage by Roncalli (1692), with the notes of the bourdons included. "Noi siamo convinti che in questo come in altri passi costituiti da note *intenzionalmente* [italics in the original] per gradi congiunti ed in cui ogni suono viene sistematicamente ricavato da corde via via diverse, i chitarristi dell'epoca intendevano ottenere dei suoni molto legati ed amalgamati con suggestiva raffinatezza timbrica. Effetto questo che, anche se non nei minimi particolari, con la dovuta accortezza nel suo insieme può venir ricreato pure sulle chitarra moderna."
7. Gill, "The Stringing of the Five Course Baroque Guitar," 370–71. Gill refers to an article by Patrizia Frosoli with new evidence from the workshop of Antonio Stradivari (which will be discussed below), "The *Museo Stradivariano* in Cremona." This was possibly the first mention of information from this source on this aspect of tuning.
8. Ibid., 370.
9. Richard Jensen, "The Development," 16. Jensen presents Giovanni Paolo Foscarini, Stefano Pesori (1648), Lodovico Monte's *Vago fior di virtu* (Venice, n.d.), and a manuscript source (I-Fr Ms.2774) in which the tuning is represented in staff notation.

10. Ibid., 10.

11. Murphy, "The Tuning," 49.

12. Jensen, "The Development," 19: "Based on the historical evidence presented above, it seems safe to conclude, as James Tyler has, that 'before 1650 most of the tablature sources required the type of tuning given by Amat (the so-called Italian tuning), and it was rare to find the more unusual one described above (i.e., Briceño's tuning) [the re-entrant tuning].' Internal evidence supports this statement, for it is only in late Italian music that the fourth and fifth courses play a melodic as well as an accompanying role." Jensen here refers to the article by Tyler, "The Renaissance Guitar."

13. Often the *repicci* from ciacconas of Pellegrini (1650) and Corbetta (1671) (audio ex. 20) are referred to as representing the tip of the iceberg. It is not so easy to tell if these more complex battuto patterns were much used outside the ciaccona genre, in other dances or in song accompaniment. What we find in battuto sources usually is very plain and straightforward (see ex. 4.3), without the obvious syncopated strumming usually heard in modern popular and Latin American styles.

14. Marin Mersenne, *Harmonie universelle*. It is sometimes supposed that Mersenne got his information about the stringing of the guitar from Hieronymus Kapsberger; however, the content of Kapsberger's correspondence with Mersenne is not known. Re-entrant tuning is also described in an early manuscript in French tablature (Fr-Psg Ms Rés. 2344) containing simple music with battuto and pizzicato elements.

15. The examples in Kircher's *Musurgia universalis* closely resemble those of Mersenne from twenty years earlier.

16. Boye, "Performing Seventeenth-Century Italian Guitar Music," 190.

17. This guitar player is also depicted together with a woman playing castanets and tambourine in a seventeenth-century picture (see fig. 2.2). The woman with tambourine also appears on a lost painting attributed to the seventeenth-century Dutch painter Hendrick Pot. It was part of the Goudstikker Collection Amsterdam in 1920.

18. This example is almost identical to the better-known charts from Foscarini's *Li cinque libri* (Rome, 1629–40).

19. From the time of Amat and Montesardo, the guitar in Italian tuning normally had high octaves on the fifth and fourth courses. It is not known if there was any tuning with a high octave only on the fifth course.

20. "À voce corista," Italian for *Chorthon* (as it was called by Praetorius), a pitch standard a semitone or a whole tone lower than the *Cammerthon* of organs and wind instruments. See Haynes, *A History of Performing Pitch*. In the tuning chart of *Quarta impressione del primo, secondo et terzo libro d'intavolatura* (1627) Pietro Millioni indicates to tune the fifth course to the third, stopping it at the second fret, probably to tune the a on the third course—the *voce corista*—to the high octave string of the fifth course. This method (already described by Amat) is also used in lute books where it is applied to the tuning of the octave-strung bass courses. For the rest, Millioni's tuning charts are almost identical to those of Pesori or Foscarini.

21. For original text, see appendix: Benedetto Sanseverino, *Il primo libro d'intavolatura* (1622).

22. Tyler and Sparks, *The Guitar*, 77: "This information could easily lead a modern player to the conclusion that the baroque guitar had bourdons on the fourth and fifth courses . . . however several manuscript sources that present precisely the same tuning chart come to an entirely different conclusion."

23. Ibid., 184, appendix.
24. For the text from Giulio Banfi's *Il maestro della chitarra*, see the appendix.
25. See Boye, "Giovanni Battista Granata," 69.
26. Only Foscarini's octave check (like the one in ex. 6.3a) is lacking, quite possibly because it would not fit on the page.
27. Giovanni Battista Granata, *Capricci armonici* (1646), preface. "Primeramente s'accordi la quinta corde, che non sia nè troppo alta, nè troppo bassa, cioè in tuono tale, che possano le altre ancora mantenersi conforme la grandezza della chitarra, e toccandola poi al quinto tasto la voce, che farà la detta quinta corda nel ditto tasto, la medesma voce, dovrà fare la quarta corda vacante similmente la voce, que sarà la terza corda al quarto tasto, la dovrà fare la seconda vacante, e similmente la voce, che sarà la seconda corda al quinto tasto, dovrà fare altresì la prima vacante."
28. There is a tuning chart in Stefano Pesori's book of circa 1675, but this is a manuscript copy of an earlier printed book.
29. For example, in the many reprints of Millioni's alfabeto books, originally from the 1620s. The tuning information corresponds largely to that from Corbetta's first book (1639) with a tuning chart and check in tablature (see ex. 6.3). In Millioni's books, they are accompanied by a verbal instruction that would result in a tuning with bourdons, but with no mention of high octave strings on the fourth and fifth courses.
30. Tyler and Sparks, *The Guitar*, 111–12.
31. See Hall, *Baroque Guitar Stringing*, 19 (and note 40). The same octave tuning on the "bass side" appears in Ribayaz's tuning instructions.
32. Tyler and Sparks, *The Guitar*, 111. The idea of playing the upper octave string alone was probably first mentioned in the literature in Tyler, *The Early Guitar* (1980).
33. Also mentioned in the vihuela and lute repertoire, by Capirola (ca. 1517), Fuenllana (1554), and Mouton (1699).
34. "In fact, most sources of mixed tablature, even those in which specific tuning instructions like Valdambrini's are not provided, tend to require a re-entrant tuning of at least the fifth course, without which the many unique effects typical of the style are difficult to achieve." Tyler, *The Guitar*, 78.
35. James Tyler, however, argues: "The reason for these re-entrant tunings becomes clear from the original tablatures: in much of the 'art' music for guitar (as opposed to exclusively strummed music), the high, re-entrant fifth course was used melodically in scale passage-work in conjunction with the other treble courses; rarely was the fifth course used as a bass. The fourth course too was used most often in the same fashion as the fifth. . . . On the whole, this music calls for the characteristic re-entrant tunings that were so important to the playing style and idioms employed during these periods and which made the guitar unique." *Grove Music Online*, s.v. "The five-course guitar" by James Tyler, accessed September 27, 2011, http://www.oxfordmusiconline.com.
36. In Foscarini's fourth book (ca. 1632), pp. 99–100, there is another (lute) type of campanela run, which does not make use of high octave strings of the fourth and fifth courses. Such runs can be compared to those in the Chaconne in *Les oeuvres de Pierre Gautier* (Rome, 1638).
37. For convenience, only the notes on the high strings of the fourth and fifth courses are given in the transcriptions.
38. There are about seven cascading scales (on pages 21, 25, 32, 35, 42, 44, and 45), in a book with 62 pages full of music. A few (on pp. 21 and 25) are A-minor scales; the rest are all in D major.

39. See Granata, *Capricci armonici*, 7 and 19. The scale run on page 19 has a "displaced" note g.

40. "Lacking information on tuning in the original sources, such as those of Granata and his Bolognese contemporaries, performers should choose a tuning and performance method that enables them to use both upper and lower octaves on the lowest two courses of the instrument." Boye, "Performing Seventeenth-Century Guitar Music," 192.

41. We also find campanela trills in Kapsberger's *Libro quarto* (1640) for chitarrone.

42. Gary Boye ("Performing Seventeenth-Century Italian Guitar Music," 191) mentions I.Bc Ms. AA 360 (c. 1660) and I:MOe Ms. Campori 612, "Regole per imparare a sonare la chitarra" (n.d.).

43. Similar anomalies can be found in Granata's *Novi capricci*, published in the same year (1674).

44. See Boye, "Performing Seventeenth-Century Italian Guitar Music," 192, footnote 21. Note the similarity between a hypothetical stringing with upper octaves on the lower three courses and the re-entrant tuning of the theorbo, an instrument that was played by several Bolognese guitarists.

45. For original text, see appendix: Sanz, *Instrucción*, Primer tratado, 8.

46. We should consider the possibility that Sanz had (at least) two guitars, one with re-entrant stringing and one strung with bourdons. See Hall, *Baroque Guitar Stringing*, 18. Hall assumes that "[professional] players may have used different instruments with different stringing for continuo playing and for solo work, and amateurs, if they took the trouble to learn how to accompany a bass line, may have done likewise." In Italian and French sources, however, this idea is never mentioned.

47. In one of the manuscripts of Jean-Baptiste de Castillion, there is a *passacaille dite Mariona* by "Lelio," loaded with campanelas. The parts for the "cythara" in his ensemble music, included in Kircher's *Musurgia universalis* of 1650, are probably for cittern, not guitar.

48. See Mischiati, *Indici, cataloghi e avvisi*, 253. In the *Indice de libri di muscia della libreria di Federico Franzini* (Rome 1676), there is a reference to the *Intavolatura di chitarra spagnola spizzicata* by Gio. Girolamo Kapsberger. My thanks to Anne Marie Dragosits for this little-known information.

49. "All exhibit the above features [well-developed melodic elements with elaborate passage work, ornamentation, campanelas, invertible counterpoint, increased use of high fingerboard positions to compensate for the loss of low notes, fourth and fifth courses minimally used, but integrated into melodic lines] to a greater or lesser degree and some may have been originally intabulated with a re-entrant tuning in mind." Hall, *Baroque Guitar Stringing*, 18.

50. Ibid., 25.

51. The same applies to Granata's first book (1646). See Boye, "Giovanni Battista Granata," 79: "This older style demonstrates that guitarists could be more concerned with chord inversions than has been previously thought. Inversions frequently found among the alfabeto chords are rarely present when the chords are written out; indeed, when using pizzicato notes in general most guitarists of the period were careful with the bass. Strummed chords, on the other hand, are frequently found in inversion, even at cadence points, and were apparently thought of as harmonic units without a true bass."

52. The French tuning is misrepresented here, seemingly by mistake, as re-entrant tuning aa,d'd',gg,bb,e'. The composers listed are Francesco Corbetta, Angelo Michele

Bartolotti, Giovanni Battista Granata, Robert de Visée, and Ludovico Roncalli. *Grove Music Online*, s.v. "The five-course guitar" by James Tyler, accessed November 9, 2008, http://www.oxfordmusiconline.com.

53. "Je vous avertis de mettre une Octave á la 4me corde de.la.re.sol [*sic*] parceque les deux unissons ne composent point d'harmonie." English translation by Hall, *Baroque Guitar Stringing*, 22.

54. In France there were probably guitarists who would have preferred the bourdon tuning. At that time there were many foreign players in Paris, including Italian actors (such as Tiberio Fiorelli, known as Scaramouche) and Spanish *chaconistas* and courtiers, associated with the guitar.

55. Pinnell, "The Role," 208. Pinnell supposed that Corbetta replaced the bourdon on his fifth course with a high a.

56. Manuscripts with Italian guitar music in French tablature (such as F-Pn Ms.Vm^7 675) generally are of a later date. Even if an individual guitarist (Gallot) started to collect music in this style in the late 1660s, we can hardly speak of a broader tradition at that time.

57. Halfway through the seventeenth century, Italian (lute) tablature was in decline. Antonio Carbonchi had his *Sonate di chitarra spagnola* (1640) printed in French tablature, saying, "Repeated requests by different students, in particular by German, French, and English gentlemen, have made me decide to publish this tablature in the French manner; I hope that in this way it will be more generally understood."

58. "Leur sotte tablature, qui met tous dessous dessus." See appendix: Huygens's letter to Sébastien Chièze of May 30, 1673.

59. See Hall, "A few more observations," 72. Hall refers to Michel Brenet, "La librairie musicale en France de 1653 à 1790 . . . ," *Sammelbände der internationalen Musik-Gesellschaft* 8 (1906–7), 414.

60. It is not known exactly when the printing of Carré's book was finished. French guitar books by composers such as Médard, Visée, Grenerin, and Campion were usually printed within a few weeks, sometimes even days, after having received royal permission. The same applies to Corbetta's second *Guitarre royalle* collection (1674). For some unknown reason, the printing of Corbetta's 1671 book was delayed for more than a year. Monica Hall remarks: "The privileges of Carré's 'Livre de guitarre' are dated 18th February 1671, and the date 1671 appears on the title page. It may therefore have appeared in print a few months before Corbetta's 'La guitarre royale.'" Monica Hall, "The Stringing of the 5-Course Guitar,' 51, *Baroque Guitar Research* (website), accessed January 29, 2015. https://monicahall2.files.wordpress.com/2012/03/stringing2012.pdf.

61. "Molti professori di chitarra, in particolare qui in Parigi, n'hanno tenuto il secondo loco dopo di me, confessato da loro medesimi." This is one of the sections left out of the French translation.

62. "J'ay voulu mettre ce livre au jour afin de faire voir en mesme temps leur ignorance par *des pièces plus belles et plus nouvelles que tout cequi a paru*, jusqu'à present, lesquelles nous paroistront faciles et gracieuses en observant les ébelissimi et les subtilités que j'ay mis dans ce livre, pour vous perfectionner dans la belle methode de iouer de la guitare." Corbetta here speaks of thieves who had stolen the plates of an earlier book, during his absence from Paris.

63. "Et parcequ'il y a tousjours des envieux qui pouroient dire que ma maniere de iouer est trop difficile, a cause qu'une partie de mes pieces aproche de la maniere du Luth." Francesco Corbetta, *La guitarre royalle* (1671), 8.

64. "Averti di mettere una piciol ottava alla seconda corda que e D sol re, perche li dui unissoni non fanno armonia, *come anche le mie sonate lo ricercano*" (italics mine). Perhaps he is saying that his sonatas require "harmony" as much as do the sonatas of other composers, such as Carré.
65. Visée, *Livre de guitarre* (1682), 50.
66. Hall, *Baroque Guitar Stringing*, 32.
67. In Nicolas de Blegny's *Livre commode des adresses de Paris pour 1692*, the following are listed as guitarists: Vizé, Cheron, Médard, le Tellier, Galet, and Poussilac.
68. "Il faut observer de mettre un octave à la quatrième corde, elle y est absolument necessaire. . . . Même il se trouve des amateurs, que j'imite, qui mettent pareillement une octave à la cinquieme corde, ils la nomment bourdon." Jean de Castillion, B-Bc Ms.S5615, preface (trans. Hall, *Baroque Guitar Stringing*, 26).
69. Pablo Nassarre, *Escuela musica* (Zaragoza, 1724), 463, http://books.google. com/books?id=oMlCAAAAcAAJ&printsec=frontcover&hl=nl&source=gbs_ge_summary_r&redir_esc=y#v=onepage&q&f=false. On p. 401 Nassarre also mentions the tuning with two bourdons.

Chapter Seven

1. *Libro de sonate diverse alla chitarra spagnola* ("Petrus Jacobus Pedruil scripsit"), I-Bc MSV 280 (Rome 1614), f. 28v. The surname is possibly a corruption of the Catalan name Pedrell.
2. Those chords have a double notation, in alfabeto and in tablature.
3. I am grateful to Thérèse de Goede for pointing me to this example.
4. To visualize the similarity, the transcription was made for a lute in A. Presumably Kapsberger played this music on a lute in G tuning. The courses 6 to 2 of the lute in A are tuned exactly like the five courses of the guitar (A, d, g, b, e′). In this example the fingering of the dissonant chords is the same for lute and guitar.
5. "Secondo, si deve avvertire, che tutte le botte notate ò in sù, ò in giù, tutte vanno battute piene; e dove si troverà qualche Lettera del Alfabeto, si sonerà quella botta, che mostrerà detta lettera, battendola tante volte in sù, o in giù, quanti saranno i Segni, che hara, ò in sù, ò in giù. Si avverti però sopra tutto di sonar qual si sia botta, cosi ben distinta, e chiara, ch'ogni corda renda il suo vero effetto."
6. "Sesto, Si osserverà la Corrente, dette Nuova Inventione, posta à car. 68, nella quale, com'anco in altre simili si dovrà avvertire di obligarsi a sonar quelli stessi numeri, che saranno notati, senza aggiungervi, ò scemarvi cosa alcuna, altrimenti invece sente; & il medismo si dovrà osservare nelle Toccate, Sinfonie, Passacagli Spagnoli passeggiati, e Ciaccone, nelle quali Sonate si dovrà porre ogni studio, e diligenza; essendo quelle, proprie à detto Instrumento, che per ciò, Io medesimo confesso di haverci usato diligenza, più, che ordinaria, per renderle maggiormente vaghe, e ricche di nuove, e varie inventioni." Translation from Boye, "Giovanni Battista Granata," 52. The corrente to which Foscarini refers is shown in example 7.8.
7. See Christensen, "The Spanish Baroque Guitar," 18. Christensen discusses the alfabeto dissonante by Foscarini: "None of these chords are intabulated with voice-leading considerations in mind, the specific function of each dissonant chord is not always immediately apparent at first glance. Spliced together, these alfabeto chords produce a nightmare of parallel perfect consonances, and dissonances that

are doubled, unprepared, and unresolved. But the point cannot be emphasised enough that it was the harmonic sonorities that were important in this guitar repertoire, not the particular voicings. Thus almost any chord inversion or dissonant harmony could be introduced, irrespective of its context." From the way Foscarini used these chords in solo music, for which they were intended, it appears that the voice leading of suspensions is certainly taken into consideration. Although Foscarini sometimes used some very unusual dissonances, the resolutions are mostly "correct" (or at least intelligible). Christensen's transcription of Foscarini's alfabeto dissonante—always including all five courses—is probably incorrect, if we keep in mind that Foscarini wrote innumerable strummed chords with fewer than five courses in his solo works. In connection with this, Christensen refers to Richard Pinnell's dissertation on Corbetta (1976), in which the rather unlikely notion is discussed that guitarists would sometimes have damped the open lower courses with the thumb of the right hand. Christensen does not say to which chords from the alfabeto dissonante this would apply. In the alfabeto dissonante it might sometimes also be necessary to exclude a higher course in strumming (e.g., in chord P^+), for which damping with the thumb would not be appropriate.

8.   This F^+ chord is identical to the lettere tagliate F from Bartolotti's *Libro primo* (1640).

9.   From the P^+ chord, the e′ of the first course may have been omitted, and maybe also the b of the second course. Several of the unusual chords like B^+, D^+, and N^+ do not appear at all in Foscarini's music. In E^+ the fourth course should probably be played. Obviously, Foscarini saw it as a modification of a D-minor harmony. One may even consider including the A of the fifth course occasionally, in a sequence E^+–E (-I^+–I).

10.   Compare the chord of A^+ to F^+ (ex. 7.7). The unmarked third and fourth courses in the middle of the A^+ chord must surely be played, but in chord F^+, it is unlikely that the fifth course should be part of the chord.

11.   Departing from this same tuning, the first chord of the third measure from example 7.10 is extremely dissonant, consisting of the tones f + g + a, d′ + e′ + f′ on the bass A ($\hat{6}$ + $\hat{7}$ + $\hat{8}$ + $\hat{1}$1 + $\hat{1}$2 + $\hat{1}$3). It is possible, however, that Foscarini never intended to use the high octave strings of the fourth and fifth course as trebles or campanelas. The octaves then would only be considered to be there to give more brightness to the timbre of the bass (we cannot even be fully sure that Foscarini used high octaves in his tuning).

12.   In example 7.11, the upper stave can be considered as the most "literal" transcription of the tablature. The standard alfabeto chords E and I are represented here with all courses included. The intervening open strings (enclosed by a left-hand fingering pattern) in non-alfabeto chords are represented in the transcription, e.g., the d′s and g′s in measures 1 and 2.

13.   Although a strum sign is lacking for this chord, it is not very likely that only f and d′ should be plucked within a battuto context like this. Besides, this same situation appears again *with* a strum sign, later on in this same passacaglia. At the beginning of the transcription on the lower stave in example 7.11, the bass-note A is in brackets. One can imagine that Foscarini left out this note (it is not indicated with a figure 0 in the alfabeto chart). As with Foscarini, so with Pedruil (ex. 7.5)—we may ask if all courses should always be played. In some of the chords in example 7.3, the fifth course should probably not be included.

14. The repeated e' could be omitted from the second chord of the second full measure, for instance. This is chord O⁺ (actually not given by Foscarini), the minor variant of A⁺. It seems justifiable to include the first course in most other chords of this example. The third measure ends with the progression I⁺-I; in these chords the e' is normally included.

15. The absolute pitch is not given, but tuned in this way, the normal tuning of the fourth, third, and second courses is preserved (d, g, and b).

16. Without the d' on the first course and the B of the fifth (two open courses) it would be a normal progression, according to the rules of counterpoint. Nevertheless, in contrast to examples 7.13a or 7.14, all dissonances are resolved, albeit in a somewhat unorthodox manner. Listen to audio example 13.

17. There are several manuscripts from the seventeenth century into which music by Corbetta was copied, such as Henri François Gallot's large manuscript (GB-Ob Ms. Mus. Sch. C94). There are sometimes "corrections" of Corbetta's notation of exactly such dissonant chords.

18. In this situation it is certainly useful to have a barre at the place where Corbetta has indicated it. This enables the E♭ on the fourth course to ring on, together with the c' on the second course in the next measure. In Carré's version, the barre can still be placed, though there is no indication in the tablature. All this does not make the section any easier for the left hand.

19. In his dissertation Richard Pinnell comments on Corbetta's confusing notation. He suggests that Corbetta wrote these letters "for convenience," and he concludes that the "nonharmonic tones" should not be played. Pinnell ("The Role of Francesco Corbetta," 226) remarks: "Since these unwanted anticipations are in rasgueado chords, and are preceded and followed by sonorities which require the left index to 'bar' or fret all the courses . . . it may have been notated only for convenience. In other words, the fifth course . . . may have been omitted by the player in the strum."

20. The idea (discussed in chapter 5, above) that the battuto chords of the guitar can sound and function as inversion-free "harmonic sonorities," regardless of the actual order of the notes, does not apply here.

21. The *Passacaille* starts at 2:27 of audio example 29.

22. Taruskin, *Oxford History*, 393.

23. Similar cadences are found with Bartolotti and Matteis. The transcription on the first stave is without the open first and fifth courses. The second stave shows the result of strumming the full five courses, in French tuning. If we use a bourdon on the fifth course, there will be a disturbing unresolved A in the strummed chords.

24. And even more if we use a fifth course bourdon. With French tuning, the A will sound as the 7 of the B-major harmony.

25. In Flamenco theory, the common Phrygian guitar cadence is A minor–G major–F major–E major (vi–III–♭II–I).

26. "Afin desviter les dissonances."

27. With the French tuning, these examples would result in chords that sound exactly the same.

28. Most likely two or more of Corbetta's books are now lost. It is impossible to tell if any of these books, published between 1648 and 1671, were in French notation. In the first "Castillion" manuscript (B-Lc Ms.245), a large number of pieces notated in French tablature are ascribed to Francesco Corbetta. Possibly these are transcriptions of works that were originally in Italian tablature.

29. Reduced H, with dots, appears once in first position, on page 10 in measure 3. In third position it appears twice: on page 10 in measure 8 (where it should be played pizzicato), and on page 37, where it is preceded by a three-part chord, also with dots.

30. As we have seen in chapter 5, in the discussion of Doizi de Velasco's chord charts and Bartolotti's lettere tagliate, sometimes three- or four-part chords were preferred over complete alfabeto patterns. As Velasco remarked (see ex. 5.1) often a four-part chord in root position was better (*mejor*) than a five-part $^6_4$ inversion. Yet Velasco also gives the five-part chord in $^6_4$ position as an alternative.

31. Most often these are harmonic progressions of non-alfabeto battuto chord patterns (from a battuto dissonance to a consonance played either battuto or pizzicato).

32. Pinnell, "The Role," 226.

33. Audio example of Francesco Corbetta's "Caprice de chacone," at 2:40.

Bibliography

Archival Sources

Manuscripts are cited by their call numbers.

A-Ila Ms. Nr. 533. Oberösterreichisches Landesarchiv, Linz. French tablature manuscript. The second part of this manuscript is in Italian tablature, probably written by another hand.

B-Bc.Ms.S5615. Conservatoire Royal de Bruxelles, Bibliothèque, Brussels. *Recueil des pièces de guitarre composées par Mr. François le Cocq / Recueil des pièces de guitarre de meilleurs maitres du siècle dixseptième.* Gent, c.1730. Manuscript compiled by Jean Baptiste de Castillion.

B-Lc Ms.245. Conservatoire Royal de Liège, Bibliothèque, Liège. Manuscript probably compiled by Jean Baptiste de Castillion.

CZ-Pnm IV.G.18. Národní Muzeum, Prague. Manuscript for ten-course lute in Italian and French tablatures.

F-Pn Ms.Vm7 675. Bibliothèque Nationale de France, Paris. Manuscript with French tablature.

F-Pn Rés.Vmf. Ms. 50. Bibliothèque Nationale de France, Paris. Early alfabeto/text manuscript.

F-Pn Rés.Vmc Ms. 59. Bibliothèque Nationale de France, Paris. Early alfabeto/text manuscript.

F-Psg Ms Rés 2344, 2349, and 2351. Bibliothèque Sainte-Geneviève, Paris. French tablature manuscripts, belonging to Monsieur Dupille, "Commissaire des guerres."

GB-Cfm Ms. Mus. 727. Fitzwilliam Museum, Cambridge. Manuscript from Spain with songs by José Marin.

GB-Cmc Ms 2591. Magdalene College, the Pepys Library, Cambridge. *Songs and other compositions light, grave and sacred, for a single voice . . . with a thorough-base on ye guitar by Cesare Morelli.* Ca. 1693.

GB-Lbl Add.Ms.31640. The British Library, London. Santiago de Murcia, *Passacalles y obras.*

GB-Ob. Ms. Mus. Sch. C94. Bodleian Library, Oxford. *Pièces de guitare de differends autheurs receuillis par Henry François Gallot.*

I.Bc Ms. AA 360. Museo internazionale e biblioteca della musica di Bologna. Alfabeto manuscript.

I-Bc MSV 280. Museo internazionale e biblioteca della musica di Bologna. *Libro de sonate diverse alla chitarra spagnola, Petrus Jacobus Pedruil scripsit.* Rome, 1614.

I-Fn MS Fondo Landau Finaly Mus. 175. Biblioteca Nazionale Centrale di Firenze, Florence. Alfabeto manuscript, probably written by Francesco Palumbi.

I-Fr Ms.2774. Biblioteca Riccardiana e Moreniana, Florence. Alfabeto manuscript.

I:MOe Ms. Campori 612. Biblioteca Estense, Modena. *Regole per imparare a sonare la chitarra.*

I-Rvat MS Chigi cod. L.VI.200. Biblioteca Apostolica Vaticana. Anonymous manuscript with Spanish texts and alfabeto (ca. 1599), which belonged to the Duchessa di Traetta.

Ms. Barb. Lat. 4059. Biblioteca Apostolica Vaticana. Includes Francesco Buti's text on which Luigi Rossi's *Orfeo* was based.

NL-DHgm MS 133. Gemeentemuseum Den Haag. Manuscript with French tablature, belonging to Isabel van Langhenhove.

Published Sources

Agazzari, Agostino. *Del sonare sopra il basso.* Siena: Falcini, 1607.

Amat, Joan Carles. *Guitarra española de cinco ordenes.* Lérida: Anglada & Llorens, 1626. Later edition of a lost print of 1596.

Anthony, James. *French Baroque Music from Beaujoyeulx to Rameau.* London: Batsford, 1997.

Aranies, Juan. *Libro segundo de tonos y villancicos.* Rome: Robletti, 1624.

Asioli, Francesco. *Concerti armonici per la chitarra spagnuola,* Bologna: Monti, 1676.

———. *Primi scherzi di chitarra.* Bologna: Monti, 1674. Facsimile edition. Florence: Studio per Edizioni Scelte, 1984.

Ayala Ruiz, Juan Carlos. "Vicente Espinel: Evidencias de una obra musical hoy desconocida." *Hoquet* 4 (2006): 5–24.

Bacci, Mina. "Lettere inedite di Baccio del Bianco." *Paragone* 14 (1963): 68–77.

Banchieri, Adriano. *L'organo suonarino.* Venice: Amadino, 1611.

Banfi, Giulio. *Il maestro della chitarra.* Milan: Banfi, 1653.

Barbieri, Patrizio. "Cembalaro, organaro, chitarraro e fabbricatore di corde armoniche nella 'Polyanthea technica' di Pinaroli (1718–32), con notizie inedite sui liutai e cembalari operanti a Roma." *Recercare* 1 (1989): 123–209.

Baron, John. "Secular Spanish Solo Song in Non-Spanish Sources, 1599–1640." *Journal of the American Musicological Society* 30, no. 1 (1977): 20–42.

———. *Spanish Art Song in the Seventeenth Century.* Madison: A-R Editions, 1985.

Bartolotti, Angelo Michele. *Libro primo di chitarra spagnola.* Florence, 1640. Facsimile edition. Geneva: Minkoff, 1984.

———. *Secondo libro di chitarra spagnola.* Rome, c. 1655. Facsimile edition. Geneva: Minkoff, 1984.

———. *Table pour apprendre facilement á toucher le theorbe sur la basse continüe.* Paris: Ballard, 1669.

Bianciardi, Francesco. *Breve regola per imparar' a sonare sopra il basso con ogni sorte d'instrumento.* Siena, 1607.

Benoit, Marcelle. "Paris, 1661–87: The Age of Lully." In *The Early Baroque Era, From the Late Sixteenth Century to the 1660s,* edited by Curtis Price, 239–69. Basingstoke: Macmillan (Man & Music Series, vol. 3), 1993.

Bermudo, Juan. *El libro llamado declaracion de instrumentos musicales*, Osuna: Juan de Leon, 1555. Facsimile edition. Madrid: Arte Tripharia, 1982.

Berti, Giovanni Pietro. *Cantade et arie*, Venice: Vincenti, 1627.

Blegny, Nicolas de. Le livre commode des adresses de Paris pour 1692 par Abraham du Pradel (Nicolas de Blegny) suivi d'appendices, précédé d'une introduction et annoté par Édouard Fournier. Paris: Daffis, 1878.

Boetticher, Wolfgang. *Handschriftlich überlieferte Lauten- und Gitarrentabulaturen.* (RISM B/VII). München: Henle Verlag, 1978.

Borgir, Tharald. *The Performance of the Basso Continuo in Italian Baroque Music.* Ann Arbor, Michigan: UMI Research Press, 1987.

Bottazzari, Giovanni. *Sonate nuove per la chitarra spagnuola.* Venice: n.p., 1663. Facsimile edition. Florence: Studio per Edizioni Scelte, 1984.

Boye, Gary. "The Case of the Purloined Letter Tablature: The Seventeenth-Century Guitar Books of Foriano Pico and Pietro Millioni." *Journal of Seventeenth-Century Music* 11, no. 1 (2005), http://sscm-jscm.press.uiuc.edu/v11/no1/boye.html.

———. "Giovanni Battista Granata and the Development of Printed Music for the Guitar in Seventeenth-Century Italy." PhD diss., Duke University, 1995.

———. "Performing Seventeenth-Century Italian Guitar Music: The Question of an Appropriate Stringing." In *Performance on Lute, Guitar and Vihuela: Historical Practice and Modern Interpretation*, edited by Victor A. Coelho, 180–94. Cambridge: Cambridge University Press, 1997.

Briçeño, Luis de. *Metodo mui facilissimo para aprender a tañer la guitarra.* Paris: Ballard, 1626. Facsimile edition. Geneva: Minkoff, 1972.

Brown, Howard M. "The Geography of Florentine Monody: Caccini at Home and Abroad." *Early Music* 9 (1981): 147–68.

Buch, David. "Style Brisé, Style Luthé and the Choses Luthées." *Musical Quarterly* 71 (1985): 52–67.

Caccini, Francesca. *Il primo libro delle musiche.* Florence: Zanobi Pignoni, 1618.

Caccini, Giulio. *Le nuove musiche.* Florence: Marescotti, 1602.

Cacho, María Teresa. "Canciones Españoles en manuscritos musicales de la biblioteca nacional de Florencia." In *Siglos dorados, homenaje a Augustin Redondo*, edited by Pierre Civil, 1:155–76. Madrid: Castalia, 2004.

Caliendo, Ciro. *La Chitarra battente. Uomini, storia e costruzione di uno strumento barocco e popolare.* San Giovanni in Persiceto: Edizioni Aspasia, 1998.

Calvi, Carlo. *Intavolatura de chitarra e chitarriglia.* Bologna: Monti, 1646. Facsimile edition. Florence: Studio per Edizioni Scelte, 1980.

Campion, François. *Addition au traité d'accompagnement.* Paris: 1730. Facsimile edition. Geneva: Minkoff, 1976.

———. *Nouvelles decouvertes sur la guitarre.* Paris: Brunet, 1705. Facsimile edition. Geneva: Minkoff, 1977.

———. *Traité d'accompagnement.* Paris: 1716. Facsimile edition. Geneva: Minkoff, 1976.

Cantù, Carlo. *Cicalamento in canzonette ridicolose, o vero trattato di matrimonio tra buffetto, e colombina comici.* Florence: Amador Massi, 1646.

Carbonchi, Antonio. *Lo dodici chitarre spostate.* Florence: Sabatini, 1643. Facsimile edition. Florence: Studio per Edizioni Scelte, 1981.

———. *Sonate di chitarra spagnola*. Florence: Massi-Landi, 1640. Facsimile edition. Florence: Studio per Edizioni Scelte, 1981.

Carré, Antoine. *Livre de guitarre*. Paris: n.p., 1671. Facsimile edition. Geneva: Minkoff, 1977.

———. *Livre de pièces de guitarre*. Paris: n.p., c. 1675. Facsimile edition. Geneva: Minkoff, 1985.

Carter, Tim. "'An Air New and Grateful to the Ear': The Concept of *Aria* in Late Renaissance and Early Baroque Italy." *Music Analysis* 12 (1993): 127–45.

———. "Artusi, Monteverdi and the Poetics of Modern Music." In *Musical Humanism and its Legacy: Essays in Honor of Claude V. Palisca*, edited by N. K. Baker and B. R. Hanning, 171–94. Stuyvesant NY: Pendragon, 1992.

———. "Caccini's *Amarilli, Mia Bella*: Some Questions (and a Few Answers)." *Journal of the Royal Musical Association* 113 (1988): 250–73.

———. "A Florentine Wedding." *Acta Musicologia* 55 (1983): 89–107.

———. "Giulio Caccini (1551–1618), New Facts, New Music." *Studi Musicali* 16 (1987): 13–31.

———. "Music Publishing in Italy, ca. 1580–1625: Some Preliminary Observations." *Royal Musical Association Research Chronicle* 20 (1986): 19–37.

———. "On the Composition and Performance of Caccini's *Le Nuove Musiche* (1602)." *Early Music* 12 (1984): 208–17.

———. "Resemblance and Representation: Towards a New Aesthetic in the Music of Monteverdi." In *"Con Che Soavità": Studies in Italian Opera, Song and Dance, 1580–1740*, edited by Iain Fenlon and Tim Carter, 118–34. Oxford: Oxford University Press, 1995.

———. "*Serate Musicali* in Early Seventeenth-Century Florence: Girolamo Montesardo's *L'Allegre Notti di Fiorenza* (1608)." In *Renaissance Studies in Honor of Craig Hugh Smyth*, edited by A. Morrogh, vol. 1, 555–68. Florence: Giunti Barbèra, 1985.

Castaldi, Bellerofonte. *Primo mazzetto di fiore*. Venice: Vincenti, 1623.

Castelli, Silvia. "Una chitarra per Scapino." In *Rime e suoni per corde spagnole*, edited by Giovanna Lazzi, 31–7. Florence: Edizioni Polistampa, 2002.

Cavalieri, Emilio de'. *Rappresentatione di Anima, et di Corpo*. Rome: 1600.

Cavallini, Ivano. "L'intavolatura per chitarrino alla napolitana dal *Conserto Vago-1645*." *Quadrivium* 19, no. 2 (1978): 227–63.

———. "Sull'opera *Gratie et affetti amorosi* di Marcantonio Aldigatti (1627)." *Quadrivium* 19, no. 2 (1978): 145–203.

Charnassé, Hélène, G. Rebours, and R. Andia. *Robert de Visée, Les deux livres de guitare, Paris 1682 et 1686* (tabulature, transcription, interprétation). Paris: Éditions Transatlantiques, 1999.

Chauvel, Claude. Introduction to the facsimile edition of Angelo Michele Bartolotti, *Libro primo et secondo di chitarra spagnola*. Geneva: Minkoff, 1984.

Christensen, Thomas. "The Spanish Baroque Guitar and Seventeenth-Century Triadic Theory." *Journal of Music Theory* 36 (1992): 1–42.

Ciancarelli, Roberto. "Modalités de réadaption de l'espace dans le théâtre Italien du XVIIe siècle." In *Les lieux du spectacle dans l'Europe du XVIIe siècle: Actes du colloque du Centre de recherches sur le XVIIe siècle européen, Université Michel de Montaigne, Bordeaux III, 11–13 mars 2004*, edited by Charles Mazoer, 133–47. Tübingen: Gunter Narr Verlag, 2006.

Coelho, Victor. "Authority, Autonomy and Interpretation in Seventeenth-Century Italian Music." In *Performance on Lute, Guitar and Vihuela: Historical Practice and Modern Interpretation*, edited by Victor Coelho, 108–41. Cambridge: Cambridge University Press, 1997.

————, ed. *The Cambridge Companion to the Guitar.* Cambridge: Cambridge University Press, 2003.

————. "The Players of Florentine Monody in Context and in History and a Newly Recognized Source for *Le Nuove Musiche.*" *Journal of Seventeenth Century Music* 9 (2003). http://sscm-jscm.org/v9/no1/coelho.html.

————. "Raffaello Cavalcanti's Lute Book (1590) and the Ideal of Singing and Playing." In *Le Concert des voix et des instruments à la Renaissance*, edited by Jean-Michel Vaccaro, 423–42. Paris: CNRS, 1995.

Congleton, Jennie. "The False Consonances of Musick." *Early Music* 9 (1981): 463–69.

Corbetta, Francesco. *La Guitarre royalle.* Paris: Bonneüil, 1671. Facsimile edition. Geneva: Minkoff, 1975.

————. *La Guitarre royalle.* Paris: Bonneüil, 1674. Facsimile edition. Bologna: Forni, n.d.

————. *De gli scherzi armonici.* Bologna: Monti, 1639.

————. *Varii capricci per la chitara spagnuola.* Milan: n.p., 1643. Facsimile edition. Florence: Studio per Edizioni Scelte, 1980.

————. *Varii scherzi di sonate per la chitara spagnuola.* Brussels: 1648. Facsimile edition. Florence: Studio per Edizioni Scelte, 1983.

————. Pirated version of *Varii scherzi di sonate per la chitarra spagnola.* Brussels, 1648. (1648). Facsimile edition. Frankfurt: Deutsche Lautengesellschaft, 2006.

Coriandoli, Francesco. *Diverse sonate recercate sopra la chitarra spagnuola.* Bologna: Monti, 1670. Facsimile edition Studio per Edizioni Scelte, 1981.

Corona-Alcalde, Antonio. "The Players and Performance Practice of the Vihuela and Its Related Instruments, the Lute and the Guitar, From c. 1450 to c. 1650, as Revealed by a Study of Musical, Theoretical and Archival Sources." PhD diss., Kings College, University of London, 1999.

————. "The Vihuela and the Guitar in Sixteenth-Century Spain: A Critical Appraisal of Some of the Existing Evidence." *The Lute* 30 (1990): 3–24.

Crawford, Tim. Introduction and Concordances to the Facsimile Edition of *The Goëss Lute Manuscripts II.* München: Tree Edition, 1993.

Daza, Esteban. *Libro de musica en cifras para vihuela, intitulado el Parnasso.* Valladolid: De Cordoba, 1576.

Danner, Peter. "Giovanni Paolo Foscarini and His *Nuova Inventione.*" *Journal of the Lute Society of America* 7 (1974): 4–18.

————. "An Update to the Bibliography of Guitar Tablatures." *Journal of the Lute Society of America* 6 (1973): 33–36.

Dean, Alexander. "The Five-Course Guitar and Seventeenth-Century Harmony: Alfabeto and Italian Song." PhD diss., University of Rochester, 2009.

Denis, Françoise-Emmanuelle. "La guitare en France au XVIIe siècle: Son importance, son répertoire." *Revue Belge de Musicologie* 32, no. 3 (1978): 143–50.

Derosier, Nicolas. *Les principes de la guitarre.* Amsterdam: n.p., c. 1690.

————. *Nouveaux principes pour la guittare.* Paris: Ballard, 1699.

Diderot, Denis. *Encyclopédie.* Vol. 7. Paris: Braisson, 1757.

Doizi de Velasco, Nicolao. *Nuevo modo de cifra para tañer la guitarra.* Naples: Longo, c. 1640.

Dunn, Alexander. "Style and Development in the Theorbo Works of Robert de Visée: An Introductory Study." PhD diss., University of California, San Diego, 1989.

Eisenhardt, Lex. "Bourdons as Usual." *The Lute* 47 (2010): 1–37.

———. "Dissonance and *Battuto*, a Hidden Practice in the Performance of Seventeenth-Century Guitar Music?" *The Lute* 47 (2010): 38–54.

———. "Nuove suonate de chitarriglia spagnuola, battute e piccicate." *Michaelsteiner Konferenzberichte* 66: 181–93. Dössel: Verlag Janos Stekovics, 2004.

Esses, Maurice. *Dance and Instrumental "Diferencias" in Spain During the Seventeenth and Early 18th Centuries.* Stuyvesant, NY: Pendragon Press, 1992.

Evelyn, John. *The Diary of John Evelyn,* edited by William Bray. London: Gibbings, 1890. http://gallica.bnf.fr/ark:/12148/bpt6k102996w/f2.image.r=.langEN.

Fabris, Dinko. "Danze intavolate per chitarra tiorbata in uno sconosciuto manoscritto napoletano (Na. Cons. Ms.1321)." *Nuova Rivista Musicale Italiana* 15 (1981): 404–26.

Failla, Salvatore. "La nuova chitarra composta da Don Antonio Di Micheli della città di Tusa." *Analecta Musicologica* 19 (1979): 244–71.

Falconieri, Andrea. *Libro primo di villanelle,* Rome: Robletti, 1616.

Fischlin, Daniel. "The Performance Context of the English Lute Song, 1596–1622." In *Performance on Lute, Guitar and Vihuela: Historical Practice and Modern Interpretation,* edited by Victor A. Coelho, 47–71. Cambridge: Cambridge University Press, 1997.

Fontijn, Claire. *Desparate Measures.* New York: Oxford University Press, 2006.

Fortune, Nigel. "Italian Secular Song from 1600 to 1635: An Introductory Survey." PhD diss., University of Cambridge, 1953.

Foscarini, Giovanni Paolo. *Il primo, secondo, e terzo libro della chitarra spagnola.* Rome: c. 1630.

———. *Li cinque libri della chitarra alla spagnola.* Rome: c. 1640. Facsimile edition. Florence: Studio per Edizioni Scelte, 1979.

Frosoli, Patrizia. "The *Museo Stradivariano* in Cremona." *The Galpin Society Journal* 24 (1971): 33–50.

Fuenllana, Miguel de. *Libro de musica para vihuela, intitulado Orphenica lyra.* Sevilla: Martin de Montesdoca, 1554. Facsimile edition. Geneva: Minkoff, 1981.

Galilei, Vincenzo. *Dialogo della musica antica, et della moderna.* Florence: Giorgio Marescotti, 1581.

Gavito, Cory Michael. "The Alfabeto Song in Print, 1610–c. 1650: Neapolitan Roots, Roman Codification and 'Il Gusto Popolare.'" PhD diss., University of Texas, Austin, 2006.

———. "Carlo Milanuzzi's *Quarto Scherzo* and the Climate of Venetian Popular Music in the 1620s." MA thesis, University of North Texas, 2001.

George, Jeffrey. *Angelo Michele Bartolotti: a Performance Edition of Suites From the Publication Secondo Libro di chitarra of 1655.* Pacific, MO: Mel Bay, 2009.

Gill, Donald. "The Gallot Guitar Books." *Early Music* 6 (1978): 79–81.

———. "The Stringing of the Five Course Baroque Guitar." *Early Music* 3 (1975): 370–71.

———. *Wire Strung Plucked Instruments Contemporary with the Lute.* The Lute Society Booklets 3. Albury: The Lute Society, 1977.

Giustiniani, Vincenzo. *Discorso Sopra La Musica.* N.p., c. 1628. Translated by Carol MacClintock, in "Giustiniani's discorso sopra la musica." *Musica disciplina* 15 (1961): 209–25.

De Goede, Thérèse. "*Del suonare sopra il basso*: Concerning the Realization of Early Seventeenth-Century Italian Unfigured Basses." *Performance Practice Review* 10 (1997): 80–115.

———. "From Dissonance to Note-Cluster: the Application of Musical-Rhetorical Figures and Dissonances to Thoroughbass Accompaniment of Early 17th-Century Italian Vocal Solo Music." *Early Music* 42, no. 2 (2005): 233–50.

Goldberg, Clemens. *Stilizierung als kunstvermittelnder Prozess: die Fransösischen Tombeau-Stücke im 17. Jahrhundert.* Heidelberg: Laaber-Verlag, 1987.

La Guitarra Española / The Spanish Guitar. Exhibition catalogue. The Metropolitan Museum of Art, New York and Museo Municipal, Madrid, 1991–92.

Goy, François-Pierre. "Three Versions of Pierre Gaultier's *Bataille* (1626, 1638, 1650)." *Journal of the Lute Society of America,* 42–43 (2009): 1–89.

Granata, Giovanni Battista. *Armoniosi toni di varie suonate musicali.* Bologna: Monti, 1684.

———. *Capricci armonici.* Bologna: Monti, 1646. Facsimile edition. Florence: Studio per Edizioni Scelte, 1978.

———. *Novi capricci armonici musicali.* Bologna: Monti, 1674.

———. *Nuova scielta di capricci armonici e suonate musicali.* Bologna: 1651.

———. *Nuove sonate di chitarriglia spagnuola.* N.p., c. 1650. Facsimile edition. Bologna: Forni, 1991.

———. *Nuovi soavi concenti di varie sonate.* Bologna: Monti, 1680.

———. *Soavi concenti di sonate musicali.* Bologna: Monti, 1659. Facsimile edition. Monaco: Chanterelle, 1979.

Grenerin, Henry. *Livre de guitarre et autres pièces de musique.* Paris: Bonneüil, 1680. Facsimile edition. Geneva: Minkoff, 1977.

———. *Livre de theorbe.* Paris: Bonneüil, c. 1682. Facsimile edition. Geneva: Minkoff, 1984.

Griffiths, John. "Strategies for the Recovery of Guitar Music of the Early Seventeenth Century." In *Rime e suoni alla Spagnuola,* edited by Giulia Veneziano, 59–81. Florence: Alinea Editrice, 2003.

———. "The Vihuela: Performance Practice, Style and Context." In *Performance on Lute, Guitar and Vihuela: Historical Practice and Modern Interpretation,* edited by Victor A. Coelho, 158–79. Cambridge: Cambridge University Press, 1997.

Grijp, Louis Peter. "The Cittern of Sweelinck and Vermeer. Contextual Information for the Excavated Zuyderzee Citterns." *Michaelsteiner Konferenzberichte* 66: 79–85. Dössel: Verlag Janos Stekovics, 2004.

Grunfeld, Frederic. *The Art and Times of the Guitar.* New York: Macmillan, 1969.

Guerau, Francisco. *Poema harmonico.* Madrid: Ruiz de Murga, 1694. Facsimile edition. London: Tecla, 1977.

Hall, Monica. *Baroque Guitar Stringing, a Survey of the Evidence.* The Lute Society Booklets 9. Albury: The Lute Society, 2003.

———. "A Few More Observations on Baroque Guitar Stringing." *The Lute* 48 (2008): 71–5.

———. Introduction to the Facsimile Edition of *Joan Carles Amat: Guitarra española (c. 1761).* Monaco: Éditions Chanterelle, 1980.

———. "Recovering a Lost Book of Guitar Music by Corbetta." *The Consort* 61 (2005).

Hall, Monica, and Lex Eisenhardt. Preface to *Francesco Corbetta und andere [Guitarra española y sus diferencias de sones].* Frankfurt/Main: Deutsche Lautengesellschaft, 2006.

Hammond, Frederick. *Music and Spectacle in Baroque Rome: Barbarini Patronage under Urban VIII.* New Haven: Yale University Press, 1994.

———. "Orpheus in a New Key: The Barbarini and the Rossi-Buti *L'Orfeo.*" *Studi Musicali* 25 (1996): 103–25.

Hanning, Barbara Russano. *Of Poetry and Music's Power: Humanism and the Creation of Opera.* Ann Arbor: UMI Research Press, 1980.

Haynes, Bruce. *A History of Performing Pitch, the Story of "A."* Lanham, MD: Scarecrow Press, 2002.

Hill, John Walter. "Florence: Musical Spectacle and Drama, 1570–1650." In *The Early Baroque Era, from the Late Sixteenth Century to the 1660s,* edited by Curtis Price, 121–45. Man and Music, vol. 3. Basingstoke: Macmillan, 1993.

———. "Realized Continuo Accompaniments From Florence c. 1600." *Early Music* 11 (1983): 194–208.

———. *Roman Monody, Cantata and Opera from the Circles around Cardinal Montalto.* 2 vols. Oxford: Clarendon Press, 1997.

Hodgson, Martin. "The Stringing of a Baroque Guitar." *Fellowship of Makers and Restorers of Historical Instruments Quarterly* 41 (1985): 61–67.

Holman, Peter. "London: Commonwealth and Restoration." In *The Early Baroque Era, from the Late Sixteenth Century to the 1660s,* edited by Curtis Price, 305–26. Man and Music, vol. 3. Basingstoke: Macmillan, 1993.

Hudson, Richard. *The Allemande, the Balletto and the Tanz.* Cambridge: Cambridge University Press, 1986.

———. "The Concept of Mode in Italian Guitar Music during the First Half of the Seventeenth Century." *Acta Musicologica* 42 no. 3–4 (1970): 163–83.

———. *The Folia, the Saraband, the Passacaglia and the Chaconne: The Historical Evolution of Four Forms that Originated in the Five-Course Spanish Guitar.* Neuhausen–Stuttgart: Hanssler, 1982.

———. "The Ripresa, the Ritornello and the Passacaglia." *Journal of the American Musicological Society* 24, no. 3 (1971): 364–94.

———. "Further Remarks on the Passacaglia and Ciaccona." *Journal of the American Musicological Society* 23, no. 2 (1970): 302–14.

Jensen, Richard. "The Development of Technique and Performance Practice as Reflected in Seventeenth-Century Italian Guitar Notation." MA thesis, California State University, Northridge, 1980.

———. "The Guitar and Italian Song." *Early Music* 13 (1985): 376–83.

Kapsberger, Girolamo. *Libro primo d'intavolatura di lauto.* Rome: 1611. Facsimile edition. Geneva: Minkoff, 1982.

———. *Libro primo di villanelle.* Rome: Flammini, 1611.

———. *Libro secondo di villanelle.* Rome: Robletti, 1619.

———. *Libro terzo di villanelle.* Rome: Robletti, 1619.

———. *Libro quarto di villanelle.* Rome: Soldi, 1623.

Katritzky, Peg. *The Art of Commedia: A Study in the Commedia dell'Arte 1560–1620.* Internationale Forschungen Zur Allgemeinen Vergleichenden Literaturwissenschaft. Amsterdam: Rodopi, 2006.

Keith, Richard. "La Guitare Royale: a Study of the Career and Compositions of Francesco Corbetta." *Recherches sur la Musique Française Classique* 7 (1966): 73–93.

Kircher, Athanasius. *Musurgia universalis.* Rome: Corbelletti, 1650.

Kirkendale, Warren. *L'Aria di Fiorenza id est Il Ballo del Gran Duca.* Florence: Olschki, 1972.

———. *The Court Musicians in Florence During the Principate of the Medici.* Florence: Olschki, 1993.

Kitsos, Theodoros. "Arpeggiated Chords in Early Seventeenth-Century Italy." *The Lute* 42 (2002): 54–72.

Landi, Stefano. *Il Sant'Alessio.* Rome: Masotti, 1634.

Le Cerf de La Viéville de Fresneuse, Jean-Louis. *Comparaison de la musique italienne et de la musique française.* Brussels: Foppens, 1705. Facsimile edition. Geneva Minkoff, 1972. http://gallica.bnf.fr/ark:/12148/bpt6k503898f.

Le Cocq, Jonathan. "A Guide to Notation in the Air de Cour for Voice and Lute (Ballard Editions, 1608–1643)." *The Lute* 39 (1999): 27–45.

Ledbetter, David. *Harpsichord and Lute Music in 17th-Century France.* Bloomington: Indiana University Press, 1987.

Leopold, Silke. "Die Anfänge von Oper und die Probleme der Gattung." *Journal of Seventeenth-Century Music* 9 (2003). http://sscm-jscm.press.uiuc.edu/v9/no1/leopold.html.

———. "Remigio Romano's Collection of Lyrics for Music." *Proceedings of the Royal Musical Association* 110 (1983): 45–61.

Lesure, François. *Pierre Trichet: Traité des instruments de musique (vers 1640).* Neuilly-sur-Seine: Société de Musique d'Autrefois, 1957.

Lospalluti, Leonardo. "Consideratione su Giovan Battista Abatessa e su manoscritto per chitarra del Seicento a Bitonto." *Il Fronimo* 67 (1989): 27–33.

Mabbett, Margaret. "Italian Musicians in Restoration England (1660–90)." *Music & Letters* 67 (1986): 237–47.

MacNeil, Anne. *Music and Women of the Commedia dell'Arte in the Late Sixteenth Century.* Oxford: Oxford University Press, 2003.

Mamone, Sara. "Most Serene Brothers-Princes-Impresarios: Theatre in Florence Under the Management and Protection of Mattias, Giovan Carlo and Leopoldo de' Medici." *Journal of Seventeenth Century Music* 9 (2003). http://sscm-jscm.press.uiuc.edu/v9/no1/mamone.html.

Marini, Biagio. *Arie, madrigali et corrente.* Venice: Gardano, 1620.

———. *Diuersi generi di Sonate Op. XXII,* Venice: Francesco Magni, 1655.

———. *Scherzi e canzonette a una, e due voci.* Parma: Viotti, 1622.

Martin, François. *Pièces de guitarre,* Paris: 1663.

Mason, Kevin. *The Chitarrone and Its Repertoire in Early Seventeenth-Century Italy.* Aberystwyth: Boethius Press, 1989.

———. "François Campion's Secret of Accompaniment for Theorbo, Guitar and Lute." *Journal of the Lute Society of America* 14 (1981): 69–94.

———. "*Per Cantare e Sonare*: Accompanying Italian Lute Song." In *Performance on Lute, Guitar and Vihuela: Historical Practice and Modern Interpretation*, edited by Victor A. Coelho, 72–107. Cambridge: Cambridge University Press, 1997.

Massip, Catherine. "Paris, 1600–61." In *The Early Baroque Era, from the Late Sixteenth Century to the 1660s*, edited by Curtis Price, 218–38. Man and Music, vol. 3. Basingstoke: Macmillan, 1993.

Mather, Betty Bang. *Dance Rhythms of the French Baroque*. Bloomington: Indiana University Press, 1987.

Mattax, Charlotte. *Accompaniment on Theorbo and Harpsichord, Denis Delair's Treatise of 1690*. Bloomington: Indiana University Press, 1991.

Matteis, Nicola. *The False Consonances of Musick*. London: 1682. Translation of *Le false consonanse della musica*. London: c. 1680.

Médard, Rémy. *Pièces de guitarre*. Paris: Bonneüil, 1676. Facsimile edition. Geneva: Minkoff, 1988.

Mersenne, Marin. *Harmonie universelle*. Paris: Cramoisy, 1636. Facsimile edition. Paris: Editions du Centre National de la Recherche Scientifique, 1963.

Mesangeau, René. *Oeuvres de René Mesangeau*. Paris: Corpus des Luthistes Français, 1971.

Meucci, Renato. "Da 'chitarra italiana' a 'chitarrone': una nuova interpretazione." In *Enrico Radesca da Foggia, atti del convegno, a cura di Francesca Seller*, 37–57. Lucca: Libreria Musicale Italiana, 2001.

Milanuzzi, Carlo. *Primo scherzo delle ariose vaghezze*. Venice: Bartolomeo Magni, 1622.

———. *Secondo scherzo delle ariose vaghezze*. Venice: Alessandro Vincenti, 1622.

———. *Sesto libro delle ariose vaghezze*. Venice: Vincenti, 1628.

———. *Terzo scherzo delle ariose vaghezze*. Venice: Vincenti, 1623.

Miller, Roark. "New Information on the Chronology of Venetian Monody: The 'Raccolte' of Remigio Romano." *Music & Letters* 77 (1996): 22–33.

Millioni, Pietro. *Corona del primo, secondo e terzo libro d'intavolatura di chitarra spagnola*. Rome: Facciotti, 1631.

———. *Prima scelta di villanelle*. Rome: Facciotti, 1627.

———. *Il quarto libro d'intavolature*. Rome: Facciotti, 1627.

Mischiati, Oscar. Indici, cataloghi e avvisi degli editori e libari musicali italiani dal 1591 al 1798. Florence: Olschki, 1984.

Montesardo, Girolamo. *L'allegre notti di Fiorenza*, Venice: Angelo Gardano & Fratelli, 1608.

———. *Nuova inventione d'intavolatura*, Florence: Marescotti, 1606.

Murata, Margaret "Guitar Passacaglie and Vocal Arie." In La monodia in Toscana alle soglie del XVII secolo, edited by Francesca Menchelli-Buttini, 81–116. Pisa: Edizioni ETS, 2007.

———. "'Singing,' 'Acting,' and 'Dancing' in Vocal Chamber Music of the Early Seicento." *Journal of Seventeenth Century Music* 9 (2003). http://sscm-jscm. press.uiuc.edu/v9/no1/murata.html.

Murcia, Santiago de. *Resumen de acompañar la parte conla guitarra*. Antwerp (?): 1714. Facsimile edition. Monaco: Chanterelle, 1980.

Murphy, Sylvia. "The Tuning of the Five-Course Guitar." *Galpin Society Journal* 23 (1970): 49–63.

Narváez, Luys de. *Los seys libros del delfin de música*, Valladolid: Hernández de Cordoba, 1538.

Nelson, Jocelyn. "Matteis and the Seventeenth-Century Guitar Accompaniment." *Lute Society of America Quarterly* 40, no. 3 (2005): 16–23.

North, Nigel. *Continuo Playing on the Lute, Archlute and Theorbo.* London: Faber, 1985.

Obizzi, Domenico. *Madrigali et arie a voce sola.* Venice: Vincenti, 1627.

O'Donnell, Aidan. "Le rôle de l'alfabeto dans le développement de la pensée harmonique en Italie, 1600–50." PhD diss., Université Paris-Sorbonne, 2011.

Oleskiewicz, Mary. "The Rise of Italian Chamber Music." In *The World of Baroque Music,* edited by George B. Stauffer, 48–77. Bloomington: Indiana University Press, 2007.

Palisca, Claude V. "Aria Types in the Earliest Operas." *Journal of Seventeenth-Century Music* 9 (2003). http://sscm-jscm.press.uiuc.edu/v9/no1/palisca.html.

———. "The Artusi-Monteverdi Controversy." In *The New Monteverdi Companion,* edited by Denis Arnold and Nigel Fortune, 127–58. London: Faber & Faber, 1985.

———. *The Florentine Camerata.* New Haven: Yale University Press, 1989.

Parisi, Susan. "Acquiring Musicians and Instruments in the Early Baroque: Observations From Mantua." *Journal of Musicology* 14, no. 2 (1996): 117–50.

Pasqual, Sandro and Roberto Regazzi. *Le radici del successo della liuteria a Bologna.* Bologna: Florenus, 1995.

Pellegrini, Domenico. *Armoniosi concerti sopra la chitarra spagnola,* Bologna: Monti, 1650. Facsimile edition. Florence: Studio per Edizioni Scelte., 1978.

Pepys, Samuel. *The Diary of Samuel Pepys,* edited by Henry B. Wheatley. New York: Bell & Sons, 1898. http://gutenberg.readingroom.ms/4/1/7/4179/4179.txt

Peruffo, Mimmo. "Italian Violin Strings in the Eighteenth and Nineteenth Centuries: Typologies, Manufacturing Techniques and Principles of Stringing." *Recercare* 9 (1997): 155–203.

Pesori, Stefano. *Galeria musicale.* Verona: Merli, 1648.

———. *Lo Scrigno armonico.* N.p., c. 1648. Facsimile edition. Florence: Studio per Edizioni Scelte, 1986.

———. *Recreationi armoniche.* N.p., c. 1675.

Piccinini, Alessandro. *Intavolatura di liuto et di chitarrone, libro primo.* Bologna: Moscatelli, 1623. Facsimile edition. Florence: Studio per Edizioni Scelte, 1983.

———. *Intavolatura di liuto.* Bologna: Monte e Zenero, 1639.

Pinnell, Richard T. "The Role of Francesco Corbetta (1615–1681) in the History of Music for the Baroque Guitar." PhD diss., California State University, Los Angeles, 1976.

———. "The Theorbed Guitar: Its Repertoire." *Early Music* 7 (1979): 323–29.

Powell, John S. "'Pourquoi Toujours des Bergers?': Lully, Molière and the Pastoral Divertissement." In *Lully Essays,* edited by John Heyer, 166–98. Cambridge: Cambridge University Press, 2000.

———. "A New Source for Lully's Music to Molière's *La Princesse d'Élide.*" In *Quellenstudien zu Jean-Baptiste Lully: Etudes des sources,* edited by Jérôme de La Gorce and Herbert Schneider, 200–22. Hildesheim: George Olms, 1999.

Praetorius, Michael. *Syntagma Musicum.* Wolfenbüttel: Holwein, 1619.

Preitano, Massimo. "Gli albordi della consezione tonale: aria, ritornello strumentale e chitarra spagnola nel primo Seicento." *Rivista Italiana de Musicologia* 29, no. 1 (1994): 27–88.

Pruiksma, Rose A. "Music, Sex, and Ethnicity: Signification in Lully's Theatrical Chaconnes." In *Gender, Sexuality, and Early Music,* edited by Todd Michael Borgerding, 227–48. New York: Routledge, 2002.

Pujol, Emilio. "Les ressources instrumentales et leur rôle dans la musique pour vihuela et pour guitare au XVIᵉ siècle et au XVIIᵉ." In *La musique instrumentale de la Renaissance: Études réunis et présentées par Jean Jacquot.* Paris: Editions du Centre National de la Recherche Scientifique, 1955.

Rasch, Rudolf. *Driehonderd brieven over muziek van, aan en rond Constantijn Huygens.* Hilversum: Verloren, 2007.

Rave, Wallace. "Performance Instructions for the Seventeenth-Century French Lute Repertoiry." In *Performance on Lute, Guitar and Vihuela: Historical Practice and Modern Interpretation,* edited by Victor A. Coelho, 142–57. Cambridge: Cambridge University Press, 1997.

Rebours, Gérard. "The Baroque Guitar in France and Its Two Main Figures: Robert de Visée and François Campion." *Michaelsteiner Konferenzberichte* 66: 195–210. Dössel: Verlag Janos Stekovics, 2004.

———. "Lully guitariste." *Les cahiers de la guitare* 38 no. 4 (1991): 14–6.

———. *Robert de Visée, catalogue thématique et concordances.* Paris: Symétrie Éditions, 2001.

Richards, Kenneth and Laura. *The Commedia dell'Arte.* Oxford: Basil Blackwell Ltd., 1990.

Roig-Francoli, Miguel. "Playing in Consonances, a Spanish Renaissance Technique of Chordal Improvisation." *Early Music* 23 (1995): 461–71.

Romano, Remigio. *Prima raccolta di bellissime canzonette.* Vicenza: Salvadori, 1618.

Roncalli, Ludovico. *Capricci armonici sopra la chitarra spagnola,* Bergamo: Casetti, 1692. Facsimile edition. Monaco: Chanterelle, 1978.

Rosand, Ellen. "Venice, 1580–1680." In *The Early Baroque Era, From the Late Sixteenth Century to the 1660s,* edited by Curtis Price, 75–102. Basingstoke: Macmillan (Man & Music Series, vol. 3), 1993.

Rudin, John and Olly Crick. *Commedia dell'Arte: a Handbook for Troupes.* New York: Routledge, 2001.

Ruiz de Ribayaz, Lucas. *Luz y norte musical,* Madrid: Alvarez, 1677. Facsimile edition. Geneva: Minkoff, 1975.

Russell, Craig H. "Imported Influences in 17th and 18th Century Guitar Music in Spain." In *Actas del congreso internacional sobre España y la música de occident, Salamanca 1985,* vol. 1, 385–403. Madrid: Ministerio de Cultura, 1987.

———. *Santiago de Murcia's "Códice Saldívar No. 4."* 2 vols. Urbana: University of Illinois Press, 1995.

———. "Radical Innovations, Social Revolution and the Baroque Guitar." In *The Cambridge Companion to the Guitar,* edited by Victor Anand Coelho, 153–81. Cambridge: Cambridge University Press, 2003.

Sanseverino, Benedetto. *Il primo libro d'intavolatura,* Milan: Lomazza, 1622.

Sanz, Gaspar. *Instrucción de musica sobre la guitarra española*, Zaragoza, Spain: Dormer, 1674. Facsimile edition. Geneva: Minkoff, 1976.

Sayce, Lynda. "Continuo Lutes in Seventeenth and Eighteenth Century England." *Early Music* 23 (1995): 667–84.

———. "The Development of Italianate Continuo Lutes." PhD diss., Open University, 2001.

Schmitz, Eugen. "Zur Geschichte der Guitarre." *Monatshefte für Musikgeschichte* 25 (1903): 133–38.

Schnoebelen, Anne. "Bologna 1580–1700." In *The Early Baroque Era, from the Late Sixteenth Century to the 1660s*, edited by Curtis Price, 103–20. Man and Music, vol. 3. Basingstoke: Macmillan, 1993.

Schulenberg, David. "Some Problems of Text, Attribution and Performance in Early Italian Baroque Keyboard Music." *Journal of Seventeenth Century Music* 4 (1998). http://sscm-jscm.press.uiuc.edu/v4/no1/schulenberg.html.

Segerman, Ephraim. "Stringing 5-Course Baroque Guitars." *Fellowship of Makers and Restorers of Historical Instruments Quarterly* 75 (1994): 43–45.

Selfridge-Field, Eleanor. "Instrumentation and Genre in Italian Music 1600–1670." *Early Music* 19 (1991): 61–67.

Sievers, Heinrich. *Die Musik in Hanover*. Hanover: Sponholz, 1961.

Silbiger, Alexander. "Passacaglia and Ciaccona: Genre Pairing and Ambiguity from Frescobaldi to Couperin." *Journal of Seventeenth Century Music* 2 (1996). http://sscm-jscm.press.illinois.edu/v2/no1/silbiger.html.

Spencer, Robert. "Chitarrone, Theorbo and Archlute." *Early Music* 4 (1976): 408–22.

Stauffer, George B. *The World of Baroque Music*. Bloomington: Indiana University Press, 2007.

Stefani, Giovanni. *Scherzi amorosi*, Venice: Vincenti, 1618.

Stein, Louise. "Accompaniment and Continuo in Spanish Baroque Music." In *Actas del congreso internacional sobre España y la música de occident, Salamanca 1985*, vol. 1, 357–70. Madrid: Ministerio de Cultura, 1987.

———. "The Origins and Character of *Recitado*." *Journal of Seventeenth Century Music* 9 (2003). http://sscm-jscm.press.uiuc.edu/v9/no1/stein.html.

———. *Songs of Mortals, Dialogues of the Gods*. Oxford: Clarendon Press, 1993.

———. "Spain." In *The Early Baroque Era, From the Late Sixteenth Century to the 1660s*, edited by Curtis Price, 349–60. Man and Music, vol. 3. Basingstoke: Macmillan, 1993.

Strizich, Robert. "L'accompagnamento di basso continuo sulla chitarra barocca." *Il Fronimo* 9, no. 1 (1981): 15–27; 9, no. 2 (1981): 8–27.

Strohm, Reinhard. "Unwritten and Written Music." In *Companion to Medieval and Renaissance Music*, edited by Tess Knighton and David Fallows, 220–36. Berkeley, University of California Press, 1992.

Strunk, Oliver. *The Baroque Era*. Source Readings in Music History, vol. 3. London: Faber, 1952.

Tagliavini, Luigi F. "The Art of 'Not Leaving the Instrument Empty.'" *Early Music* 11 (1983): 298–308.

Taruskin, Richard. *The Oxford History of Western Music* vol. 2. Oxford: Oxford University Press, 2005.

Tomlinson, Gary. *Monteverdi and the End of the Renaissance.* Berkeley: University of California Press, 1987.

Tonazzi, Bruno. *Liuto, vihuela, chitarra e strumenti similari nelle loro intavolature. Con cenni sulle loro letterature.* Ancona, Italy: Bèrben, 1971.

Treadwell, Nina. "The 'Chitarra Spagnola' and Italian Monody 1589 to circa 1630." MMA thesis, University of Southern California, 1995.

———. "Guitar Alfabeto in Italian Monody: The Publications of Alessandro Vincenti." *The Lute* 33 (1993): 12–22.

———. "She Descended on a Cloud 'from the Highest Spheres': Florentine Monody 'alla Romanina.'" *Cambridge Opera Journal* 16, no. 1 (2004): 1–22.

Tyler, James. *The Early Guitar: A History and Handbook.* London: Oxford University Press, 1980.

———. "The Renaissance Guitar 1500–1650." *Early Music* 3 (1975): 341–47.

———. "The Role of the Guitar in the Rise of Monody: the Earliest Manuscripts." *Journal of Seventeenth Century Music* 9 (2003). http://sscm-jscm.press.uiuc. edu/v9/no1/tyler.html.

Tyler, James, and Paul Sparks. *The Guitar and Its Music.* London: Oxford University Press, 2002.

Valdambrini, Ferdinando. *Libro primo d'intavolatura di chitarra a cinque ordini,* Rome: 1646.

———. *Libro secondo d'intavolatura di chitarra a cinque ordini,* Rome: 1647.

Vecchi, Giuseppe. "La monodia da camera a Bologna e *I pietosi affetti* (1646) di Domenico Pellegrini." *Quadrivium* 18 (1977): 97–106.

Viadana, Lodovico. *Li cento concerti ecclesiastici.* Venice: Vicenti, 1605.

Visée, Robert de. *Livre de guitarre.* Paris: Bonneüil, 1682. Facsimile edition. Geneva: Minkoff, 1973.

———. *Livre de pièces pour la guitarre,* Paris: Bonneüil, 1686. Facsimile edition. Geneva: Minkoff, 1973.

———. *Suite in G Minor.* Vienna: Universal Edition, n.d.

Walker, Thomas. "Ciaccona and Passacaglia: Remarks on Their Origin and Early History." *Journal of the American Musicological Society* 21 (1968): 300–20.

Ward, John M. "The Relationship of Folk and Art Music in 17th-Century Spain." *Studi musicali* 12 (1983): 281–300.

Weidlich, Joseph. "Battuto Performance Practice in Early Italian Guitar Music." *Journal of the Lute Society of America* 11 (1978): 63–86.

Wenland, John. "Madre non mi far Monaca: The Biography of a Renaissance Folksong." *Acta Musicologica* 48 (1976): 185–204.

Williams, Peter. "The Harpsichord Acciaccatura." *Music Quarterly* 54 (1968): 503–23.

Wistreich, Richard. *Warrior, Courtier, Singer: Giulio Cesare Brancaccio and the Performance of Identity in the Late Renaissance.* Aldershot, UK: Ashgate Publishing, 2007.

Wolzien, Charles. "Early Guitar Literature: Baroque Song Literature." *Soundboard* 20, no. 3 (1993): 77–80; 20, no. 4 (1993): 67–70; 20, no. 5 (1993): 79–82.

———. *Early Guitar Anthology II, the Early Baroque.* www.EarlyGuitarAnthology.com. Accessed June 26, 2015.

Yakely, June. "New Sources of Spanish Music for the Five Course Guitar." *Revista de musicologia* 21 (1996): 267–86.

——. "The Life and Times of José Marin." *The Lute* 39 (1999): 16–26.

Yakely, June, and Monica Hall. "El Estillo Castellano y Estillo Catalan: An Introduction to Spanish Guitar Chord Notation." *The Lute* 35 (1995): 28–61.

Zappulla, Robert. "Figured Bass Accompaniment in France c. 1650–c. 1775." PhD diss., Universiteit Utrecht, 1998.

Zuluaga, Daniel. "Spanish Song, *Chitarra alla Spagnola,* and the *a.bi.ci.* Matheo Bezón and his 1599 *Alfabeto* Songbook." *Resonance* (Spring 2013): 1–31. http://www.resonancejournal.org/current-issue/spr-2013/spanish-song-chitarra-alla-spagnola-and-the-a-bi-ci-matheo-bezon-and-his-1599-alfabeto-songbook.

Index

An italicized page number indicates a figure or music example.

In the seventeenth century, like today, the guitar was often used for chord strumming ("battuto" in Italian) in songs and popular dance genres, such as the *ciaccona* or *sarabanda*. In the golden age of the baroque guitar, Italy gave rise to a unique solo repertoire, in which chord strumming and lute-like plucked ("pizzicato") styles were mixed. *Italian Guitar Music of the Seventeenth Century: Battuto and Pizzicato* explores this little-known repertoire, providing a historical background and examining particular performance issues. The book is accompanied by audio examples on a companion website.

Lex Eisenhardt is one of Europe's foremost experts on early guitar. He teaches both classical guitar and historical plucked instruments at the Conservatory of Amsterdam. He has produced a number of highly acclaimed CD recordings, and has given concerts and masterclasses in Europe, the United States, and Australia.

Printed in the United States
By Bookmasters